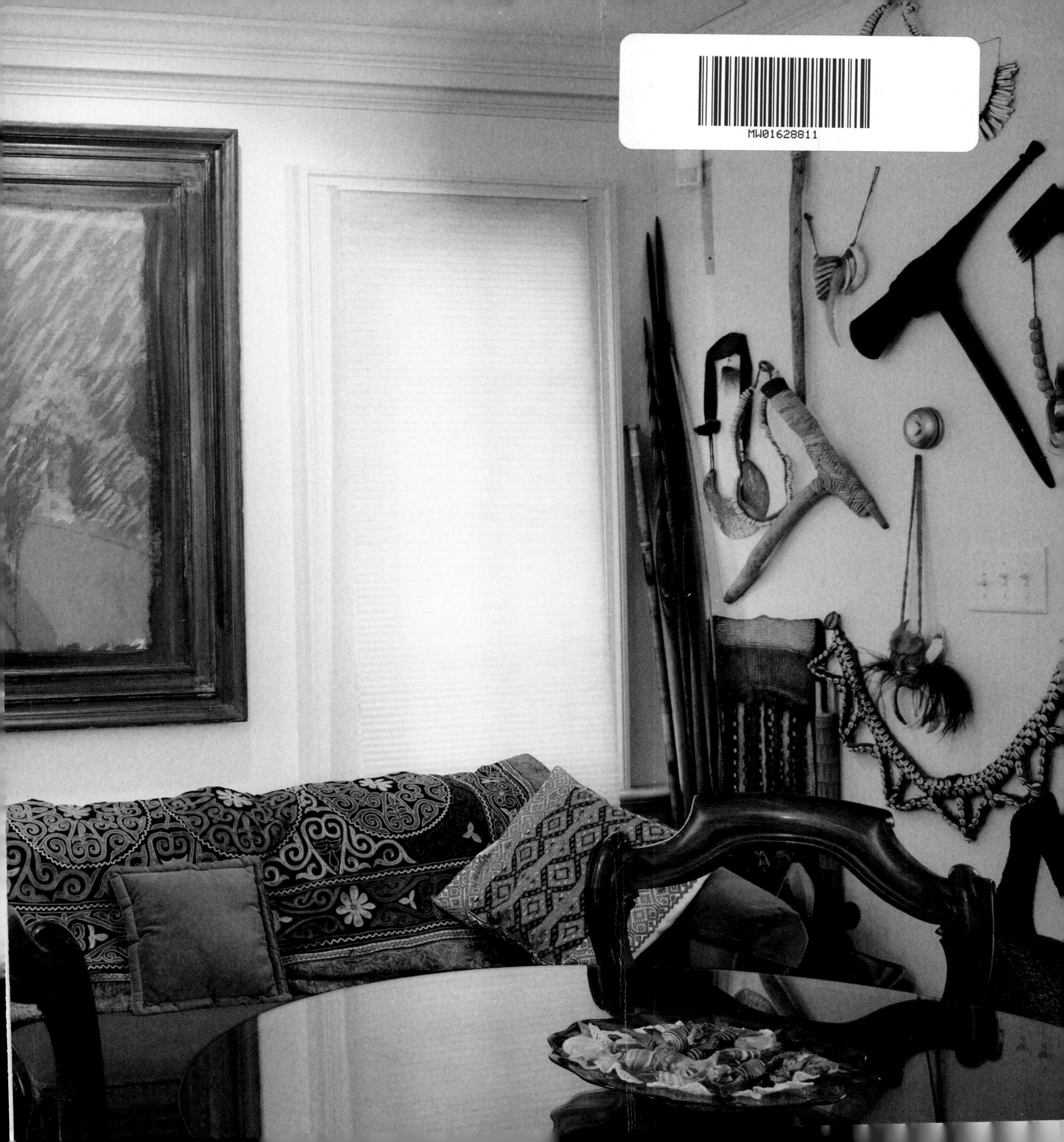

HOWARD HODGKIN

PAINTINGS 1992–2007

with essays by
Richard Morphet
Anthony Lane

edited and curated by
Julia Marciari Alexander
David Scrase

The Yale Center for British Art
The Fitzwilliam Museum

Yale University Press
New Haven & London

This publication accompanies *Howard Hodgkin: Paintings 1992–2007*, organized by the Yale Center for British Art and the Fitzwilliam Museum, on view at the Center from 1 February to 1 April 2007 and at the Fitzwilliam from 24 May to 23 September 2007.

Support for the exhibition was provided by The British Council.

Endpapers: *Afternoon Flowers* (no. 2, front) and *A Visit to Paul and Bernard* (no. 6, back) in situ, Private collection.

Library of Congress Control Number: 2006939809

Designed by Sally Salvesen
Printed in Italy by Conti Tipocolor

CONTENTS

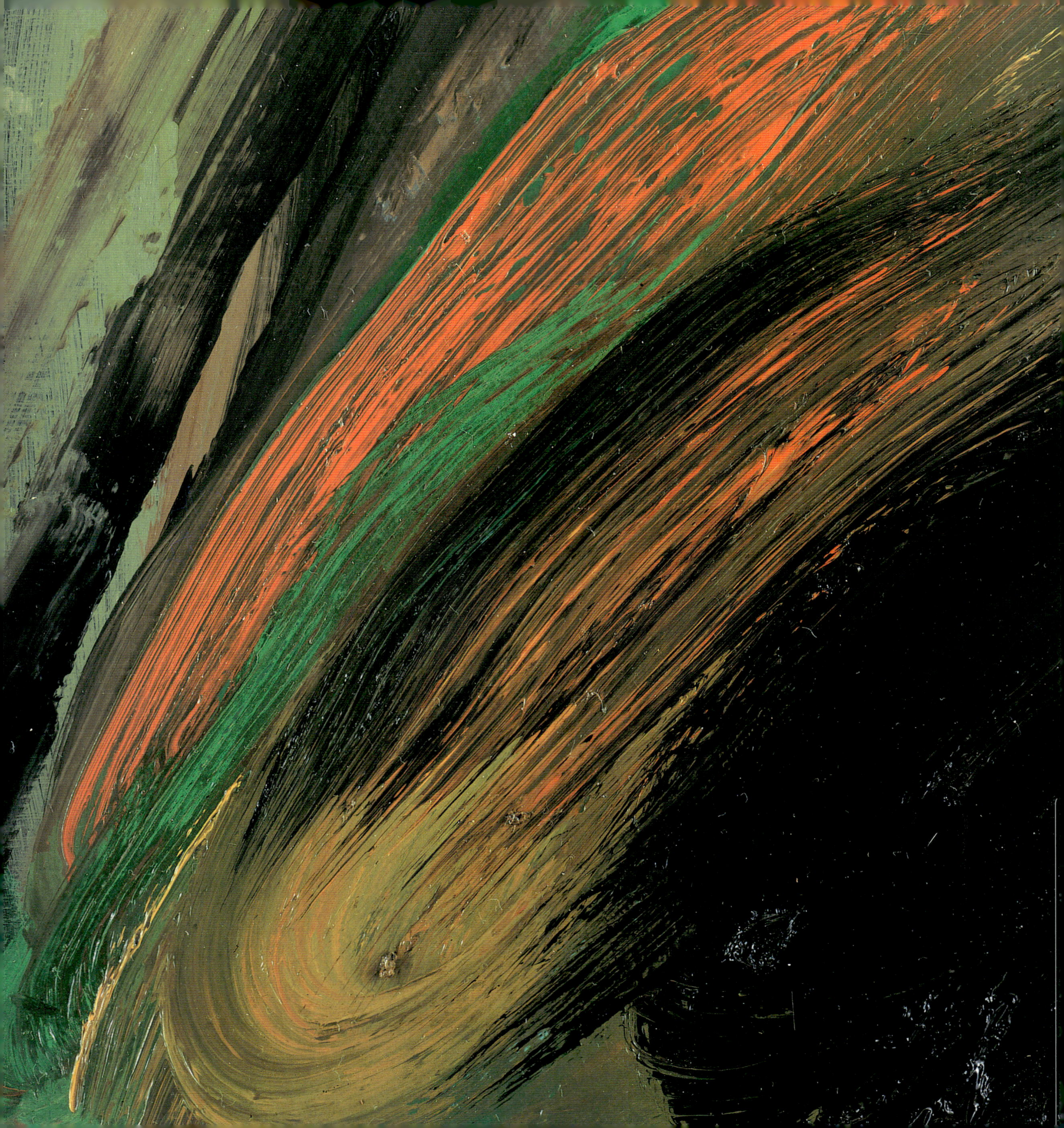

DIRECTORS' FOREWORD

The Fitzwilliam Museum and the Yale Center for British Art are delighted to present selected paintings by Howard Hodgkin from the past fifteen years. The two, closely related exhibitions in New Haven and Cambridge and the accompanying book result from longstanding collaborations. Indeed, it is wonderful to see the return of Hodgkin first to the Center, just over twenty years after an exhibition of his work organized by the British Council here, and then to the Fitzwilliam, an institution the artists has long enjoyed.

Although his life and career have taken place almost exclusively in Britain, Hodgkin's ties with the United States are strong. Spending three years from 1940 to 1943 as a wartime evacuee on Long Island, New York, determined his future: it was then he decided to become an artist. That *Howard Hodgkin: Paintings 1992–2007* celebrates the artist's transatlantic relationships is entirely appropriate: in nearly equal proportions, the works in this selection (the majority of which are in both exhibitions) belong to private collectors and institutions in either the United States or the United Kingdom.

Howard Hodgkin: Paintings 1992–2007 will have been conceived and realized in just over a year. We would like to thank the curators David Scrase and Julia Marciari Alexander for bringing these complementary projects to fruition at our two institutions. Our colleagues at Gagosian Gallery, Robin Vousden and Ealan Wingate, with the assistance of Alexandra Robinson, have provided the curators with invaluable and timely advice, practical help, and support at all stages of the process. We are grateful to

Howard Hodgkin, **An Autumn Leaf**, detail of no. 29.

The British Council, which has given support for the exhibition at Yale. In New Haven the lion's share of the exhibitions' implementation has fallen, as always, to the staffs of the Center's departments of Exhibitions and Publications, Registration, Installation, Design, and Public Relations, and it is to them that we must extend our gratitude. At the Fitzwilliam, we thank Thyrza Smith, Sean Fall, Andrew Bowker, Jane Sargent, Fiona Brown and Sue Rhodes. We owe the production of the book to its editor and designer Sally Salvesen of Yale University Press, London; she has once again proved to be among the most valuable members of our transatlantic team.

The recent retrospective that traveled in 2006 from Dublin to London to Madrid has served to reinforce Howard Hodgkin's importance among twentieth-century British arts. While only two works in our exhibition were included in it, many of the lenders are the same. It is a measure of the strong personal bond between the artist and his collectors, and of their appreciation for his paintings, that they are willing to part with them for a further prolonged period of time. We are indebted to them and to our colleagues at museums who have generously lent to our institutions. Most of all, we are proud to be able to continue our partnership with Howard Hodgkin. We trust that our exhibitions will reflect and deepen understanding of this extraordinary artist's work.

Amy Meyers, *Director, Yale Center for British Art*
Duncan Robinson, *Director, The Fitzwilliam Museum*

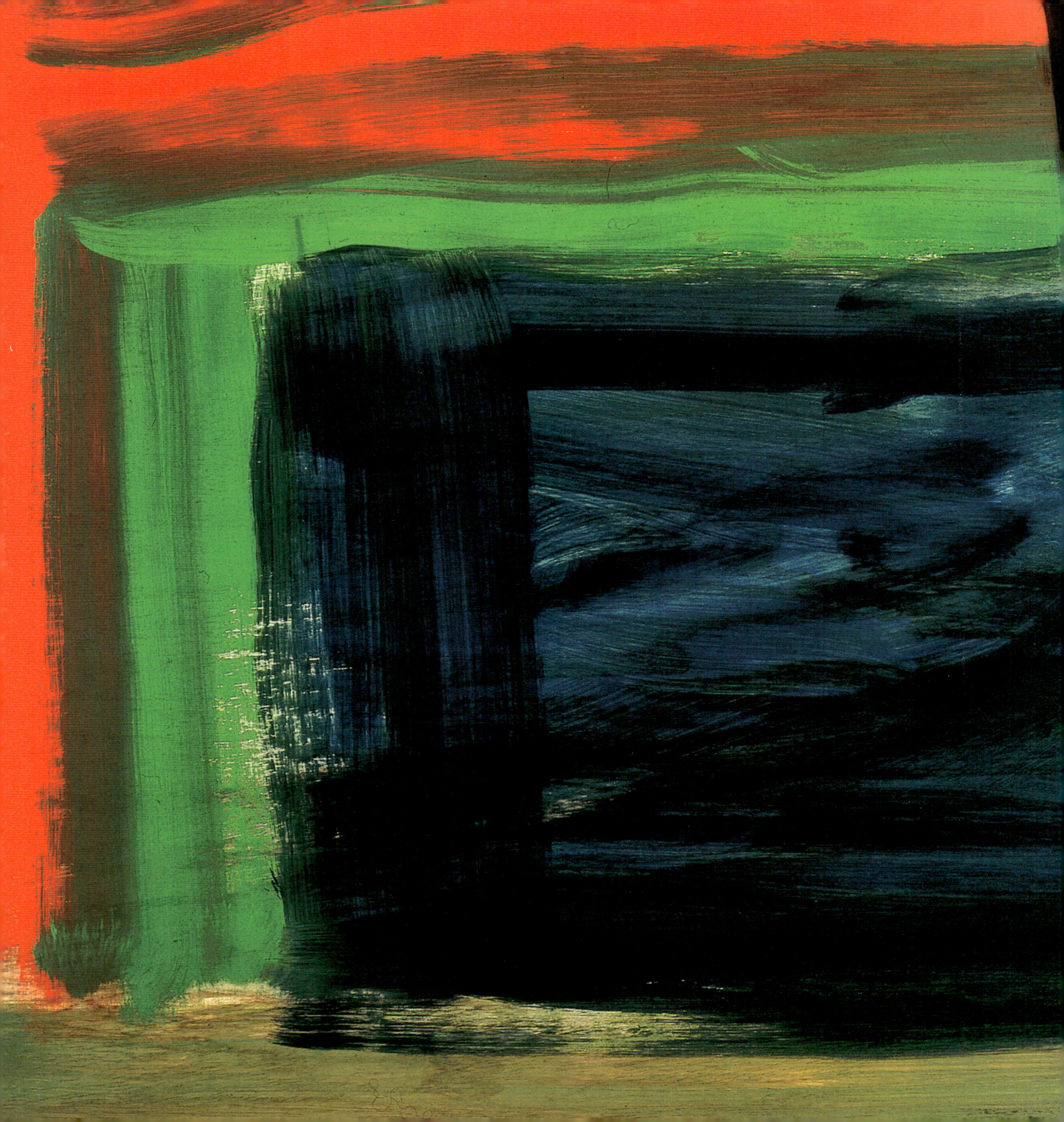

Perhaps the most often repeated description of Howard Hodgkin's art is that in which he designated his paintings as "representational pictures of emotional situations." Evocative, certainly, this phrase is nonetheless tantalizingly vague. Indeed, when looking at his body of work, one is struck by the ostensible lack of "representational" motifs; accordingly, art historians and critics alike have discussed the role of figuration and abstraction in his work. This debate, while elegant and intriguing, seems to miss the point. Layering paint on his surfaces and frames (sometimes over the course of years), Hodgkin creates—and recreates—intense experiences for his viewers.

The scale of the two exhibitions at the Fitzwilliam and the Yale Center for British Art is different, one small, the other larger, but they share a core repertoire of the same paintings. They range from small paintings that draw the viewer into intimate encounters, such as *Small Chez Max* (no. 61) and *Theatre* (no. 43), to large ones whose presence is often imposing, such as *Performance Art* (no. 21; detail, facing page) and *Autumn* (no. 39). For Hodgkin, an intense intellectual and physical process goes into making each work, as each painting is built up from a series of interlocking elements: the event or situation that inspires the artist; the evolution of that inspiration as the painting is created; and the impact of the finished object on those who experience it.

Often, the artist makes teasing reference in his titles to past artists and artistic conventions, as in *After Degas* (no. 44), *After Samuel Palmer* (no. 1), and *Ultramarine* (no. 13). But Hodgkin is

COMMENT

Howard Hodgkin, Performance Art, detail of no. 21.

adamant that these associations are only ever allusive—in fact, they are sometimes decidedly deceptive and even playful (*Ultramarine*, for example, which refers to Malcolm Lowry's first published novel, is painted in cobalt). The titles may pay homage to an encounter, an instance, or an object that sparked the artist's creativity, but they do not describe or proscribe individual encounters with the painting. Howard Hodgkin's ability to confound discussion of his work is legendary. Yet, the particular quality of his paintings that frustrates articulate description of their subjects or meaning is precisely that which engages artist, object, and audience.

A major retrospective Hodgkin's paintings opened in February 2006 in Dublin at the Irish Museum of Modern Art, went next to London where it was shown at Tate Britain, and closed at the Museo Nacional Centro de Arte Reina Sofía in Madrid; this exhibition was curated by Sir Nicholas Serota and Enrique Juncosa. As with any retrospective, no one period was the focus of the show. The selection represented a sharply honed encapsulation of the artist's oeuvre. In order to succeed, such a retrospective must be—or appear to be—objective. *Howard Hodgkin: Paintings1992–2007*, by contrast, aims at subjectivity. Making the selection for this exhibition and its accompanying publication has provided the artist with the chance to speak through his paintings and the opportunity to craft a visual statement about his work of the last fifteen years. The selection presented in the book brings form to an ideal that differs only slightly from the two related exhibitions (whose contents are recorded in the checklist at the volume's end); this publication is meant to complement rather than copy the exhibitions to which it attends.

Howard Hodgkin: Paintings 1992–2007 is the result of an ongoing dialogue between colleagues and friends. For the Fitzwilliam, the exhibition came out of a longstanding bond between artist and curator; for the Yale Center, discussion began—rather aptly—beneath Sir Joshua Reynolds's extraordinary portraits of the Society of Dilettanti, themselves visual testaments to the affective power of art among individuals. The selection has shifted and changed through our mutual discussions with Howard, but it has also been productively influenced through conversations with Robin Vousden, Ealan Wingate, Matthew Rutenberg, Antony Peattie, and John Marciari. Without their passion for and insights into these paintings, neither the exhibitions at Cambridge and Yale, nor the accompanying book could have happened. The installation has benefited from Ealan Wingate's expertise, and Andy Barker has provided invaluable support for the project.

We are also grateful to the writers in this volume, whose essays are significant contributions to Hodgkin scholarship. Richard Morphet wrote the first major essay on the artist's work thirty years ago, introducing the catalogue for his first retrospective, *Howard Hodgkin: Forty-Five paintings 1949–1975* (Museum of Modern Art, Oxford, 1976). Anthony Lane returns to the subject having published a previous essay on Hodgkin in *The New Yorker* in 2003.

Meetings and exchanges with the many lenders have enriched our appreciation for the paintings as objects that "live" with their owners. One lender, in particular, lamented that parting with his painting would leave him in an unfathomable state of "Hodgkinlessness." For those who possess them, Hodgkin's paintings are not simply static "representational pictures of emotional situations;" rather, they are part of the continual staging of everyday experience. The shifting form of the exhibitions has made us realize that the works finally chosen will create yet another pattern of reflected and lived interactions.

For curators whose academic specialties nominally rest in past centuries, there is nothing more potentially daunting than working with a living artist. Precisely because of his erudition, both artistic and personal, Howard Hodgkin is an ideal subject for such curators; in particular, the process of installation has been collaborative, which was not possible for either Barocci at Cambridge or Canaletto at Yale. Experiencing Hodgkin's paintings in the context of both our collections reveals their intimate connections and, yet, demonstrates that the relationship between his work and that of his predecessors is often taunting, frequently elusive, and sometimes illusory. It has been a delight to experience the ways in which, both with Hodgkin and his art, eloquence is found in silence.

Julia Marciari Alexander, *Yale Center for British Art*
David Scrase, *The Fitzwilliam Museum*

PARA-
DOX &
PLENI-
TUDE

RICHARD MORPHET

HODGKIN NOW

Howard Hodgkin's paintings of the past fifteen years are among the most direct and forthright painted anywhere. In their surprising invention, their sensuous abundance, and their richness of suggestion, the fullness of the experience they offer invites comparison with the work of some of the key painters of the recent and more distant past. As is often the case with art that evokes such a response, Hodgkin's is the site of many paradoxes.

Prominent among these paradoxes is the fact that the means Hodgkin employs frequently stand received notions of "good painting" on their head, yet he makes an important contribution to the continued vitality of painting. In conventional terms, his pictures are at times almost insulting. The way they are painted accords maximum prominence to every mark made. Thus marks—along with other key factors such as texture, color, and the interrelation of all of these on a surface and in a "space"—carry exceptional weight in a picture's effect. Yet these marks are not only unusually simple, they are often (in orthodox terms) inconsequential to an extreme degree. At first sight they can seem extraordinarily casual or slight, even purposeless. Other no less puzzling effects are of a contrasting kind. Towards their outer edges many works have features (painted or made of wood) that are akin to frames. Such configurations direct special attention to what is going on in the spaces they enclose, but Hodgkin repeatedly seems to blot out or cancel anything that might be happening there with a bold swathe of paint, applied in what appears to be a single brutal gesture. Neither Hodgkin's "negligible" marks, nor his vehement "obstructions" are usually descriptive. Yet they are major elements in paintings, each of which (as both its title and our knowledge of the nature of Hodgkin's project tell us) is a representation of particular content, for which its surprising form is the precisely judged vehicle.

Strangely, however, these peculiarities are no impediment for the viewer. Each work is perceived first as a whole, and it is striking how widespread is the experience that, far from seeming weakly felt, pointless, or blocked, a Hodgkin painting communicates both a forceful emotional charge and even a strong, tangible sense of people, objects, and nature. Far from deflecting attention from its material constituents, each painting encourages detailed scrutiny, yet it simultaneously places the viewer in an environment of heightened physical, imaginative, and affective sensitivity—and does so very directly.

Since 1992 Hodgkin has been working with enhanced freedom and audacity. As his attitude to the conventions has grown more cavalier, the breadth of his expression has increased. Landscape has assumed ever-greater prominence. People represented in his interiors have long been conceived in more than purely visual relationship to their usually very particular settings. Correspondingly, human presence amid the atmospheric and light conditions of Hodgkin's outdoor scenes often seems more complex in nature than mere occupation of these environments. Though some of Hodgkin's landscapes are straightforward embodiments of what he saw, more have the character of inward or psychological topographies that are fused with a perennial astonishment at the effects of nature. However improbable this might seem in the context of characterizations of Hodgkin's art till recently, something of the very different sensibilities of Friedrich or late Watts comes to mind, or even aspects of Van Gogh or Munch.

In a notable related trend, any sense of Hodgkin's pictures as reports on other people's lives has given way to a sense of Hodgkin's own close and often deep involvement in the encounters and relationships his pictures represent. This is a matter of developing emphasis rather than of categorical change, since all Hodgkin's early mature pictures of people in their settings involved his own memories and feelings, called forth by occasions in which he was a participant. However, there is almost certainly a link between increased independence from descriptive necessity in terms of observation and the enhanced degree to which human presence is felt in the work of recent years. In a very broad generalization, some figures seen in Hodgkin's work of the 1960s and 70s seem trapped, in an interesting way (whether in their represented settings or in the structures that represent these), whereas now human presence seems to be *in* the paint itself, blatantly *there*.

There are more ways in which Hodgkin's paint is imbued with human presence. Most obviously, it was he who placed his paint marks where we see them. Deep though his attachment is to the idea of anonymous marks, every mark brings us close to him. Through his choices of shape, juxtaposition, and type of touch (the latter an extensive vocabulary) his unique identity is declared. Furthermore, he makes his marks in such a way as to seem to bring to life for the viewer the very actions he performed to give them the form we see. As he guards his privacy while painting we cannot, of course, be sure that any given mark really was made in the way it appears unambiguously to have been. Some certainly were not. Nevertheless, each painting has the character of being a narrative of the physical acts that produced it, with all the extreme deliberation of a process that encompasses both the repetitive application of standardized marks and an almost abandoned spontaneity.

That narrative is compelling, irrespective of the subject that generated it (even though, as will be discussed, the two cannot properly be separated). But the dance of movements and action, into which the viewer seems to enter, is coterminous with another. This is because in each picture Hodgkin's marks create an extraordinary scene, compounded at once of the materials he has fashioned and of the representational illusion he creates. Thus we not only follow the movements of Hodgkin's hand and arm but also explore the invented world that is set before us. In this process it is as though one's own body is in the scene. This operates with works of all sizes, because the scale of the view being contemplated is not restricted by the literal size of the picture that presents it.

In *Fog* (no. 49), which is only 14½ inches wide, the roughly rectilinear arrangement of bands, in various shades of blue, has the mass and depth of a stage-surround that dwarfs us, but this is unnervingly in motion, both up and down, and in the fast-moving directional impetuses of the individual bands. The nearest of these is low in the field of vision but another one is bent through ninety degrees; both seem to be in process of being formed. That everything is unstable is further indicated by the gap visible at the base. Nevertheless, we gaze at the view through the main aperture. This could be of the fog of the title, for wisps of gray occupy the left side and brilliant but veiled light struggles to penetrate the atmosphere. But, in a Wonderland shift characteristic of Hodgkin's pictures, its rosy cream might equally be that of a closely-seen smudged plaster wall, thus dramatically altering the understood scale. Even as we think this, however, we perceive the grain of wood and feel, instead, that we are peering into an intimate box.

In *Navy Blue* (no. 23) a massive curtain of that color blocks two-thirds of the extensive view that draws the eye beyond it. We long to pull it aside, but wonder if we dare, since at its foot the blue of the curtain passes straight into an aqueous zone of indeterminate depth and extent. To the left of the view, no fewer than seven drop curtains recede into the distance, the farthest two actually in the land- (or heaving sea-) scape, beyond which the sun is setting.

You are my Sunshine (no. 56) is on fire. Flames eddy, yet in the paint that blurs the boundary between inside and out we slither about, experiencing primitive sensations induced by the viscous mud-colored material. Some of this lodges on the serrations of the "window frame" through which we view what might or might not be a strangely close-up figure (itself fluid in form).[1]

When in Rome (no. 5) telescopes the extreme proximity of a rough, bread-like form (or it might be two) in front of an oval aperture, a purer upright in the chamber we see through it, and the far, azure empyrean. Still in Italy, can a single swell and slap of water ever have been conveyed with such focus and proximity as in the image that is enclosed by four thickly spread rectangles in *Venetian Landscape* (no. 54)? As mentioned earlier, Hodgkin sometimes occludes the traditional picture area at the center of his "framed" images. Both *Venetian Landscape* and the *trompe l'oeil* stretch of sunlit russet seen through the wildly contrasting "frame" in *Walking on Water* (no. 42) remind us how opposite to an occlusion can be the picture that Hodgkin places in that space.

The descriptions in the previous four paragraphs are one person's take. Another viewer might contradict them. Moreover, if one knew in detail what Hodgkin was representing here, some or all of these interpretations might seem ludicrous. Yet they are valid because the pictures call them forth. The conundrum is illustrated by one of the larger pictures in this exhibition, *Clarendon Road* (no. 50). The subject is a location known to both Hodgkin and me (to him from childhood, and to me for the last twenty years of its occupation by members of his family, during which its appearance remained broadly similar). The "scene" is at the London house of cousins of Hodgkin, the principal rooms in which were filled with fine and applied art by the Bloomsbury artists.[2] One of these rooms led into another, which overlooked (and in turn led to) first the garden of the house itself and then the larger, enclosed garden shared by the house and many of its neighbors. Insofar as this image is an account of things seen (which is not always so, and is, in any case, only part of what a picture represents), I cannot tell by looking at it what is shown, even though the remembered setting is so particular. In recent years, Hodgkin's broad vocabulary of swathes of paint and smaller, individual splotches has been augmented by wandering, often aimless-seeming drawn lines that, in a characteristic paradox, play a strong role in a painting. Here, as in other works where they appear, these are not descriptive, despite the viewer being tempted to read them in such a way. *Clarendon Road* cannot, therefore, be read in a straightforward way either as a view from interior to garden, or as a view of interior or garden individually, or as a fusion of the two. Instead, one is struck by a deluge of variously colored ticks. Though corralled according to their hues, these seem unusually susceptible to natural forces. The fat green ones have a luxurious succulence, yet the entire image is alive with flickering motion. It is as if a violent wind is flinging out the grays, in particular, yet also as if much of the image is being consumed by fire. Here, both these natural forces are of emotion, with which the whole work is charged.

How different is this *mouvementé* work, painted on an expansive, flat board, from the enigmatic *Silence* (no. 26). Small in its outer measurements, yet block-like in the structure of its support (which is made of visibly discrete parts, fitted together), this comes out towards the viewer like a truncated pyramid seen from above. Though the three broad swatches of color that provide the sole "figuration" on an orange ground assert "three", they become at least six. For they are variously affected

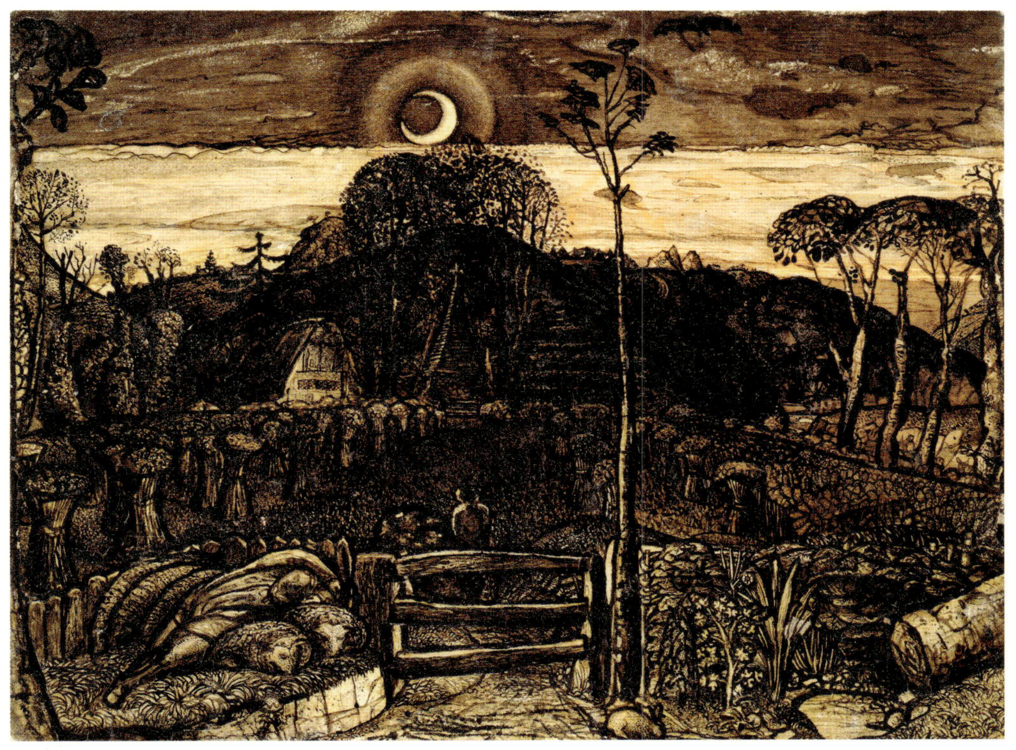

1. Samuel Palmer, Late Twilight, 1825, brown ink and sepia mixed with gum arabic, 7½ x 9³⁄₁₆ in. (18 x 23.8 cm). Ashmolean Museum, Oxford

by transparent over-painting at the left, by the blending of wet on wet in the middle and by the change in perceived hue that is caused by the fall of light on the beefy diagonal plane at right.

The selection includes three of Hodgkin's homages to great painters of the past. The most recent, to Samuel Palmer (no. 1), improbably uses tar-like paint to separate, on three sides, an almost playful border from the rich, still mood of Palmer's central sunset landscape (fig. 1). The power of this vision again attests the Romantic sense of man in nature that is now recurrent in Hodgkin's art, and which in the 1960s would have seemed

so unlikely a preoccupation. A contrasting example is *Evening Sea* (no. 12). Luminous, wistful, and springing, like Palmer's landscapes, from something seen and felt, this image, in which an architectural firmness complements delicious, attenuated floating smears, seems like a world of dream. Yet it is tough.

Hodgkin's work reminds us of this duality in numerous ways. In the climate of Modernism, many would have questioned until recently whether it was possible for a painter to be considered serious if the subjects of paintings included *Chinoiserie* or *Chintz* (nos. 4, 17). The truth, of course, is that no kind of material or field of interest is in principle inadmissible for serious art, and also that there are many ways of looking at any of these. The taste and the type of fabric, respectively, of these titles recall substantial achievements in art and design; these can have functions of many kinds in people's lives, from the elevated to the base.

In *Chinoiserie* no fewer than fourteen stepped bands separate the outer edge of the work from the image at its center. All are painted a rich and assertive red, which except in the innermost band is pitted by the myriad decorative incisions on a former frame or frames. As so often in Hodgkin, the outer paint spills into the picture within a picture—in this case another seductive dialogue between near and far. A striking aspect of the composition is the juxtaposition of the "static," if vibrant, surround with the sweeping inner movements that are initiated by the innermost rank of "frame." In the slightly smaller *Chintz*, enormous-seeming discharges of paint at once contradict the conventional structure beneath and accentuate its presence. One of Hodgkin's aptitudes is to make paint intensely physical for the viewer, in however small a compass. Notable here, for example, are the dynamic overlapping of at least five layers in the restricted space of the top left corner and the immediacy of the way in which the loaded brush has been sharply pulled away at lower right.

Almost overflowing with action, *Chintz*, at just over fifteen inches wide, is nevertheless far from the smallest of Hodgkin's recent paintings. Typically, such a work can, by itself, hold strongly a wall many times its own width. Yet over the past decade and a half Hodgkin has also painted pictures of exceptional size and, indeed, grandeur. The small works might seem private, yet they are bold public statements. The very large ones resonate with inward meanings yet expose their making as never before. On each scale, Hodgkin is without protection. When his work as a painter began, even he could not have imagined such pictures.

SIXTY YEARS OF ART

Hodgkin has stated that "my real career as a painter began by looking at pictures in New York."[3] This was when he lived in the USA in 1940–43, and on a return visit in 1948. His earliest published paintings are of American subjects (fig. 2). They employ a strange but effective language of exaggerated formal clarity to represent situations of human interaction. Already the viewer's curiosity is engaged as to what exactly is going on in these scenes, but, though the appearance of figures and objects is described in considerable detail, the matter is never resolved. Nevertheless, the power of the subject remains compelling. At

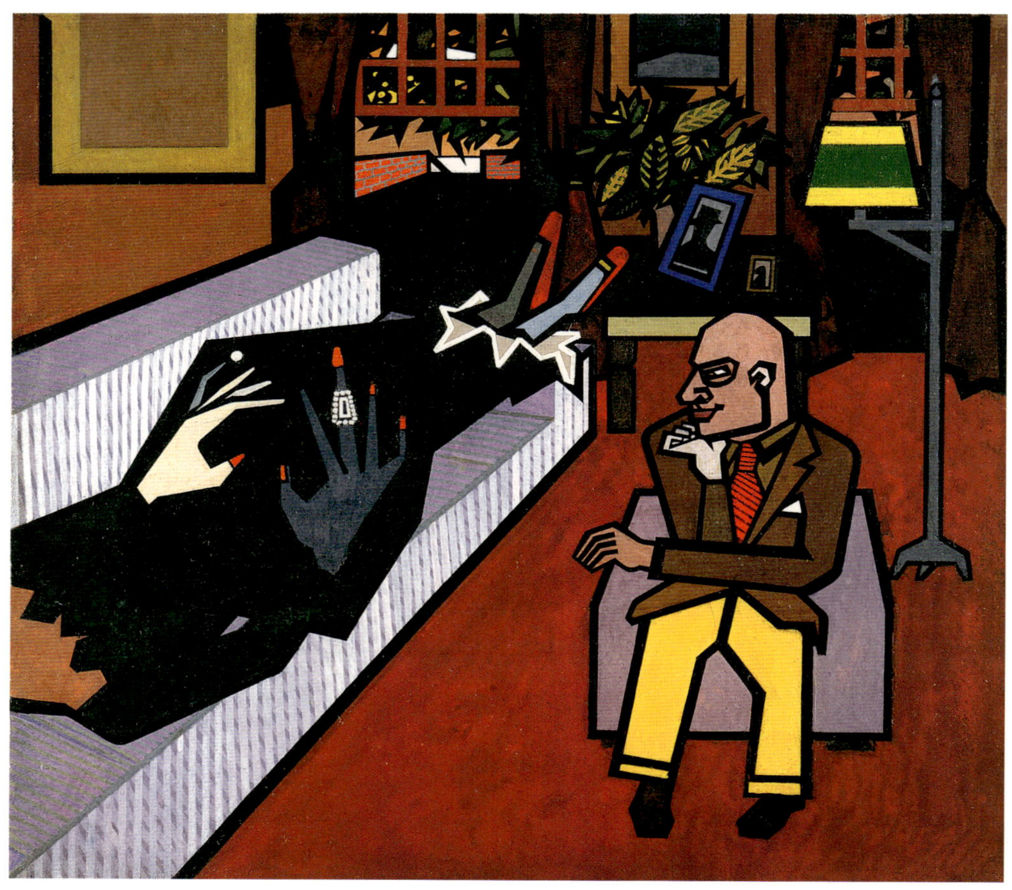

2. Howard Hodgkin, Memoirs, 1949, gouache on board, 8⅝ x 9⅞ in. (22 x 25 cm). Collection of the artist.

the heart of Hodgkin's achievement across nearly sixty years is the fact that while soon abandoning literal description and instead according marked prominence to paint itself and to its application, he has not just maintained the force of the subject for the viewer but has intensified it. Comparison between the early work and that of the present decade shows how surprising Hodgkin's development has been (fig. 3). Its objective, however, has remained consistent.

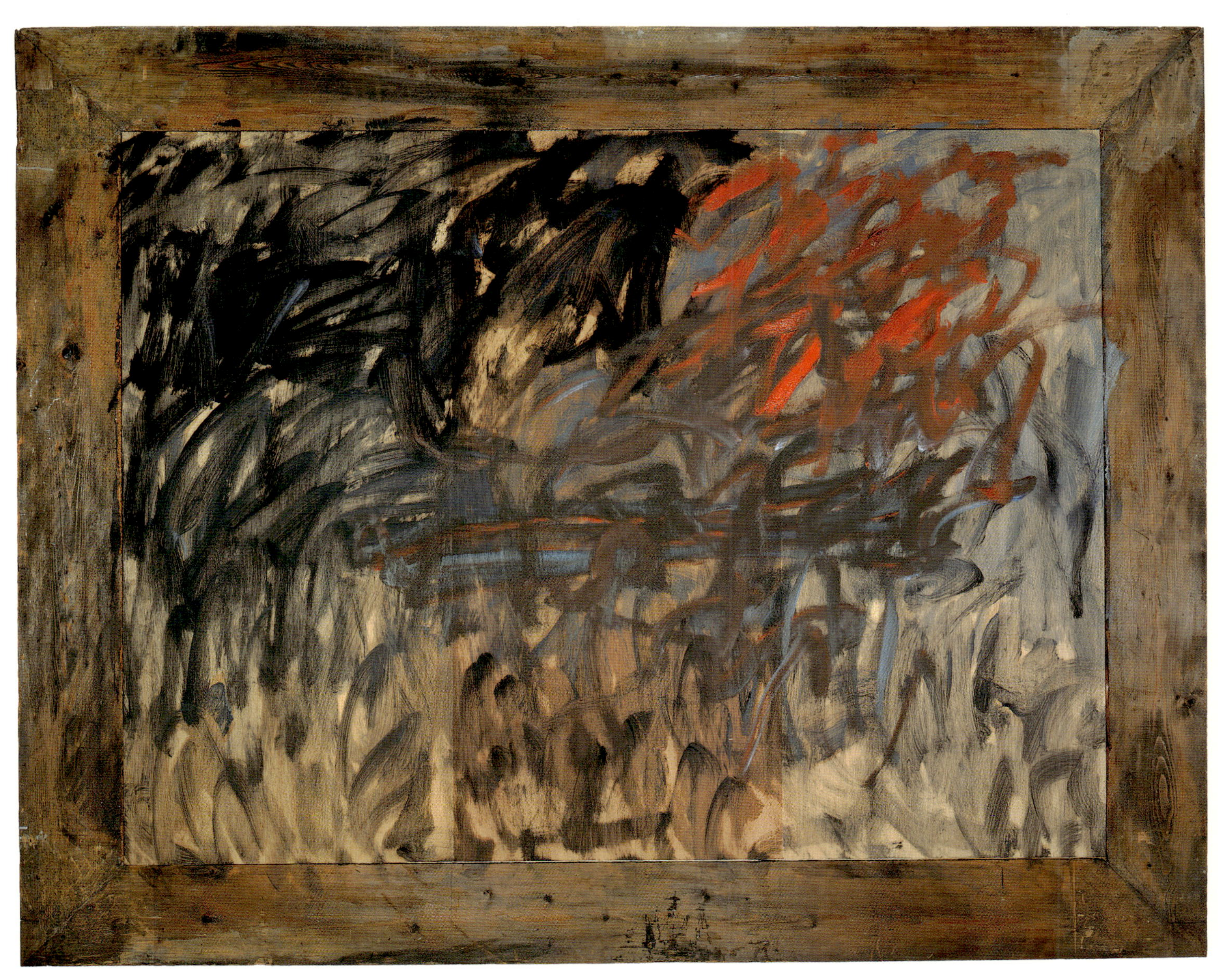

3. Howard Hodgkin, Undertones of War, 2001–03, oil on wood, 81 x 100 in. (205.7 x 254.1 cm). Lhoist Group Collection.

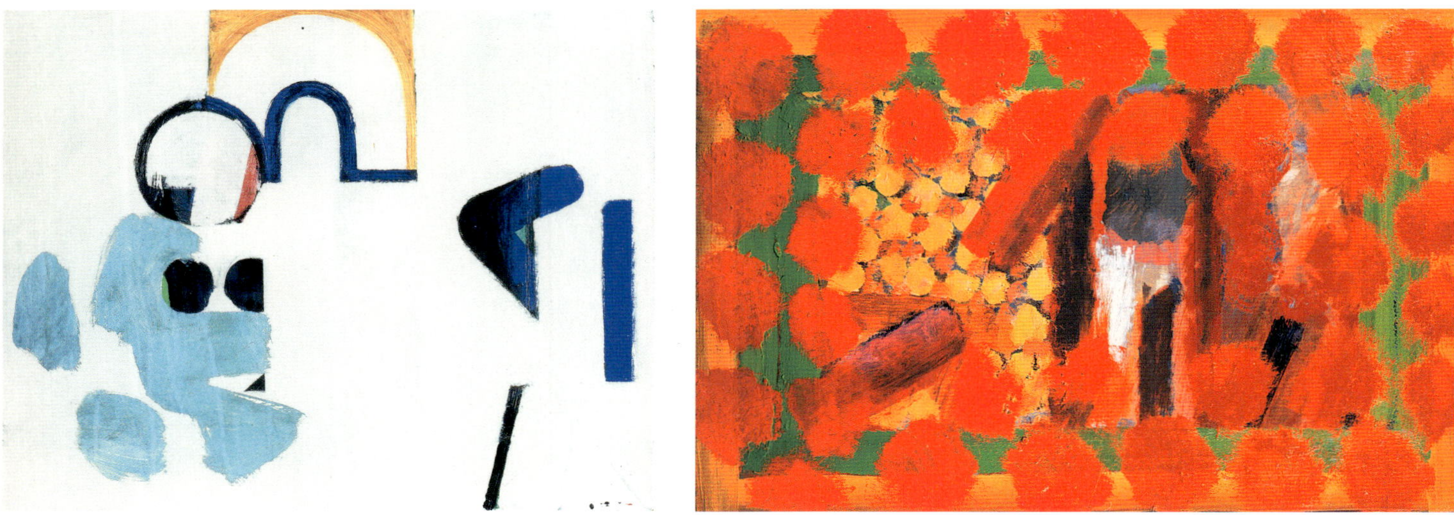

4. Howard Hodgkin, The Second Visit, 1963, oil on hardboard, 16 x 20 in. (40.5 x 51 cm). Southampton City Art Gallery, UK.

5. Howard Hodgkin, Lawson, Underwood & Sleep, 1977–80, oil on wood, 24 x 36 in. (60.9 x 91.4 cm). Private collection, on loan to the Fitzwilliam Museum, Cambridge.

About fifty years ago Hodgkin began to apply paint in a manner that, though actually more sophisticated, was in conventional terms more crude. At the same time, descriptive particularity loosened dramatically. As a result, a representational reading became still more enigmatic, even as the urge to "read" a picture grew stronger, owing to the insistence with which the work itself conveyed the artist's deep engagement with the subject. Much of the motif was blocked out, perplexing a viewer seeking to understand it and often rendering ambiguous the distinction between people and things. In a picture such as *The Second Visit* (fig. 4), such marks as there are lie exposed on the surface. Representing an interior scene in this way seemed so vestigial, rudimentary, and awkward as to make the viewer wonder what kind of thing this cryptic tablet might be. Yet it seemed insistently charged.

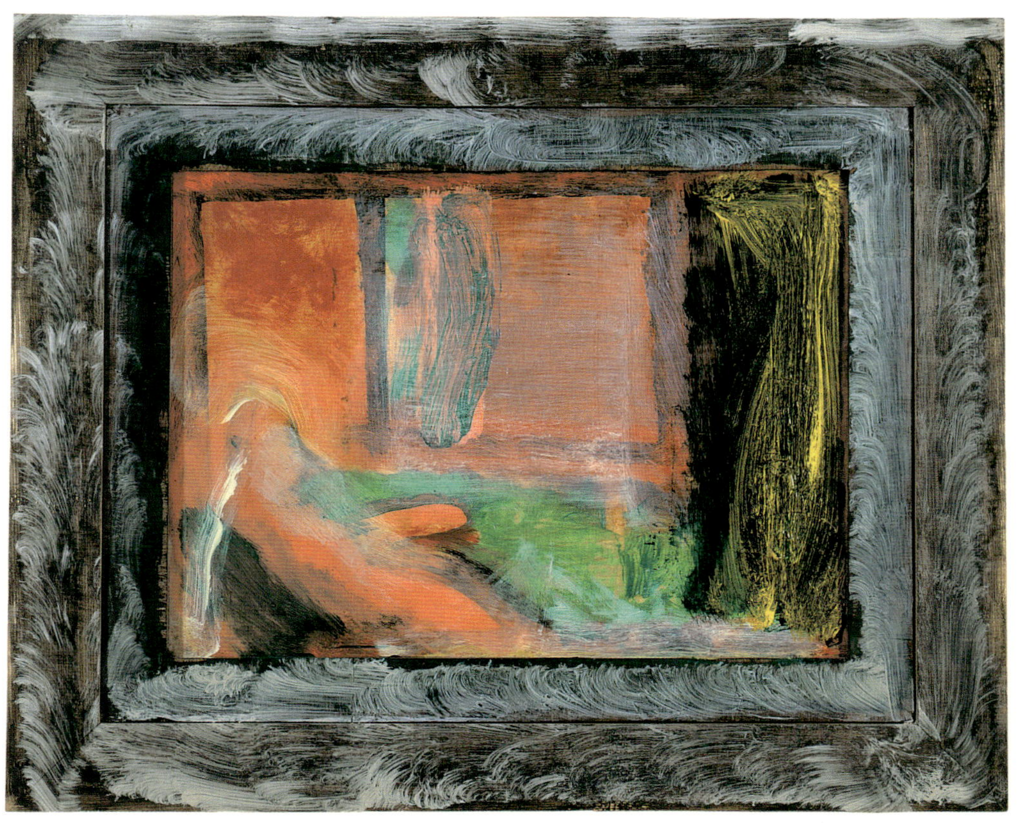

6. Howard Hodgkin, None But the Brave Deserves the Fair, 1981–84, oil on wood, 24¾ x 30 in. (62.8 x 76.2 cm). Private collection, New York.

In the 1960s and 1970s, more than before or since, many of Hodgkin's titles named particular friends, such as *Lawson, Underwood & Sleep* (fig. 5) or married couples. Any impression that Hodgkin's purpose was to document or comment on a stratum of the English art world is, however, misleading. Indeed, as mark, shape, and the viscosity of paint took on ever-greater freedom it could be sensed increasingly plainly that his work accorded primacy to his feelings. While the representation of people grew less explicit both in delineation and in titling, their

presence grew more palpable. Despite many instances of an almost Turner-like adumbration of physical intimacy (fig. 6), there was (and has remained) a strong complementary tendency for human presence and passion to be immanent in the very paint, through judgment of its hues and the eloquence of touch. The more "abstract" a picture, the more full it can often be, at once in human terms and in those of the alchemy of art.

On the face of it, the viewer of Hodgkin's recent pictures might have difficulty when confronted by what are at first sight substantially abstract works, of which the titles can be as specific as *Double Portrait*, *Pyjamas,* or *An Autumn Leaf* (nos. 14, 53, 29), or as intriguing as *You are My Sunshine* or *Hide and Seek* (nos. 56, 58). With their bold daubs and deliberated splotches, these paintings not only highlight abstract shapes but compel attention, no less strongly, to the frank physical reality of all materials employed in making a work. Found or fabricated supports are deployed in such a way as themselves to become major actors in the pictorial drama. One could be forgiven for concluding that this pronounced physical dialogue is the very subject of these paintings (and all the more so because that dialogue is so full and satisfying in its own right), yet this is not the case. Instead, in an ever-stronger insistence on the blunt material facts of the autonomous crafted object before one's eyes, Hodgkin's purpose is to give lasting form to the intensity of his feelings about a given experience (whether recent or long ago). The concentration with which these objects are imbued is sometimes all the greater for being achieved through kinds of gesture that, whether seemingly casual or, by contrast, methodical, might have been expected to preclude such a condition. Each object is obviously a separate thing from the subject that occasioned it, yet the urgency of Hodgkin's representational intent is the generator of its form. The richness of sensation—sensuous, intellectual, emotional, and referential—thus opened for the viewer cannot replicate the impulses that led to its appearance, but the object that is their vehicle is their extraordinary equivalent.

In statements that are by now widely familiar, Hodgkin has given the following explanations, among others, of his work and aims:

> I am a representational painter but not a painter of appearances. I paint representational pictures of emotional situations.[4]

> My pictures are finished when the subject comes back. I start out with the subject and naturally I have to remember first what it looked like, but it would also perhaps contain a great deal of feeling and sentiment. All of that has got to be somehow transmuted, transformed or made into a physical object, and when that happens, when that's finally been done, when the last physical marks have been put on and the subject comes back—which, after all, is usually the moment when the painting is at long last a coherent physical object—well, the painting's finished.... My pictures really finish themselves.[5]

> The only way an artist can communicate with the world at large is on the level of feeling. I think the function of the artist is to practice his art to such a level that like the soul leaving the body, it comes out into the world and affects other people.[6]

Though he studied at art schools in England, Hodgkin was particularly resistant to one of the dominant approaches to painting of the time, associated with the teaching of William Coldstream (1908–87). This attached special importance to painting from observation with careful accuracy and tonal sobriety. To Hodgkin the method was weak in feeling and severely constrained in its use of color. Despite exposure to many tendencies, he was essentially self-taught. He developed his own language of marks, the down to earth character of which seemed at first an unlikely vehicle for the breadth of expression to which he aspired.[7] By 1972 he had abandoned canvas, as support, in favor of wood, preferring both the resistance of its surface and its reinforcement of the object-quality that he sought in any picture. Accentuating this quality had the further advantage of emphasizing the fact that a finished work was a thing separate from himself. It was important to him that it should communicate to each viewer with unmediated directness. The centrality of a work's subject meant that a picture's title was also important. Though characteristically straightforward Hodgkin's titles, like the individual paintings they identify, suggest experience on many levels.

As with most distinctive artists, there are illuminating parallels between Hodgkin's daily life and the nature of his art. From an early age he has been fascinated by the artifice underlying the fabrication of objects, especially works of decorative and fine art, and is alert to the historical context of their creation and use. In his home environments the past seems alive. Its insistent presence in the here and now feels entirely natural. There is a continuum between Hodgkin's sensibility and the character of his paintings, carefully crafted objects in which a sense of the past (alongside a powerful one of the present) is increasingly pervasive. The highly personal form of his pictures comments on the history of the made object and also extends it. Changing and informal, his interiors have an un-smart straightforwardness and an unpretentiousness of use. Hodgkin's inclination towards singular artefacts (sometimes exceptional, but often of a utilitarian character) combines with his sense of space and color to make each thing in his surroundings unusually visible.[8]

Not surprisingly, the directness, exposure, and lack of fuss that characterize Hodgkin's spaces and the presence of objects within them are central qualities of his art (even though their function and effect there are necessarily different). Also evident in his painting, as in life, is his keen interest in the vagaries of human behavior, especially between people and in relation to literature, objects, and art. It encompasses the impassioned and the inconsequential, the recherché and the popular, the intimate life and issues of general concern. As he grows older the longstanding fragility of his personal boundary between relaxation and emotion seems to grow more pronounced, so that one can give way to the other in an instant. There is a direct link between the two, for he is generous both in friendship and in response to the potency of art, yet easily overwhelmed by others' appreciation of what he is trying to achieve, or on the other hand by disregard of art's seriousness. He asserts the artist's commitment as a moral imperative. This, along with the primacy of feeling in the making of any work, means that for him (as for so many artists) the act of creation is both unavoidable

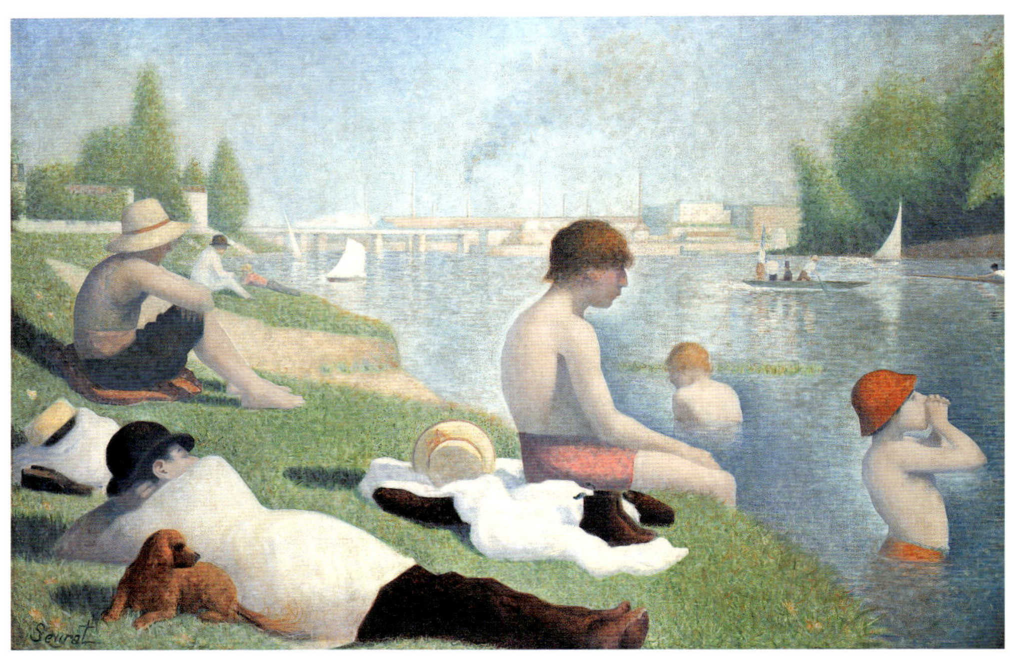

7. Georges-Pierre Seurat, Bathers at Asnières, 1884, oil on canvas, 79 x 118 in. (201 x 300 cm). National Gallery, London.

and often agonizing. Hodgkin's predisposition towards directness affects all aspects of his painting. Equally keen in art on extravagance and on austerity when their expression is unmitigated, he is against good taste and averse to half measures. Though active in complex ways, his pictures are articulated with rigor.

A painting by Hodgkin is a direct expression of memories and feelings. The form of the object through which that subject is expressed is also very direct; and the viewer experiences with equal directness both the object and the emotion that is integral with it. Yet paradoxically, there is no means of ensuring that the particulars of the originating memory and emotion are

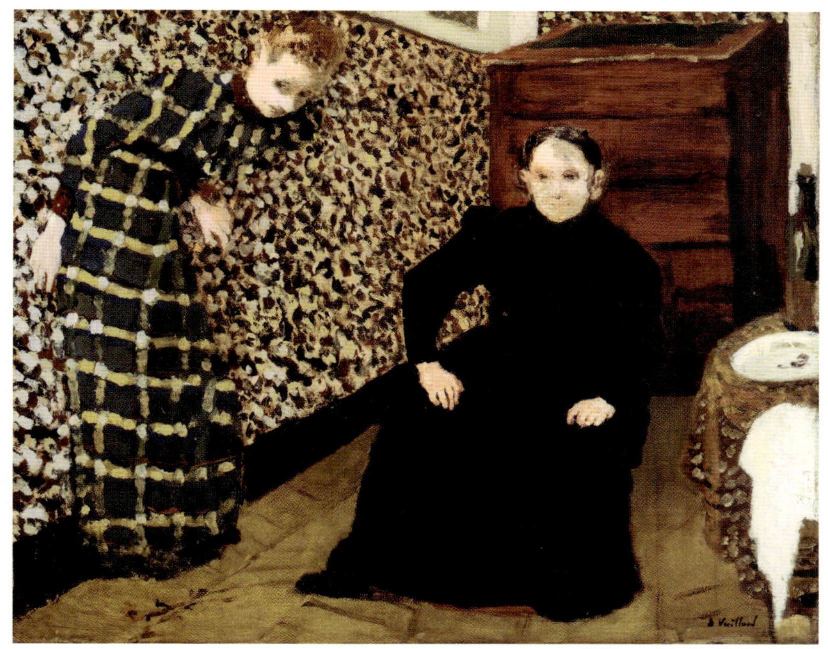

8. Edouard Vuillard, Interior, Mother and Sister of the Artist, 1893, oil on canvas, 18¼ x 22¼ in. (46.3 x 56.5 cm). Gift of Mrs. Saidie A. May (141.1934), Museum of Modern Art, New York.

communicated to the viewer directly, or even at all. On occasion this may happen, but on other occasions a seemingly clear grasp of their nature may actually contradict it. Still more paradoxically, however, this is not a problem.

For the viewer of Seurat's *Bathers at Asnières* (fig. 7), Degas's *Hélène Rouart in her Father's Study*,[9] Vuillard's *Interior, Mother and Sister of the Artist* (fig. 8), or Matisse's *The Moroccans*[10] (all paintings Hodgkin admires deeply), the powerful effect, though bound up with the subject of the title, goes far beyond it. Though each picture is plainly imbued with emotion for the artist who made it and, like Hodgkin's works, conveys emotion directly, we have no means of defining the emotion the artist felt. Though

often rich in specific suggestions, painting is multivalent by virtue of one person fusing not only appearance but also feeling, with paint.

TWO ENGLISH AFFINITIES

All the artists just named were French, and it is perhaps not surprising that one of the English painters with whose work Hodgkin's has numerous affinities is (the German-born) Walter Sickert.[11] As Hodgkin would do, he looked to French example, is associated with Degas and Vuillard, and opened new territory for English art, while also transcending it. Like Hodgkin, Sickert lived and worked at various times in London, Normandy, and the vicinity of Bath and always painted with a strong sense of the art of

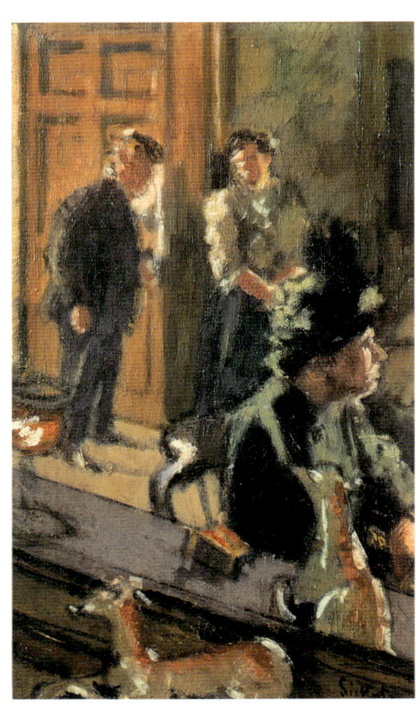

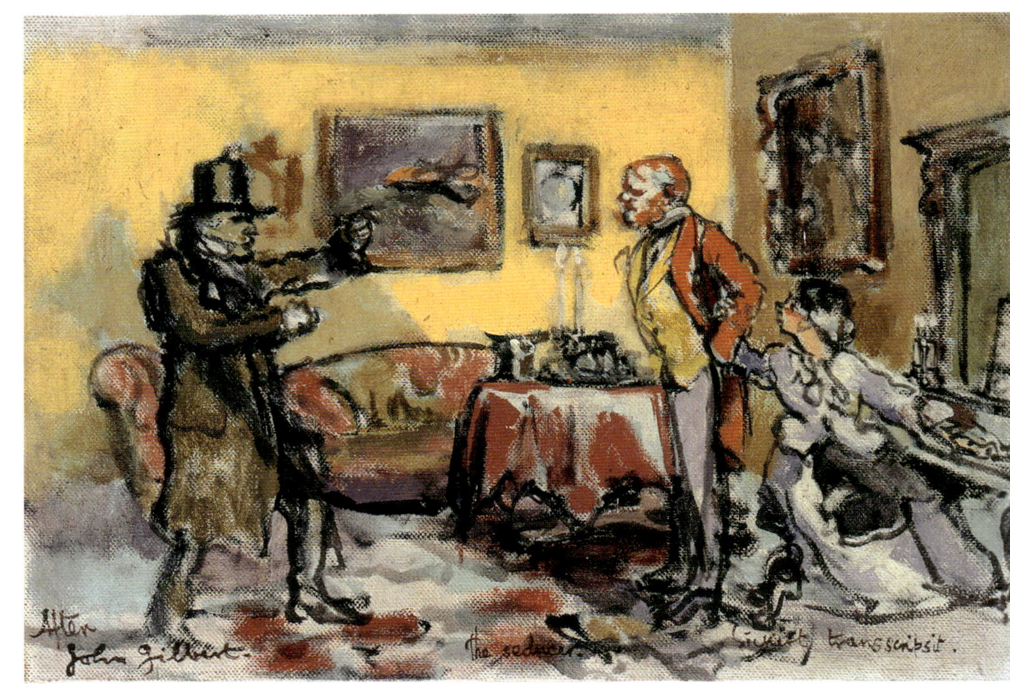

the past. Venice was vital to Sickert, as to Hodgkin. Unlike Hodgkin's, Sickert's pictures were developed not from memories but from visual documents (themselves permeated with memories, recent or distant). For many years these immediate sources were drawings from observation (on which, for example, fig. 9 depends). Later in his career they were nineteenth-century engravings, of which fig. 10 (inscribed "Sickert transscripsit") is a typical outcome, and contemporary photographs (ranging from snapshots to news and theater photographs and studio portraits), as used for fig. 11. As is the case with Hodgkin's memories, it was what Sickert did with his sources that counted. By acts of selection, he greatly concentrated the presence of the subject,

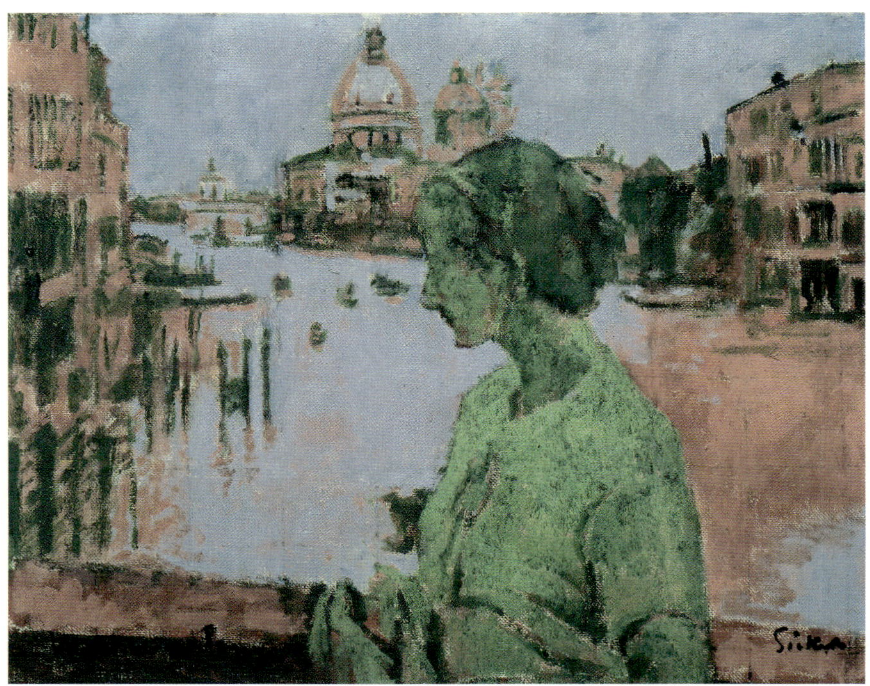

Facing page, left:
9. Walter Sickert, A Few Words: Off to the Pub, ca. 1912, oil on canvas, 20 x 12 in. (50.8 x 30.5 cm). Private Collection.

Facing page, right:
10. Walter Sickert, The Seducer, ca. 1929–30, oil on canvas, 16½ x 24 in. (42.5 x 62.5 cm). Tate, London.

This page:
11. Walter Sickert, Variation on Peggy, 1934–35, oil on canvas, 22¾ x 28¼ in. (57.8 x 71.8 cm). Tate, London.

giving the viewer the sense of entering into the represented scene. Where (as often) the subject was a person or an interpersonal situation, narrative and psychological interest was heightened. At the same time paint as a material, and its exposed physical handling, were accorded prominence; as Hodgkin would do, Sickert combined great deliberation and control with painterly freedom. As his career progressed, he increasingly created color relationships and effects of startling originality, while also drawing frank attention to the roughness of his supports (unusually coarse canvas). Sickert imbued low-life subjects with new life and in his late paintings used color and touch to transform amateur snapshots or snatched press photographs into resonant human presences, as if from some stranger and more colorful world. When one considers these metamorphoses, or Hodgkin's of "banal" individual marks on discarded breadboards or worm-eaten wood, one is reminded of Sickert's observation that: "The artist is he who can take a piece of flint and wring out of it drops of attar of roses."[12]

With Sickert's pictures, as with Hodgkin's, the work declares the artist's engagement with its subject, but for the viewer there is often a degree of ambiguity as to the nature of the artist's role in the situation that is the work's focus. Is he just a keen observer or is he a participant in a fuller sense? A major difference is that with Hodgkin we are at least clear as to the artist's identity. With Sickert this shifts, in a restless change of self-created personae (and of costume) that links to his experience as an actor and to his continuing obsession with the stage. Analogy with the theater, however, provides parallels between the two artists. The subject of each work by Hodgkin is the artist's emotion. The place in which we not only observe it but participate in it (as in the special conditions of the theater) is a concentrated arena (the art object), from which the action is transmitted with great intensity. This calls to mind the heightened human interaction of opera, loved by Hodgkin and framed by a proscenium arch. In many of Hodgkin's emphatically "framed" pictures the "actors" are, indeed, people in settings, but sometimes (as when the curtain rises) they are landscapes. Irrespective of the subject (or of a picture's size or its degree of pictorial excitement), however, a Hodgkin painting has the character of a dramatic statement or act. This, too, obtained increasingly in Sickert's work as he grew older.

Hodgkin's titles are specific and to the point. However, they not only identify individual works but rouse interest in their meanings, and for the viewer their effect is often enigmatic. Sickert's titling practice can pose similar problems (compounded, in his case, on occasion, by a mischievous willingness to provide alternative titles, and thus "meanings," to a single picture). With both artists, alongside a picture's undeviating purpose, an element of enigma is often associated with one of humor. This connects with their shared interest in colloquialisms and specifically in popular entertainment, finding particular common ground in responsiveness to the words of popular songs, with their *double-entendres* and often a power of sentiment for which their succint words are the vehicle. With each artist, material that may be light in itself (and delighted in, on that level) is employed in an artistic process upon the seriousness of which both insist, and that can take the artist to instinctual extremes.

Hodgkin's obsession with language embraces his titles and his entire system of mark-making. In each area, his concern with precision is complemented by one with multiple meaning. It might be thought easy to divide Hodgkin's titles between categories of subject (still life, conditions of weather, landscape, states of being, fragments of conversation, aphorisms, popular song titles, etc.). When this is attempted, however, it rapidly becomes evident how difficult it is to confine a title to a single category. Often this is because a title can be interpreted simultaneously as referring to a material fact and to an emotional state; or a commonplace figure of speech can read as reminiscence of an event. Of course many titles are incapable of more than one meaning, in themselves; attached to a painting, however, they can function like the opening of a story.

Some Hodgkin titles are of the utmost banality or are catchy phrases that have become empty through over-use. The typical effect of his choice of such a phrase is simultaneously to reinforce its hackneyed character and to open it up as if it had never been thought about before. This is one of the many ways in which Hodgkin works like a poet. Willing to draw his material from anywhere, his instinct is to express complexity through simplicity. He is also like a novelist. As he observed in 1981: "My work is entirely sustained by experiences of one sort or another. Somebody once said, 'well, you must have to live like a novelist to paint pictures like this.' Which is true."[13] More recently he stated that: "I've never had any real colleagues as a painter. My artist colleagues are writers."[14] The remarkable *Writers on Howard Hodgkin*, published in 2006, does nothing to undermine this view.

Hodgkin was familiar from childhood with Bloomsbury painting and applied art. While this was stimulating, it probably did not encompass until the 1960s the boldly colored paintings made by Vanessa Bell and Duncan Grant around 1914, which for many years were little known. His art was in any case not influenced by theirs. A key Bloomsbury figure with whom perhaps he has closer affinities (but never knew) was Bell's sister, Virginia Woolf. Six years before publishing a biography of her close friend (and Hodgkin's cousin) Roger Fry, Woolf wrote her memorable text on one of Fry's chief sparring-partners in art, *Walter Sickert: a Conversation* (fig. 12). The text makes one feel that had she been alive today Woolf would have been keenly interested in Hodgkin's art. Fascinated by the silent world of the painter, she acknowledges the power of his or her art to convey without words how something is in life, and she praises the perception by Sickert, in particular, of the whole circumstances of a particular past moment. Woolf has been reported by Frank Kermode to have described her task as a writer as being:

> to cut away all superfluity and 'give the moment whole....Say that the moment is a combination of thought; sensation; the voice of the sea.' At the time she was working on *The Waves*. It was a task to be performed only by the act of writing: 'nothing makes a whole,' she remarked in 1933, 'except when I am writing.'[15]

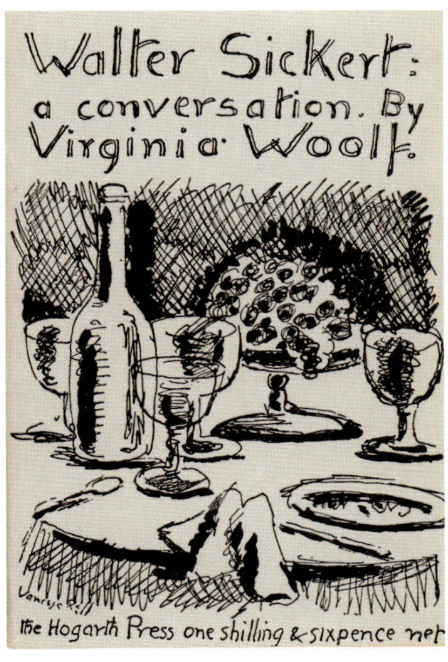

12. Vanessa Bell, Cover design for Virginia Woolf, *Walter Sickert: a Conversation* (London: Leonard and Virginia Woolf at the Hogarth Press, 1934). Beinecke Rare Book and Manuscript Library, Yale University.

These last nine quoted words of Woolf's are analogous to Hodgkin's impulse to make a whole of a remembered moment, in terms of *his* kind of art.[16] Kermode goes on to enumerate the multiple levels of reference that are present in a characteristically simple and straightforward-seeming passage in a novel by Woolf. Noting her concern, all at once, with matter of fact detail, with existential issues, and with the complex interaction of the very elements (words) of the "simple" medium she employs, he observes: "This is work for the reader, and the demands on the reader are almost exorbitant." So they are in a painting by Hodgkin, for all its initial appearance of ease.

Clive Bell wrote of Virginia Woolf that: "almost painterlike vision...is what distinguishes her from all her contemporaries."[17] As Lily Briscoe considers the painting on which she is working, Woolf gives her these thoughts:

> Beautiful and bright it should be on the surface, feathery and evanescent, one color melting into another like the colors on a butterfly's wing; but beneath the fabric must be clamped together with bolts of iron. It was to be a thing you could ruffle with your breath; and a thing you could not dislodge with a team of horses.[18]

CONTAINER, OBJECT & PLACE

Hodgkin's important debts to Seurat, Degas, early Vuillard, and Matisse have been widely explored in interviews and by commentators. He has painted explicit tributes to all four. Hodgkin's admiration for each of these painters for forging a language of his own is of a kind that extends backwards through art, applying, for example, to Poussin and to David and forward

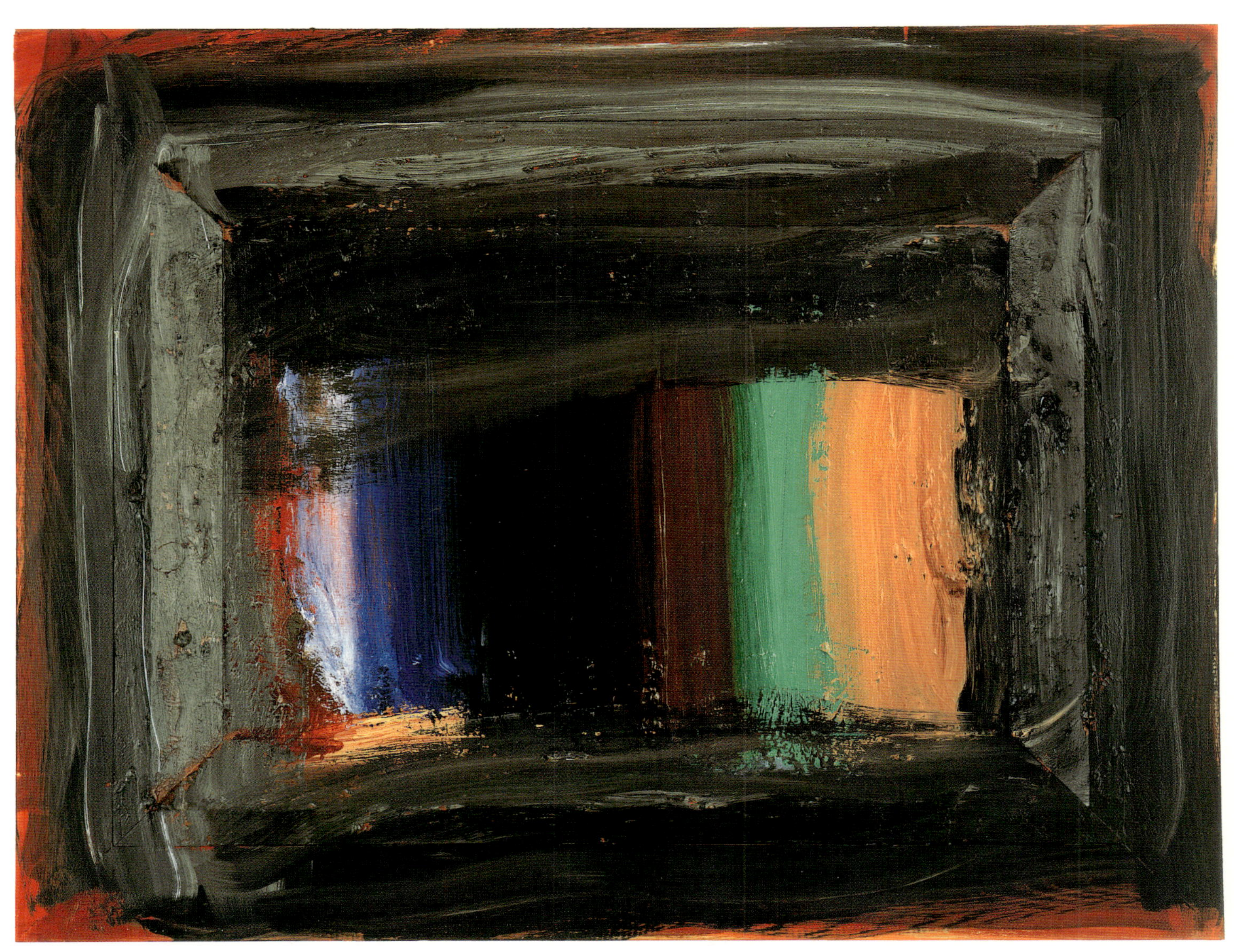

13. Howard Hodgkin, After Morandi, 1989–94, oil on wood, 21 x 27 in. (53.3 x 68.6 cm). Collection of James H. Duffy, New York.

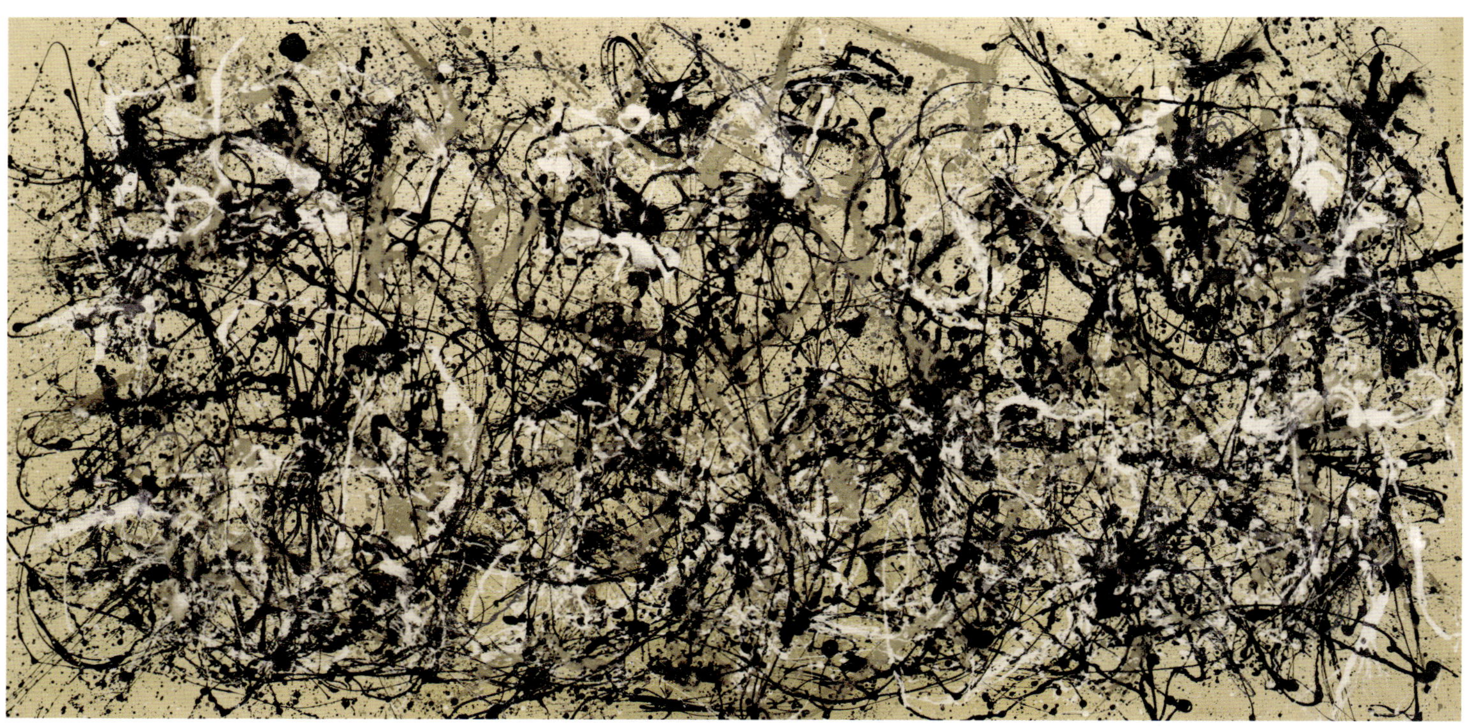

14. Jackson Pollock, Autumn Rhythm (Number 30), 1950, enamel on canvas, 105 x 207 in. (266.7 x 525.8 cm). The Metropolitan Museum of Art, George A. Hearn Fund, 1957 (57.92).

to later Mondrian, and to Morandi (fig. 13) and Ellsworth Kelly. Several of these artists helped intensify perception of a painting as a physical object, another of Hodgkin's central concerns.

A key stage in this story was Abstract Expressionism, of which Hodgkin had vivid experience in the famous Tate exhibitions of 1956 and 1959 and in the intervening Pollock retrospective at the Whitechapel Art Gallery in 1958. Despite interesting suggestions of affinity between Hodgkin and Surrealism (itself a strong thread in Abstract Expressionist painting, including Pollock's), it was perhaps the enhanced prominence of the picture surface in the work of Pollock, in particular, that had the strongest long-term impact on him (fig. 14). Crucially, he experienced this in conjunction with Pollock's extraordinary gestural control, his jettisoning of inessentials and his willingness to go the whole way, painting with the whole person.

By 1992 (when the period covered by the present selection begins) Hodgkin had been painting for some fifteen years in a manner sympathetic—in his own distinct language—to the touch of de Kooning or late Picasso; yet his work also relates, of course, to that of his contemporaries. In their very different formats, the paintings of Jasper Johns and Robert Ryman as well as Minimal sculpture, such as that of Judd, took the focus on material fact further still.[19] In such a context it was natural to attend in a heightened degree to any painting's support and to exactly what was laid on it (and in what way). Hodgkin's pictures, however, positively provoked a more searching scrutiny. In that examination the location of every fraction of deposited material counts, as do hairline divisions between abutted boards or individual beads of paint enduringly fixed in the declivities where they lodged when a loaded brushstroke crossed the raised bands of a "framed" periphery. His pictures encourage the eye to journey across the terrain of a painted surface in detail, alert to the fact that it is anything but a plain. This brings increased awareness of braces or other structural reinforcements, of wood having been distressed in an earlier existence, of nail holes, of the raised filigree beneath old gilding on plaster mouldings, and not least of the different abutting gradients of "framing" slips (old or new) in the carpentered construction on which he paints.

Pictures of recent years present innumerable variations in the topography of the route from a work's extreme outer edge to the plane surface that customarily lies at the center.

Indeed, to a greater degree than is normal for paintings, each Hodgkin picture establishes itself as a *place*. It is a world of its own, in two senses at once. It offers both the world that it represents—the particular moment or memory, which is of one substance with the painter's emotion about it—and the tangible, measurable object before one's gaze, about the real nature of which there can be no ambiguity. Though each of these interdependent worlds is of compelling immediacy in its own right, they, too, are of one substance; as one is explored, so is the other. In this process there can even be strange kinds of cross-over. The work is both a picture and a place, but the picture may be *of* a place. Even more oddly, it is possible for the nature of the represented content to communicate to the viewer in one, as indisputable fact—as Hodgkin intends—while the literal physical facts of the painting's component parts read, in their interaction, as an exotic invention that it is difficult to believe anyone could have thought of giving the form it takes.

There is a close connection between these ways in which a painting by Hodgkin is a world of its own and the importance of its frame-like component. This can be an actual former frame or a purpose-made frame-like structure or marks painted by Hodgkin in a frame-like configuration (or any combination of these). The frame-like element does not, of course, perform the normal function of a frame, since even if it once was an actual frame it is now subsumed into a picture, of which it is itself an equal part. Not only does it accentuate the illusionism of the configuration it encloses[20] (which constitutes another thing within a thing) but also helps mark off the phenomenon that is the painting from whatever else is in the room where it is seen. The need to do that is one reason why Hodgkin chooses strong wall colors for the display of his pictures (from which surfaces the pictures stand out with emphatic individuality). It is also a contributory factor in his need for substantial constructs on which to paint.

Though many pictures flaunt the previous function of the frames that now form part of Hodgkin's support (and of a picture's imagery), quite a number of his works are, less evidently, painted on the backs of former frames. However, when the identity of a former frame is clear, the place of the picture it previously framed is taken by something else. A fresh support has to have been fitted into the former frame (or that frame altered to fit the new element). Both the satisfying character of the "fit" and the atmosphere of Hodgkin's work as a whole, with its keen evident interest in the design and history of frames, make individual works speak—however much else is going in them—of a whole subculture of frame-making and connoisseurship. While some of the former frames are special, others are grandiose or run-of-the-mill. In a strange paradox, however, though Hodgkin is undermining the purpose for which these frames were made, his works convey a certain affection for the convention that they recall. They even give the vestige of an after-life to the former ensemble of picture and frame of which they were once a part.

In subverting the original purpose of a former frame by dissolving the distinction between frame and picture, Hodgkin introduces further creative contradictions. The "picture" it now "frames" is in reality only part of a picture. In some works, moreover, the seemingly-framed picture is not a "picture" at all, being substantially a monochrome expanse. But even when the central, "framed" picture surface bears animated marks, it is often the case that Hodgkin cannot have known, when painting, quite what configuration that surface would finally present, since vigorous, seemingly free brushstrokes travel over "frame," "slip," and "picture plane" indiscriminately. Typically of the ambiguities that abound in these works, it is strangely satisfying that these purposeful-seeming former or specially mocked-up frames should enclose something that both is and is not an accident. Whether taking the form of a conventional frame or of bands of paint he has applied, the frame-like forms in a Hodgkin do indeed frame elements of the painting; yet, in their capacity as part of the work, they simultaneously break down the barriers between the viewer and the action.

SOME KINSHIPS

Frames are, of course, meant to serve the images they display. In attracting so much attention to themselves in Hodgkin's art those frames that did once serve earlier paintings by other artists do, as suggested earlier, connect with many post-1960 artists' concern to expose all the elements of a work with maxi-

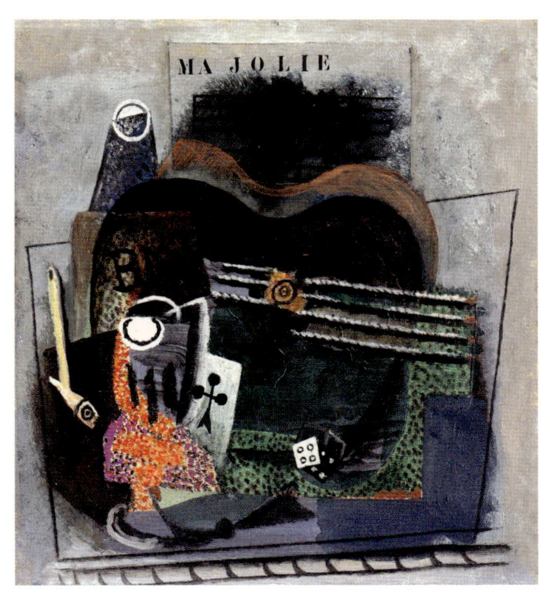

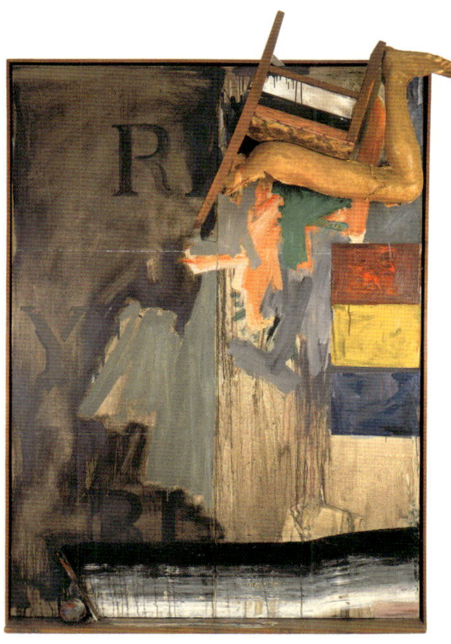

15. Pablo Picasso, Ma Jolie, 1914, oil on canvas, 17¾ x 16⅛ in. (45 x 41 cm). Nationalgalerie, Museum Berggruen, Staatliche Museen zu Berlin, Berlin.

16. Jasper Johns, Watchman, 1964, oil on canvas with objects (two panels), 85 x 60¼ in. (215.9 x 153 cm). Location Unknown.

mum frankness. They also remind one of Picasso's paintings of around 1913–15, in which materials that had earlier lives are brought together with paint, while in others such an effect is suggested illusionistically (fig. 15). They remind one, too, of the complex paintings-with-objects of Jasper Johns (fig. 16). All three artists introduce non-art material that previously had another kind of function into the enclosed, "non-functional" world of a work of art, while reflecting on human experience outside art, as well as on art itself. Their ways of doing so combine arresting public statement with strong private content. The resulting work is at once assertively frank and richly mysterious.

There are interesting parallels with the work of Cy Twombly, who is of the same generation as Hodgkin and Johns. He, too, introduces previously non-art materials, chiefly in his sculpture,

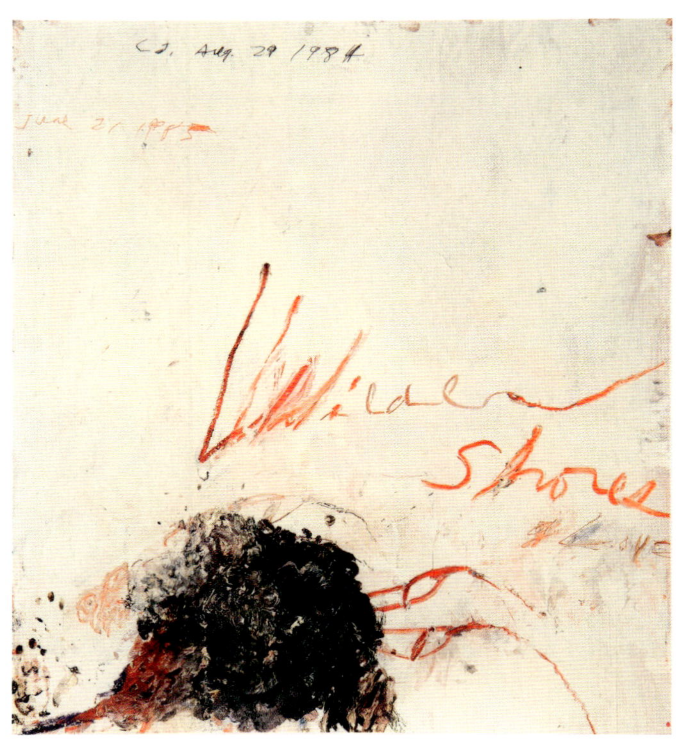

17. Cy Twombly, Wilder Shores of Love, 1985, oil, crayon and pencil on plywood, 55⅛ x 47¼ in. (140 x 120 cm). Private collection.

while as a painter, affected by Abstract Expressionism, he works, as does Hodgkin, in a world of sensation that embraces spareness and extreme luxury. For both artists, past art and literature is alive now. Each lives surrounded by artefacts from the past and is drawn to the Mediterranean world. The erotic is a key element in the work of each, as is a sense of human relationship, of nature, of place and of the seasons. For each, directness in the act of applying paint is vital. Paint itself takes on extraordinary life in their hands. Mark-making that some would consider offhand and inconsequential is the medium of engagement and urgency (fig. 17).

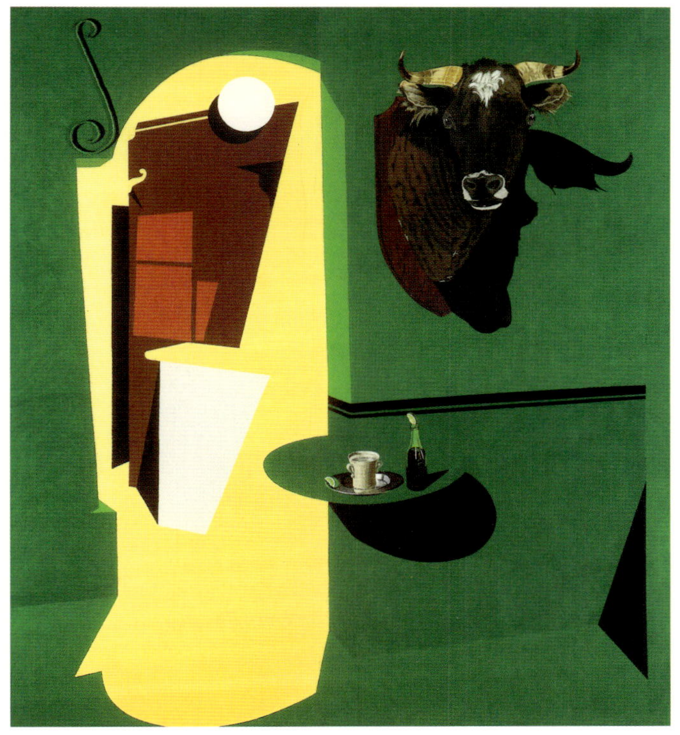

18. Patrick Caulfield, Hemingway Never Ate Here, 1999, acrylic and collage on canvas, 84 x 75 in. (213.5 x 190.5 cm). Tate, London.

In a final comparison, it is helpful to return to painting of a contrasting kind of refinement. Hodgkin has already been quoted saying he has had no real colleagues as a painter, but he has long expressed a special regard for the work and person of Patrick Caulfield (fig. 18). Idiomatically, Caulfield's work is strikingly unlike Hodgkin's of recent decades (though there are significant affinities with Hodgkin's work up to the mid-1970s), but an inner sympathy runs throughout.[21] This is seen in a powerful feeling of human presence (even though both artists depict figures only infrequently); in a fascination with styles of design and decoration and their use in daily life; in the concentrated use of

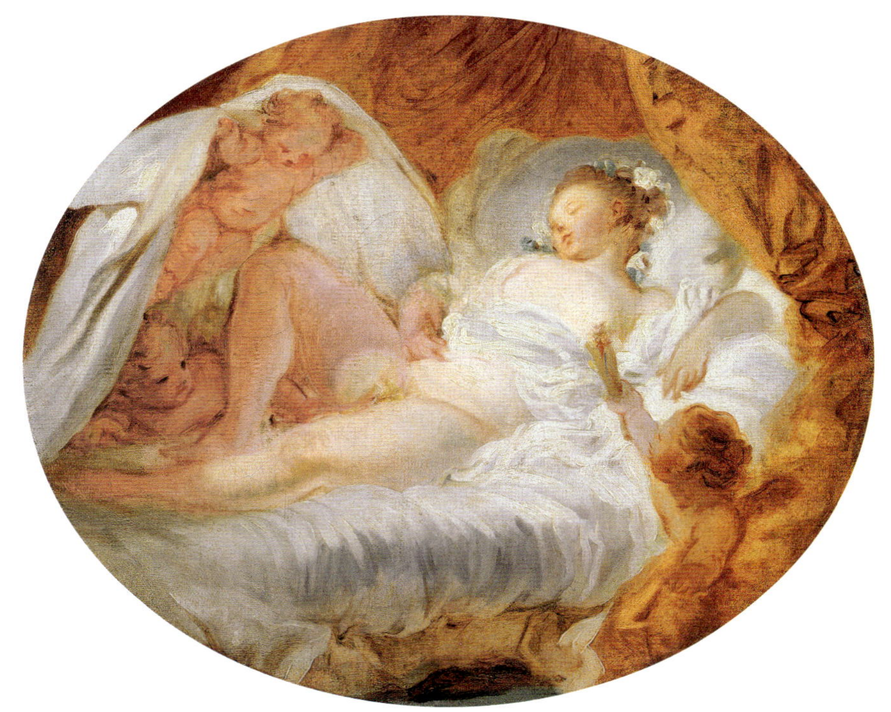

19. Jean-Honoré Fragonard, Le Feu aux poudres, ca. 1764, oil on canvas, oval, 14½ x 17¾ in. (37 x 45 cm). Musée du Louvre, Paris.

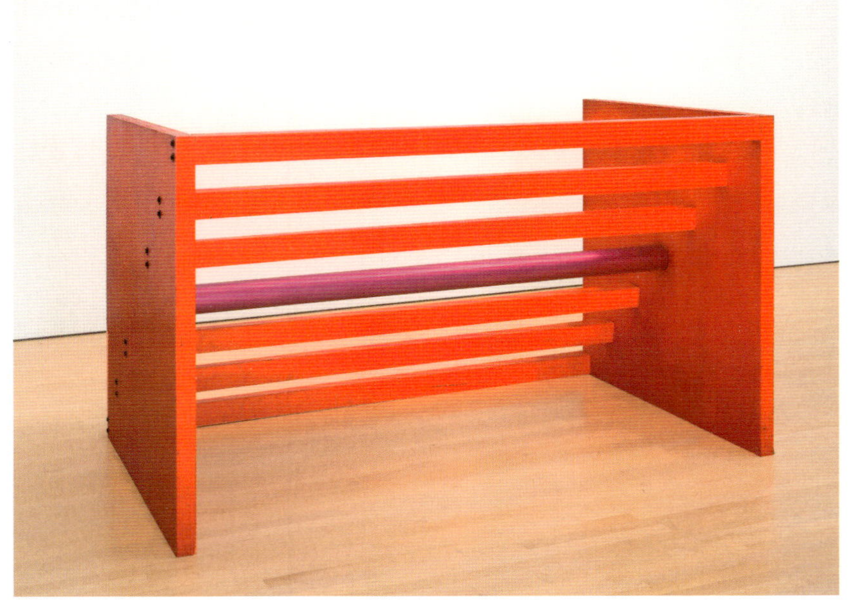

20. Donald Judd, Untitled, 1963–75, light-cadmium-red oil on wood and purple lacquer on aluminium, 48$\frac{1}{16}$ x 83 x 48$\frac{1}{16}$ in. (122 x 210.8 x 122 cm). National Gallery of Canada, Ottawa.

color in often surprising ways; in extreme deliberation; and above all in the evocation of a moment, imbued with atmosphere and with the painter's strong emotion. It was probably with fellow feeling that, in a published conversation between the two artists, Caulfield twice described Hodgkin's painting as "tightrope walking."[22] When one compares Caulfield's fastidiously lucid images with the dramatically more free though actually no less lucid images of Hodgkin, one gains further perspective on Hodgkin's observation that he always wanted to be "a classical artist . . . where all emotion, all feeling, turns into a beautifully articulated anonymous architectural memorial at the other end."[23]

Hodgkin being *sui generis*, none of these comparisons can be at all exact. Still less precisely, a recent Hodgkin can call forth extraordinary musings, as if, for example, a Fragonard bedroom scene (fig. 19) were fused with an early, pre-industrial sculpture by Judd (fig. 20). But such imaginings are on the side, for a Hodgkin recalls the viewer directly to the paradoxes that the work itself declares. Marks are at once banal and sophisticated. The awkward and the slight prove to be considered, exact, and rich. Rawness and opulence combine. A past moment and resulting later studio acts (also past) together yield something that—however long its gestation—we experience with great immediacy, in a permanent present.

Notes

1. In this and many other pictures, a sense of figural presence does not hinge on the accuracy of any guess at how the picture represents a figure or figures (if, indeed, it does so at all).
2. Hodgkin first knew it when it was occupied by his cousin Margery Fry, who lived there from the year before he was born until her death in 1958. Chairman of the Howard League for Penal Reform, and a campaigner for the abolition of capital punishment, she brought Marion Richardson in to teach painting to young prisoners. Fry was unconventional, uncompromising, and direct (perhaps family traits). After her death the house was occupied by Pamela Diamand (d. 1985), daughter of Margery's brother, Roger Fry.
3. "How to be an Artist," *The Burlington Magazine*, September 1982, pp. 552–4.
4. Quoted by John Elderfield, "Mystery in Method," in Marla Price, *Howard Hodgkin: The Complete Paintings* (London, 2006), p. 14.
5. "Howard Hodgkin interviewed by David Sylvester," in *Howard Hodgkin: Forty Paintings 1973–84*, ed. Nicholas Serota (London, 1984), pp. 97–106, published on the occasion of Hodgkin's exhibition in the British Pavilion, XLI Venice Biennale and tour to USA, Germany, and Britain.
6. Quoted by Timothy Hyman, "Howard Hodgkin: making a riddle out of the solution," in *Art and Design*, vol. 1, September 1985, pp. 6–11.
7. See Hodgkin in his 1984 interview with David Sylvester, (note 5 above): "To be an artist now, you have to make your own language.... Gradually, as you make your own language, the more you learn to do the more you can do, and the more you include." See also "Howard Hodgkin on Seurat," interview with John-Paul Stonard in Courtauld Institute of Art e-publication *Art & Architecture*, 2006, "What I admire most [in Seurat] is his instant ability, in the face of nature... to make a language of his own," www.artandarchitecture.org.uk.
8. In his 1984 interview with David Sylvester (see note 5 above), Hodgkin said: "It's the moods, the way people live in India, that has probably influenced my painting very much... everything is visible, somehow, there." Hodgkin has been visiting India since 1964 and has painted many Indian subjects. Past and present are evident in his own surroundings through Eastern as well as Western art. In the 2006 interview with John-Paul Stonard (see note 7 above), Hodgkin said: "the physical control one sees in Seurat is so relaxed, so simple, so straightforward and so visible that the effect is breathtaking."
9. The National Gallery, London.
10. The Museum of Modern Art, New York.
11. While this essay addresses the nature of Hodgkin's painting, it does not attempt a detailed account of his connections with the British or foreign art of his time, or earlier. Among many authors on this subject see James Meyer's impressive "Hodgkin's Body" in *Howard Hodgkin*, ed. Nicholas Serota, exh. cat., Irish Museum of Modern Art, Dublin; Tate Britain, London; Museo Nacional Centro de Arte Reina Sofía, Madrid (London, 2006), pp. 19–60.
12. Walter Sickert, "A Perfect Modern" [S.F. Gore], in *The New Age*, April 2, 1914.
13. "Howard Hodgkin: the wild card in the post-modernist pack talks to Edward Lucie-Smith," in *Quarto*, no.19, July 1981, pp. 15–17.
14. Interview with Ann Temkin in *Contemporary voices: works from the UBS Art Collection*, exh. cat., the Museum of Modern Art, New York (New York, 2005), pp. 66–75.
15. Frank Kermode, "Introduction" to Virginia Woolf, *Between the Acts* (Oxford, 1992), p. xviii.
16. John Elderfield has described Hodgkin's painting process as "one of continual layering until a point is reached where the multiple fragments appear to collapse onto each other and coalesce, as if what we see had been painted in one go. This restoration of unity to heterogeneous, disconnected instants is, literally, making the past present in the sticky continuum of the paint. But, because we are shown the fragments as well as their

coalescing, we can see the fissures in the fabric as well as the continuum, the temporality as well as the simultaneity." ("Mystery in Method", in Price, *Complete Paintings*, p. 22).

17. Clive Bell, "Virginia Woolf," in *The Dial*, vol. 77, December 1924, p. 459. Reprinted in Robin Majumdar and Allen McLaurin, eds., *Virginia Woolf: the Critical Heritage* (London, 1975).
18. Virginia Woolf, *To the Lighthouse* (London, 1927, reprinted Oxford, 2000), p. 231.
19. In January 1968 it was Hodgkin, then in the middle of the "Mr & Mrs" phase of his imagery, who first urged me, enthusiastically, to view one of Richard Long's early floor sculptures, *A Circle of Sticks*, on show in *Young Contemporaries*, Royal Institute Galleries, Piccadilly, London, January–February 1968 (not catalogued).
20. As Hodgkin has often pointed out, it also "protects" the memory / emotion that is represented.
21. And both artists admired the work of Stuart Davis from an early age (Hodgkin from when he was a child in the USA).
22. "Howard Hodgkin and Patrick Caulfield in conversation," in *Art Monthly*, July–August 1984, no. 78, pp. 1, 4–6.
23. Interview by David Sylvester (see note 5 above), p. 105.

AFTER WORDS

ANTHONY LANE

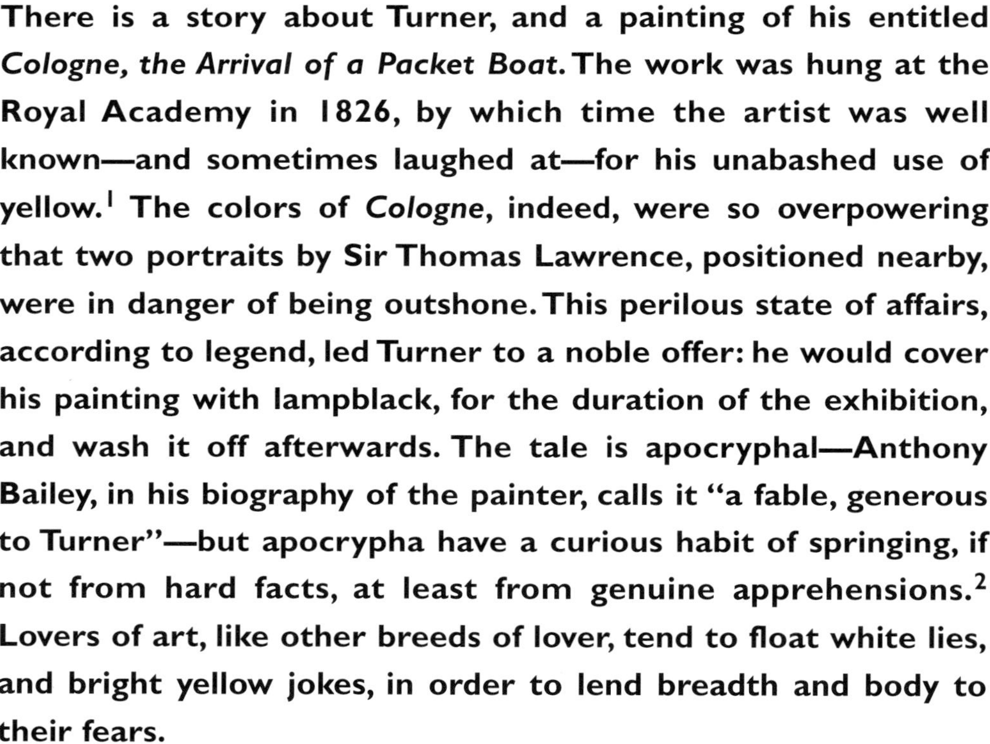

There is a story about Turner, and a painting of his entitled *Cologne, the Arrival of a Packet Boat.* The work was hung at the Royal Academy in 1826, by which time the artist was well known—and sometimes laughed at—for his unabashed use of yellow.[1] The colors of *Cologne*, indeed, were so overpowering that two portraits by Sir Thomas Lawrence, positioned nearby, were in danger of being outshone. This perilous state of affairs, according to legend, led Turner to a noble offer: he would cover his painting with lampblack, for the duration of the exhibition, and wash it off afterwards. The tale is apocryphal—Anthony Bailey, in his biography of the painter, calls it "a fable, generous to Turner"—but apocrypha have a curious habit of springing, if not from hard facts, at least from genuine apprehensions.[2] Lovers of art, like other breeds of lover, tend to float white lies, and bright yellow jokes, in order to lend breadth and body to their fears.

What lingers around this fable, after almost two hundred years, are two related thoughts. First, there is the thought of Turner himself, swinging his pot of lampblack; to shadow and shroud your achievement, so as to allow the work of another, less tumultuous talent to have its time in the sun, is an act both of vast assurance, bordering on arrogance, and of literal self-effacement. It says out loud, "No, please, after you," and also, in a whispered aside, "Yet I am what they have really come to see; I cannot help my yellows; I am solar-powered." This leads us directly to the second thought, which concerns the tangle—inextricable long before Turner, and still not teased apart even now—

of British social mores and British art. To what purpose, precisely, and in whose service, does the painter toil? Is ferocity of color, or strength of form, something of which to be proud, or something for which one is obliged, at least in company, to apologize? To put the matter at its bluntest and most archaic: what happens when the artist and the gentleman collide?

This is not a question, I hasten to add, that would have troubled Jackson Pollock. He had quite enough collisions in his life already. Nor, on the other hand, would it have made any sense to Van Dyck; he knew better than anyone what a gentleman consisted of, and painted as many examples of the species as any other painter of his rank, but the idea of a tension, let alone a violence, disturbing the relation between his calling and his status would have struck him as absurd. As a youthful prodigy, he worked as an apprentice in an Antwerp guild; he was employed by James I in 1620, knighted by Charles I a dozen years later, and married shortly afterwards to the daughter of an English peer. That is an upward path, not a tussle, and Henry James glanced beautifully at the collusive aspect of Van Dyck's art when he noted a portrait of the Duke of Richmond that hung in Burlington House in 1877. "The gentleman's yellow hair falls upon his satin mantle, and his face, which is not handsome, is touchingly grave. Such a give-and-take of gentlemanliness between painter and model is surely nowhere else to be seen."[3] Giving and taking: as so often in Britain, the social ideal is tinged with the mercantile, as if those on the make were tacitly trading portions of their soul. It is a fruitful arrangement that can

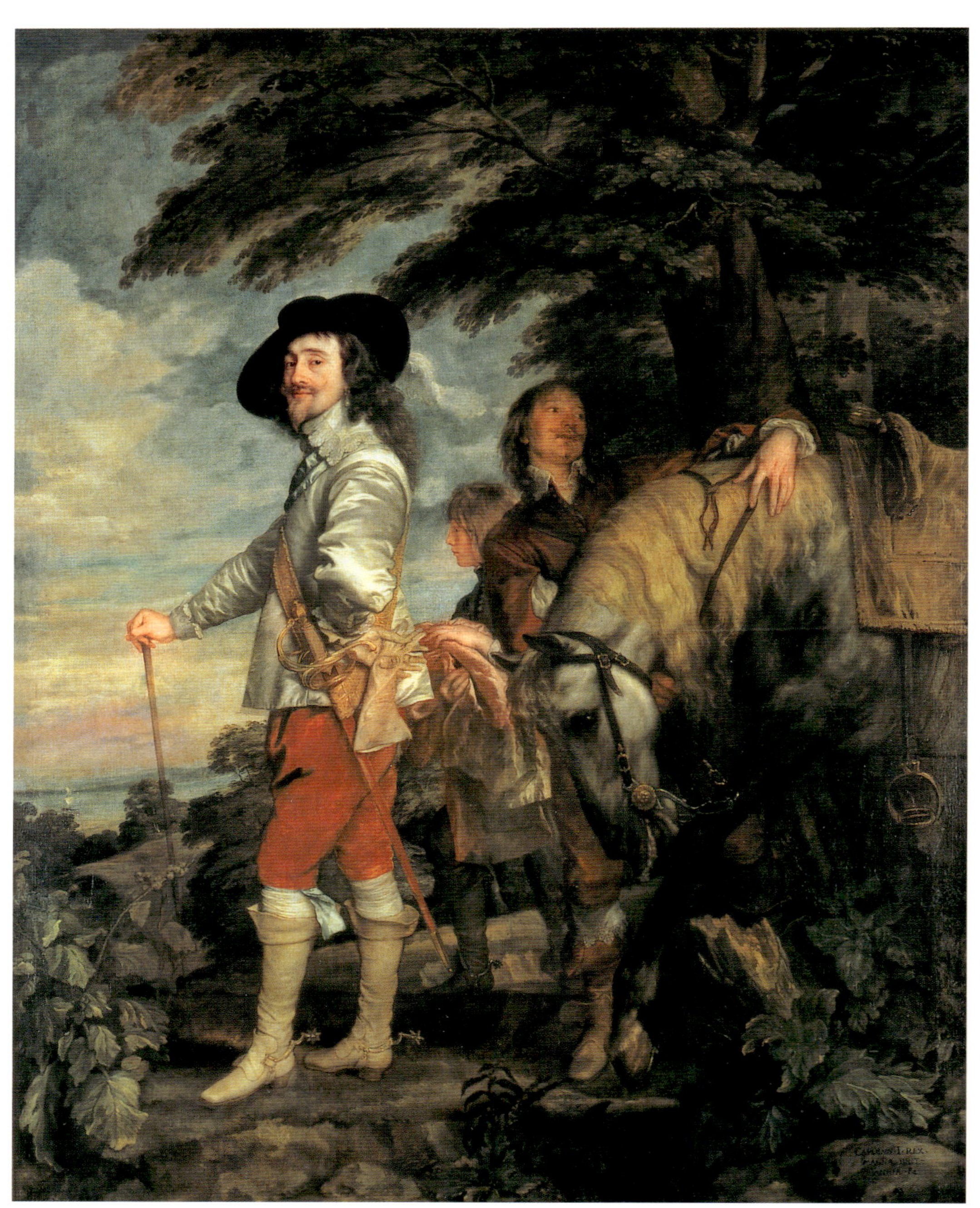

21. Anthony Van Dyck, Charles I, ca. 1635, oil on canvas, 104¾ x 81½ in. (266 x 207 cm). Musée du Louvre, Paris.

survive anything, perhaps, except the rise of a more ravenous ideal—the ideal of the romantic artist, for instance, in which the painter, or the poet, redrafts the contract between himself and the rest of society. His position within it is now more precarious, as is his financial security. (In his later, debased incarnations, he may even take to wearing his penury as a badge of pride.) Nevertheless, something in his art now insists that, in his transactions with the perceptible world and its inhabitants, he is bargaining from a superior position. We inspect Van Dyck's picture of Charles I, in the Musée du Louvre (fig. 21), not merely to learn about Van Dyck, but to furnish ourselves with a matter of record; every detail is taken on trust as an index to the character and taste of the king, from the autumnal gold of his saddlecloth to the artlessly rolled tops of his boots. Whereas by the time that John Constable, say, paints Salisbury Cathedral, all is changed utterly.

As Constable turns, time and again, to that same building, what consumes the viewer is not so much the finely rendered grandeur of the spire, or the ways in which so majestic a place of worship seems to be both rooted and re-rooted within a shifting landscape, as the presence of the artist himself. He, or at least his eye, is now king of all it surveys. Architectural historians may still console themselves that a painting such as *Salisbury Cathedral from the Meadows*, first exhibited in 1831 and now hanging in the National Gallery, London (fig. 22), is still, like the depiction of Charles I, a matter of record. It may be, too, that what is at stake here is not one church but the survival of the

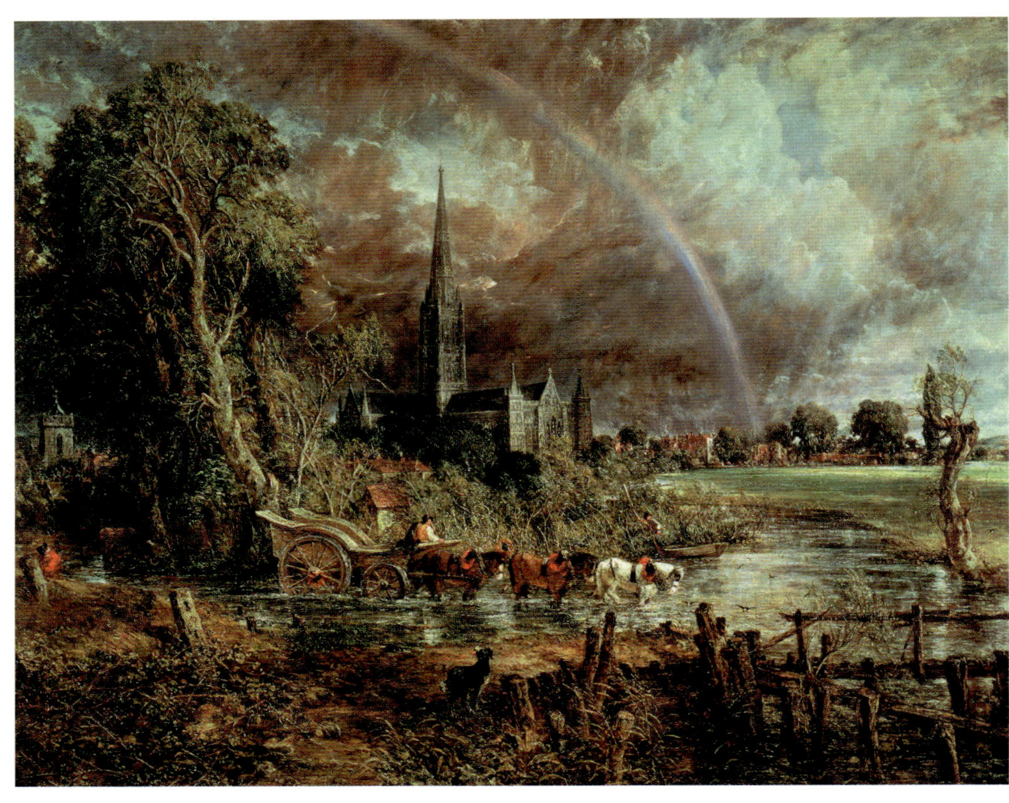

22. John Constable, Salisbury Cathedral from the Meadows, 1831, oil on canvas, 59¾ x 74¾ (151.8 x 189.9 cm). Private collection, on loan to the National Gallery, London.

entire Anglican communion, under pressure of reform, and that, as Graham Reynolds suggests in his catalogue of the artist's works, "Constable's introduction of the rainbow, which only occurs in the last, exhibited version, suggests that he had begun to take a more optimistic outlook of the outcome."[4] To most of us, however, whatever is being contested here is far from being settled. The ash-tree on the left continues to cower; the spire is half in darkness, as if darkness were a guarantee of shame; and that bruised violet arc—as unpretty a rainbow as has ever been

depicted, a wounded rebuke to Wordsworth's leaping heart—seems not to herald the advent of sunshine, but to bend itself back and prepare for the assault of fresh storms. The fight is in the paint.

There are many rainbows in the work of Howard Hodgkin. Many are on view in the present exhibition, and none of them, it should be noted, includes all the colors of the rainbow. Hodgkin, like Constable, does not concern himself with a prismatic effect; whether you read that refusal as bravado or caution, you can safely say that neither man wishes to be caught up in the sentimental associations of the rainbow *tout court*, as painted—and delighted in—by a child. Another peculiarity: Constable's rainbow, in Salisbury, sweeps down from left-of-centre towards the bottom right, whereas the majority of Hodgkin's tend in the opposite direction, thrusting upwards and to the right, like an acute accent. That is certainly the case with the burning leaf-gold of *After Degas* (no. 44), a russet bonfire of all the green vanities that surround it. It is thrice true of *Rain at Il Palazzo* (no. 7), with a slant of black and blue on one side, sandwiching silver-gray; above it, a small crowd of reddened curves, like an ambitious young rainbow that wants to be a rising sun; and, top left, scrapings of blue, exhausted now, with little left to say. There are green half-rainbows in *Torso* (no. 16), bending like a spine; a mean and inky quarter-circle, rumbling in the lower planes of *Thunder* (no. 30); bunched varieties of apple in *An Autumn Leaf* (no. 29), hardly tilted on their journey, not quite daring to leave the straight and narrow, and thus all too clearly heading for a fall; a long, lurking comma of black in *After Vuillard* (no. 45), which would frighten that fastidious Frenchman out of his wits; the desperate loveliness of *Spring Rain* (no. 31), with a thin whip of blue making a break for it, through the massed ranks of darker shades; a citric segment in *Chintz* (no. 17), rising and shining over a grassy bank; wave upon wave of possible rainbows, in *Memorial* (no. 22), stacked in parts as tight as bicycle wheels; the strokes of dawn in *First Light* (fig. 23, no. 35), which could be the wheeltracks left by Aurora; the ardent intrusion of *Visitors* (no. 19), where the arc starts to split in two halfway up the frame, as if divided by an argument; the trunk of wood and sepia that grows up the left-hand side of *Moonlight* (no. 47), swaying slightly at its peak, like the very base of a bow; and finally, *After the Storm* (no. 18), with its mournful, lowering, but never quite despairing burdens of deep blue, nocturnal and submarine—echoes of Whistler, you might say, were it not for the sudden swipe of green in the lowest third, springing its verdant surprise.

All these rainbows, as I say, point towards the uppermost right of the picture. (If there are pots of gold at the end, they are smuggled well out of sight.) Only rarely does Hodgkin follow Constable's cue and veer the other way. He does it in *Falling Down* (no. 57), a painting alive with unhappy black comedy, as the curve describes the passage of a body—an ageing or infirm one, for example—as it trips and tumbles, amid stripes of jagged panic. *Autumn Foliage* (no. 11) is a work of sad largesse, offering us two rainbows for the price of one, as the lemon and auburn

23. Howard Hodgkin, First Light, detail of no. 35.

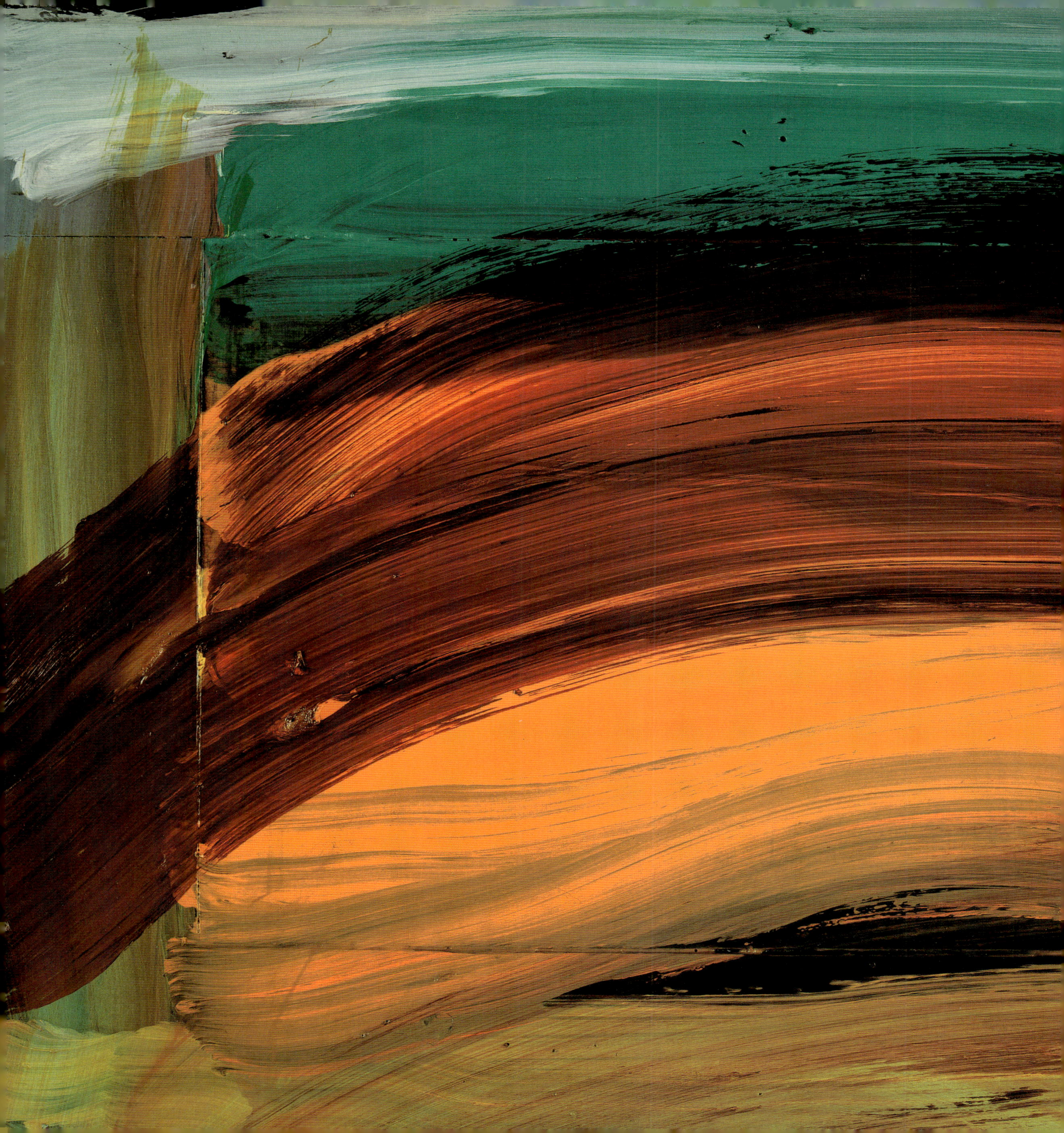

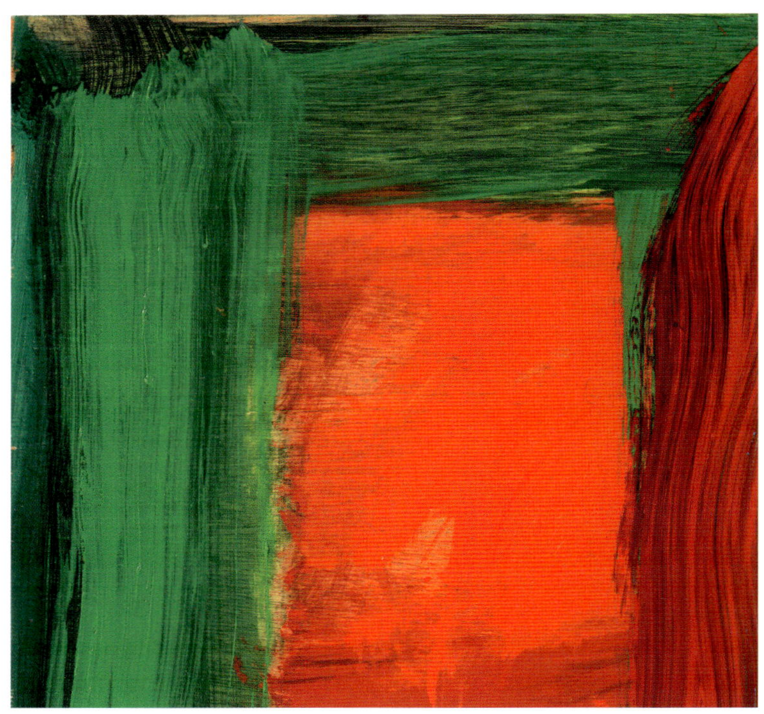

24. Howard Hodgkin, Pyjamas, detail of no. 53.

left-leaner washes lightly over the pale, rightwards specter beneath. Most unstoppable of all, deriding all our efforts to withstand it, is *Grief* (no. 33, see fig. 29), in which Constable's slender rainbow of defiance and doubt has thickened into a tsunami, the color of militant despair, craning over tiny patches of white and red like the head of an infuriated god.

It would be blunt and naïve, especially when confronted with an art as intricate as Hodgkin's, to proceed on the principle that there is some universal feeling-chart that corresponds to the color-spectrum; that red betokens wrath, or that an empurpled

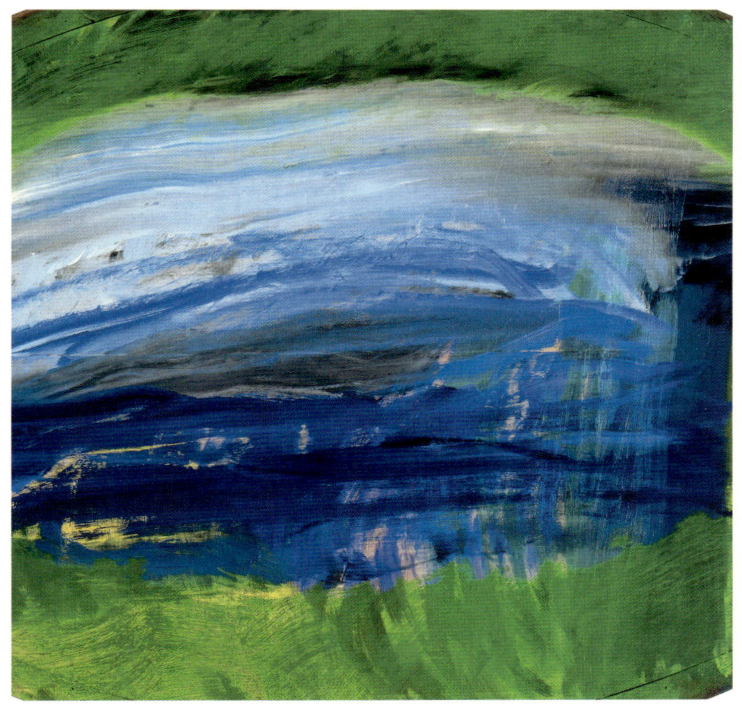

25. Howard Hodgkin, Evening Sea, detail of no. 12.

black should strike as intrinsically hostile. He of all people is attuned, as the Old Masters were, to the fact that a color changes tone, and thus what we may helplessly call its meaning, according not just to its extent and density but to the company in which it finds itself. The greens of *Pyjamas* (fig. 24, no. 53) are at best second cousins of the greens in *Evening Sea* (fig. 25, no. 12), completed two years before, even though, on the palette, they may have been closer kin; the first must stand up straight, like cotton bolts, laid against the warmth of navy and red, while the second lap around strata of calmative blue, as if an island and

its encircling waters had changed places on a whim. Nevertheless, for all the delicacy of this calibration and counterpoise, it does appear that the Hodgkin of the past decade and a half has set out—more like a traveler, as always, than like a man with a plan—to complicate and, on occasion, to challenge the notion that his is an art of small pleasures.

Was this ever really the case? It seemed to be so, and with good cause, when Robert Hughes, an admirer of Hodgkin, wrote about a show at Knoedler and Company in 1982. He cast a line that hooked the artist to the largely French school of Intimism—"closeness of feeling, modesty of scale, and a witty accuracy about place and character."[5] All these virtues are there to be unearthed in Hodgkin, often from close to the surface, amid what Hughes describes as "controllable realms of pleasure."[6] The theme was taken up again, a dozen years later, by Andrew Graham-Dixon, whose fine, book-length encomium to Hodgkin harps on his radiant recreations—or, as Graham-Dixon argues, improvements—of the sensible world. At one point our attention is drawn to a work labeled, simply, *Rainbow* (fig. 26), a painting that "aims undisguisedly at beauty, that wants to ravish the eye."[7] This sounds indisputable, but "undisguised"? One should always be careful of ascribing blatancy and transparency to an artist such as Hodgkin. Those who find a magical loveliness in his pictures should remind themselves that one of the duties of a magician is to pull the wool over our eyes, or to pull one color over another. There are endless sleights in Hodgkin, minute glimpses of distant paint viewed through cracks and gaps

26. Howard Hodgkin, Rainbow, 1983–85, oil on wood, 22⅞ x 21 in. (58 x 53.5 cm). Private collection.

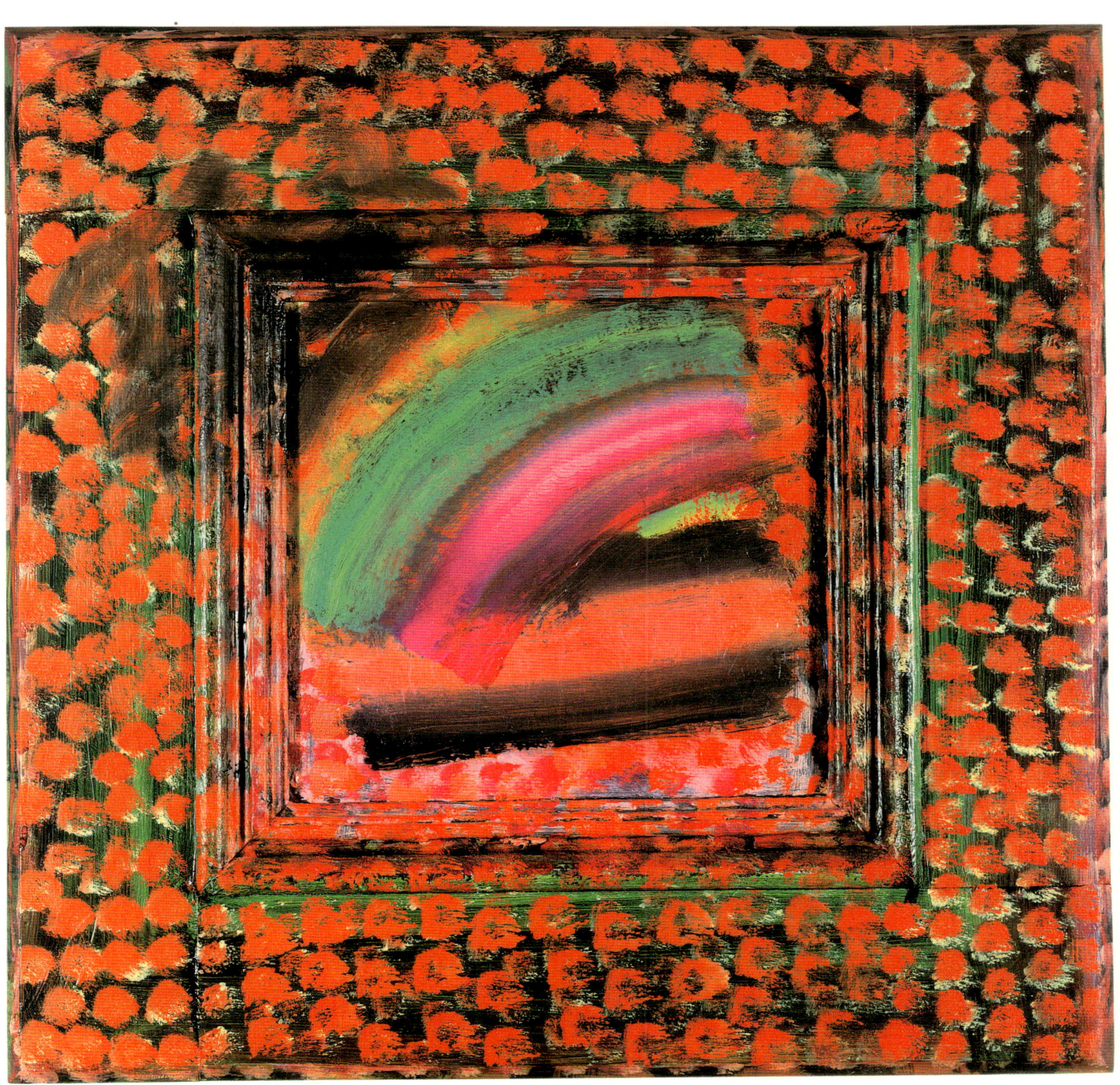

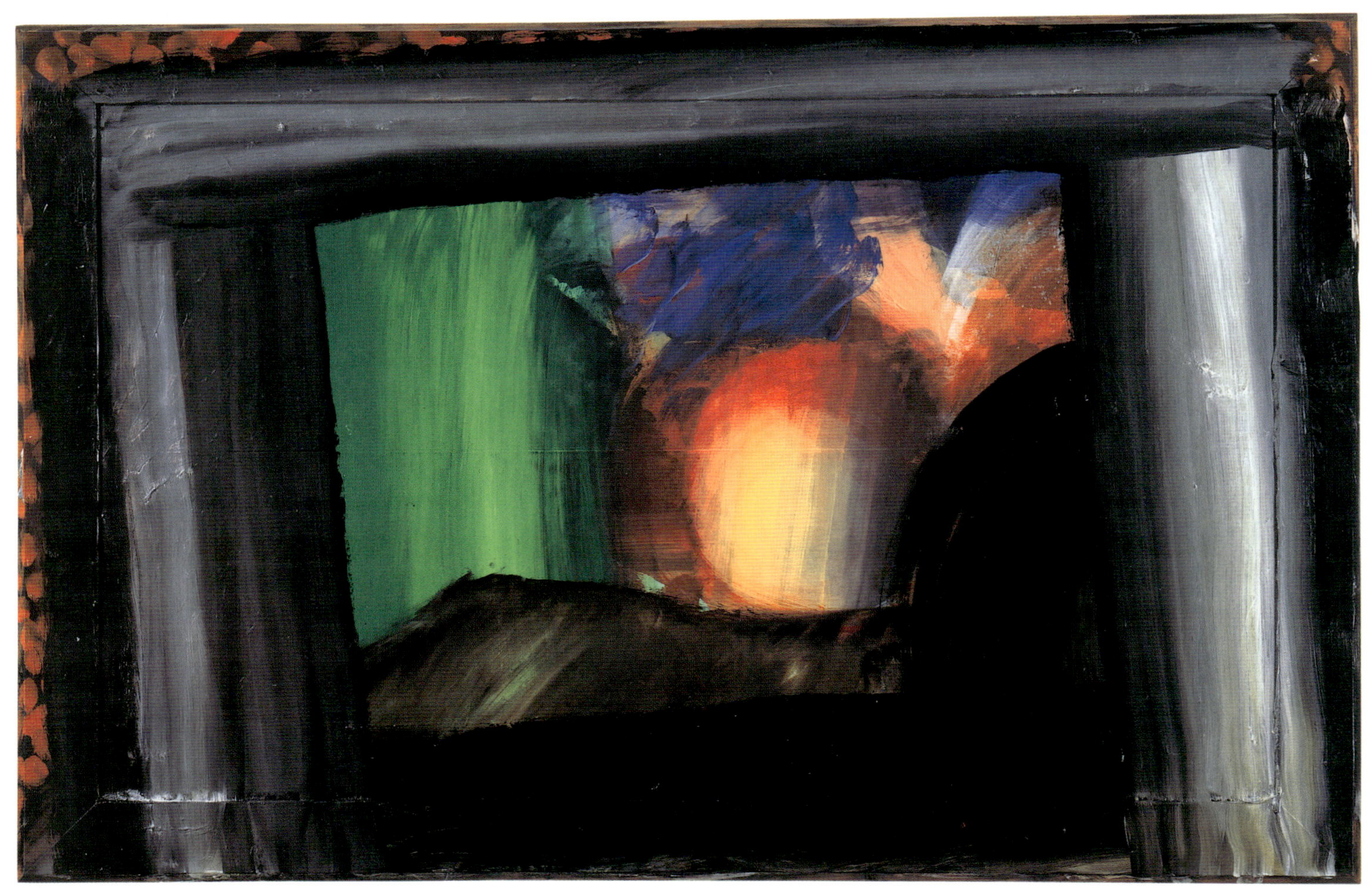

27. Howard Hodgkin,
Snapshot, 1984–93, oil on wood,
59 x 88¾ in. (150 x 225.4 cm).
Private collection, London.

in a landscape; none of his contemporaries has investigated so thoroughly what "depth of field" entails, and it is vulgar of us to presume that so generous a purveyor of rapture can not also be a master of disguise.

That *Rainbow*, for instance: if it is nothing but distilled joy, a jewel-box of unearthly delights, what is that scuffed patch of dirty brown-black, like a bootmark, doing in the upper left? Did the artist stamp on it in frustration before it left the studio? And the stuttering, green-backed blobs of red that frame the whole conceit: if they reek of poppies, are they more like the poppies of Monet or like the poppies that cover the battlefields of the First World War, copies of which are still worn in the lapels of the British once a year? The point is this: just because a painting (or a poem) is taut and compact, we should not rush to assume that the emotional range that it enshrines is comparably small. The color that Hodgkin lays along the base of his rainbow, for instance, is in part a cheerful, un-British joke, as if the solemnity of the pastoral can be stuck together with bubblegum; but, in retrospect, the very stridency of the hue is faintly disturbing. Intimism tells of polite conversations, of voices lowered not in fear but because there is nothing to shout about. That hot pink is a yelp.

When Hughes wrote his appreciation, he was able to declare with confidence that most Hodgkins were no larger than the page of a book. No one could follow the progress of Hodgkin over the last twenty years and make the same claim. I first saw *Snapshot* (fig. 27) in reproduction and assumed that its formidable arrangements—a half-rosy sun, a curtain of green, other blockish forms imprisoned within a tough parallelogram the color of battleships—were all laid out in miniature. Then I came upon the work itself, and that gray frame, I gathered, was not like the viewfinder of a camera; it was more like a shot of Stonehenge. The sun had swelled to a giant peach, straight out of Roald Dahl. The whole construction, on wood, was just shy of sixty inches by ninety, and that was the only shy thing about it; even Hughes, with his muscular prose, would have had trouble picking this thing up like a book. It would be wrong to say that, since then, Hodkgin has been liberated from the constraints of the smaller picture—not least because those were constraints that he imposed on himself, and which, like the heavy pruning of a rose, bore a surfeit of fruit. Let us simply say that he has inquired, with accelerating vigor, into the yields that might be promised by a larger domain. How else would he have arrived at *A Rainbow* (fig. 28), which is only seven inches narrower than Constable's vast panorama of the rainbow over Salisbury? Much of the Hodgkin is bare wood, stubbled with green that could have been jabbed on with a shaving brush. As for the arc itself, it barely bends. (It is more like an outsized piece of striped candy, kinked from chewing, whatever sweetness it had long gone.) There is no ground from which it might have been launched, and no upper atmosphere where it might lose itself in glory. Although *A Rainbow* is by no means a cynical piece of work, it finds transcendence awfully hard to come by. If happy little bluebirds fly beyond the rainbow, it demands, then why the hell can't I?

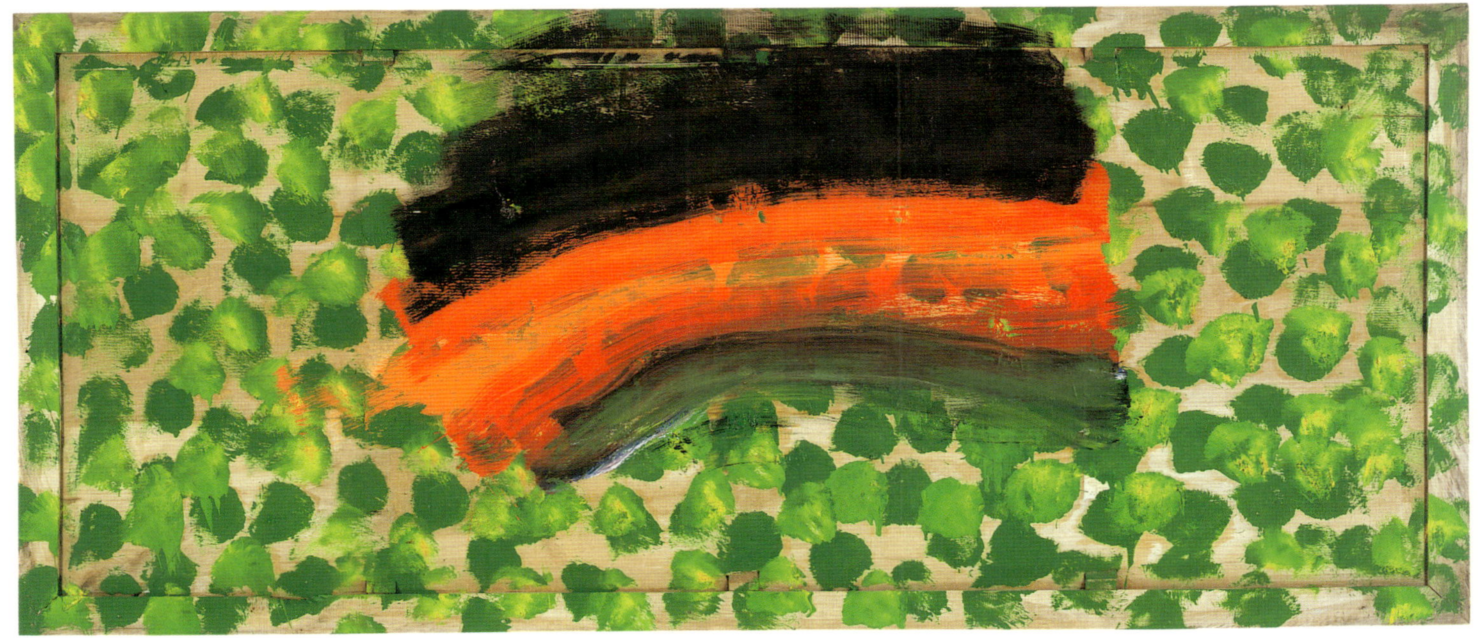

28. Howard Hodgkin, A Rainbow, 2004, oil on wood, 30 x 67⅝ in. (76.2 x 171.7 cm). Private collection, Sydney.

All of which is more than a question of physical dimension. As the present selection proves, Hodgkin has in no way abandoned the smaller frame altogether. But the elasticity of his later work, the stretch and squeeze of recent compositions, should help us to restate a central question: is Howard Hodgkin an artist of the small scale? That is what both his fans and his detractors like to claim; he is, on the one hand, applauded as a Chardin *de nos jours* and, on the other, scorned as a kind of advanced interior decorator. What has become increasingly evident, however, is that the emotional climate in which he deals is not, and never has been, temperate, milky, or mild. If *Grief* is not an easy or attractive painting (see fig. 29),

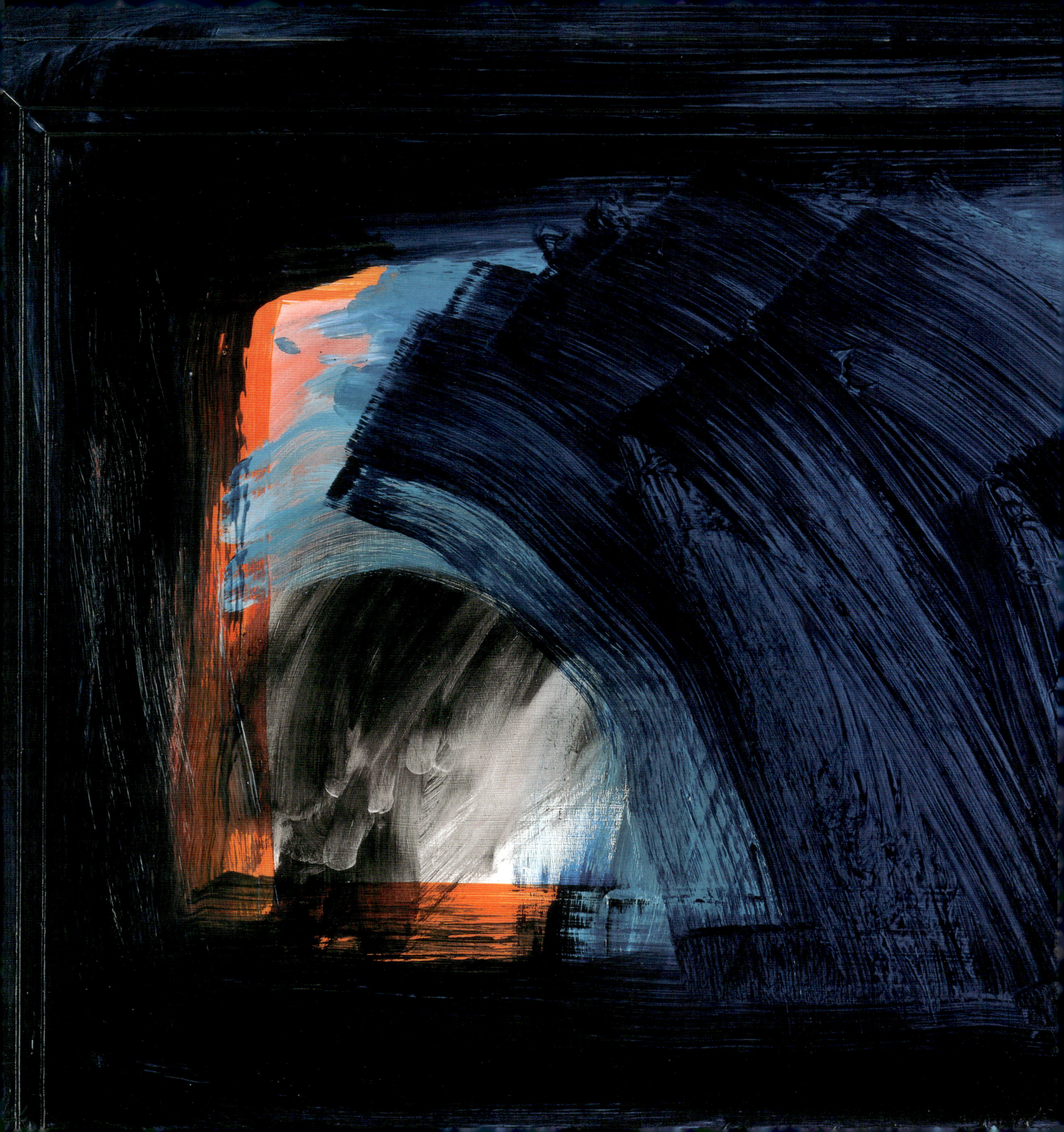

that is because the act of grieving, as anyone who has dwelt among the bereaved can testify, is not a pretty sight; it is spiky and bitter, and, as Tennyson would say, "wild with all regret."[8] The Victorian British, whose grasp of mortality was by definition more educated than ours, were under fewer illusions about the urge and need to lament; they codified the chronology and the costume of mourning in a full realization that grief, left unmarshalled, could easily spiral and spill out of control. Hodgkin is in fact a good Tennysonian: he is possessed by feelings so intense that only in the exquisiteness of their ordering can their deepest and most abiding impact be made plain. The frame of the painting performs a task not dissimilar to the stanza, (the room, in its Italianate root): it limits what might otherwise escape. Hodgkin is not, by this light, an Intimist; he is an extremist, operating under necessary pressure. And he is not a Frenchman *manqué*, refurnishing the tea-table and the still life; he is closer to Tennyson, to Turner, and to Constable—to the bloodline of the nervously sturdy, striving to quell a bursting heart, or at least to find consolation in a regular beat. To the outside world, there is no paradox more amusing, or more likely to surprise: the impassioned Englishman.

That *Howard Hodgkin: Paintings 1992–2007* should be opening at the Yale Center for British Art is more than good fortune. It is also a neat fit, offering to the inquisitive viewer a distinct path, along which one's approach to Hodgkin can be paced out. Who is the author, for instance, of the imbroglio in figure 30? If it is not

29. Howard Hodgkin, Grief, detail of no. 33.

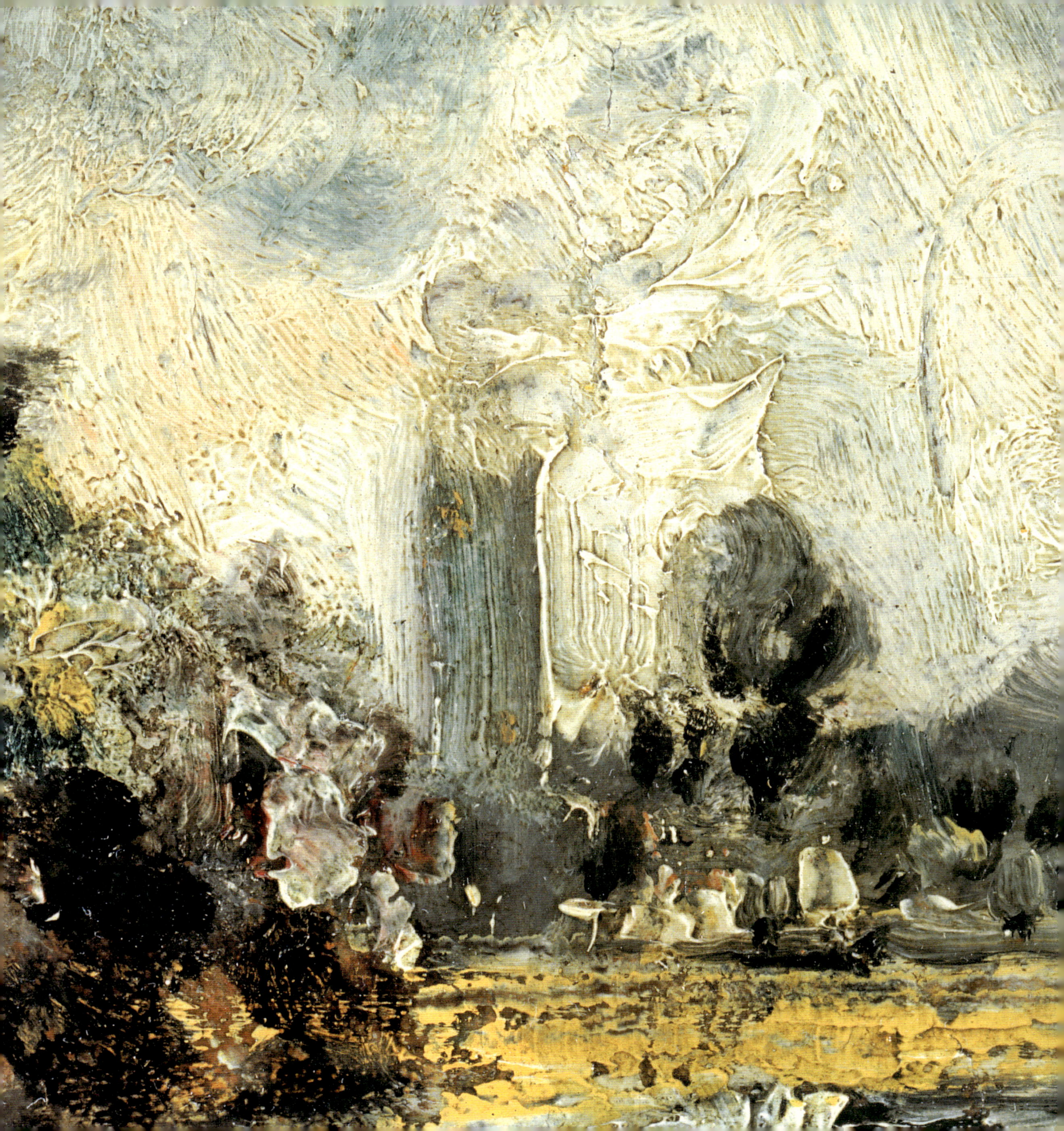

Hodgkin, it is someone with his near-gastronomic appetite for oil paint. You want to scrape that creamy scoop of white from the canvas and lick it off your finger. And what exactly is that central vertical brushstroke, blue-sage, melting at the top? It could be a typical swipe from Ivon Hitchens, say, who could turn almost anything, at any angle, into a mini-waterfall. It could be a signature flourish of Hodgkin.

The detail comes, in fact, from *Dedham Lock* (fig. 31), an oil sketch made by Constable about 1819–20, and given to the Yale Center for British Art by Paul Mellon in 1981. The upward stroke is a church tower. In the finished painting, which exists in three versions—the most tranquil being at the Currier Gallery of Art in Manchester, New Hampshire—we are able to make out everything about that tower, from the tracery of its window up to the crenellations and the flagless pole.

The tower reappears in another oil sketch, also held at the Center. It dates from the same period and addresses the same subject—or, at any rate, the same rural view, more tightly massed and bunched (fig. 32). Here we are, still in the growing pains of the nineteenth century (only four years, say, since the publication of *Emma*), and already we seem to be at the limits of expressive energy. Some of these furious roilings are all but indecipherable. The church tower may be clearer than it was in the previous sketch, but, if so, then what is that solid jet thrusting up from the river bank to the right of it? How to account for the squiggles of blue that snake from the river's surface, on the left, and lose themselves between the trees? Are they actually the

30. John Constable, Dedham Lock, detail of fig. 31.

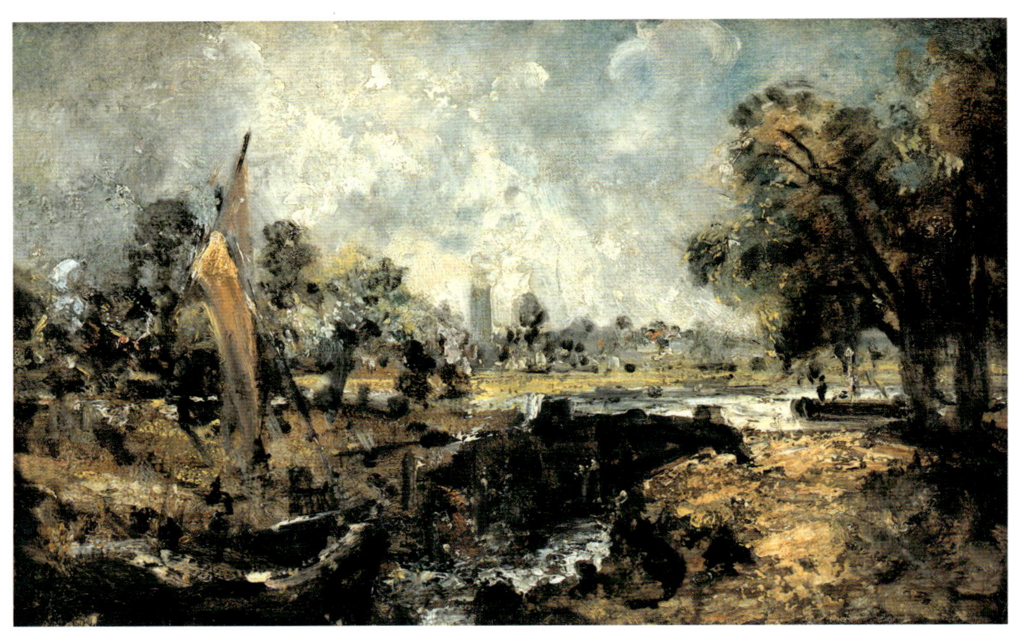

31. John Constable, Dedham Lock, ca. 1819–20, oil on canvas laid on board, 13¼ x 19⅝ in. (33.7 x 49.8 cm). Yale Center for British Art, Paul Mellon Collection.

the scraps of a tributary that feeds the river? They could equally be smoke, uncoiling from a lit pipe. So where is the smoker?

As we make these guesses, struggling to forge the links between object and representation, what we sound like, of course, is a practiced art-gazer of today, standing in eager semi-bemusement before a Kandinsky, or a De Kooning, or a Hodgkin—before any of those artists who have plied their trade, with its mysterious blend of revelation and concealment, along those friable borders where the figurative dissolves into abstraction. To Constable, of course, the task held no mystery; he was sketching fast, and with concrete purpose, in the open air. He was producing *aides-mémoire*, and nobody would have

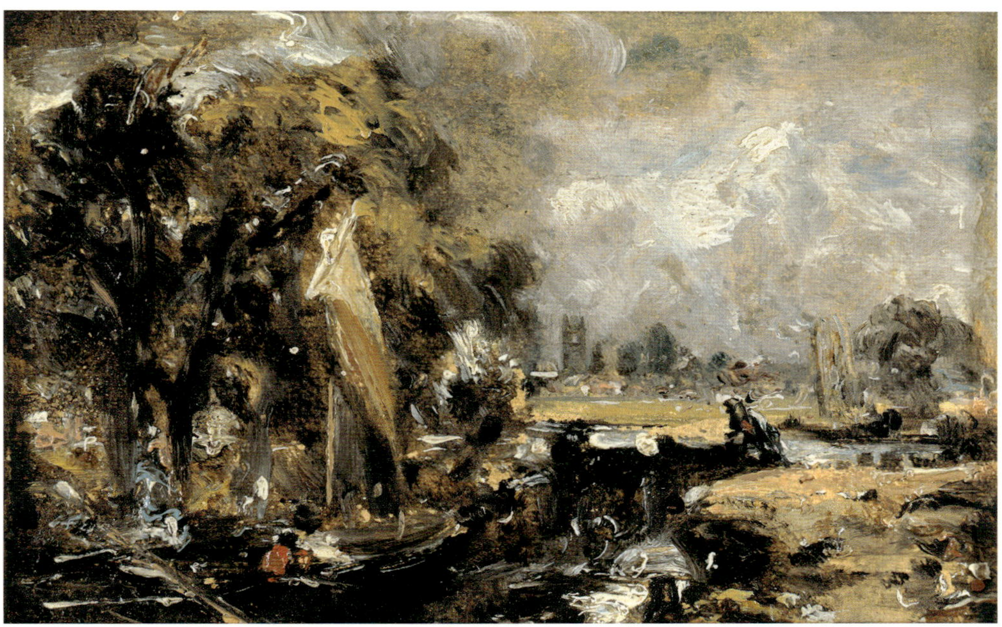

32. John Constable, Dedham Lock, ca. 1819–20, oil on paper laid on canvas, 5¼ x 7⅜ in. (13.3 x 18.7 cm). Yale Center for British Art, Paul Mellon Collection.

been more taken aback than himself to learn that the results are treasured and scrutinized, in our own age, with the same measure of attentiveness that we lend to the finished oils. Indeed, there are many modern eyes which prefer what they perceive as the roughness and readiness of the sketch, and which glaze over at the poised formality of the end product. That is part of the history of taste, a treacherous tale by any standards, and the question of why, and how, and precisely when the twentieth-century developed a sweet tooth for the unfinished, and sometimes for the barely started, deserves a book to itself. We may, for the moment, content ourselves with noting that the second of these small oils was probably bought by a

French collector named Cheramy, early in the last century, and that the first was definitely owned by Albert Hecht, who had connections with Degas and Manet; as Graham Reynolds points out, Constable's sketch "must therefore be one of the earliest works of its kind to be available for inspection by the Impressionists in a French collection."[9]

Contact is made: a single footnote hints at a line of footsteps, from the Englishman on the river Stour to a later generation in Paris, and from there all over the world—the world, that is, of those who made it their business to interrogate nature, and to read its innumerable clues. One of the aspects of the oil sketch, presumably, that appealed to the conscientious Impressionist was its air of spontaneity; to this day, and to a fault, we value the unmediated and unrefined, often neglecting in our enthusiasm the sheer industry required for such annotation of the immediate. On a practical level, Constable did not dream of completing—and could not physically have completed—one of his "six-footers" *en plein air*, whereas to do so became a point of Impressionist pride. So, where does that leave an artist like Hodgkin, who somehow forges his own, alchemical combination of the two styles? His manner is prefigured in the church tower of the first sketch, and in the tall, folded canvas of the riverboat's sail in the second—in the blurt of lighter paint on the spar and the clever twist into brown-sugar tones further down. But these, for him, would not be memoranda, scrawled onto the canvas against the clock, or the dying day, or the boiling of those rainclouds above. The dates for Hodgkin's *Afternoon Flowers*, say, are given as 1989–95 (no. 2), which is about as far as you can get from a single afternoon. Like the Impressionists, he is happy to retain, within a completed painting, signs of vehemence and verve, of shadow-patterns or light-falls that had to be captured before they flickered away, as if he were grabbing at the coat-tails of a flamboyant dream; on the other hand, those signs are illusions, patiently maneuvered over time. Like Constable, he thinks the studio the proper arena for the fulfillment of art. He does not paint in the open, but in the closed set of his studio, working on one painting only and hiding the faces of the others with covers of white scrim. His pictures are Dedham Locks, immaculately done, but with the lock-gates opened, and the waters flooding in.

Thus we come full circle, back to Turner and his lampblack. Hodgkin has sought, and continues to seek, solutions to the enduring dilemma: as our own age devises ever more noxious mockeries (technological as well as social) of the private soul, what is left for the gentleman artist? The phrase sounds impossibly musty, and mildewed with traces of the amateur; all I mean by it, however, is the creative spirit, of either sex, that wishes to articulate its experience without simply giving vent. It maintains the artist's essential nerve and gall, going public with his or her elaborate responses to the world, but, it still knows the importance of retiring from the fray, even within the confines of a painting. Those who decry Hodgkin as a decorative artist are perhaps making an understandable mistake, for they are misreading his unfashionable attachment to decorum. Take a painting like *Low Tide* (no. 41), which might seem, at first blush, to revel and roll too easily in its own murk—in the loveliness of its late-Victorian gloom. But the blush-tones of the paint, all clayey mud and sunset, are held within a proscenium arch, and transmuted into a kind of quotation, as if the artist were a theatergoer, attending the performance of a nocturne from another era, and asking himself, with as much rigor as melancholy, what has ebbed away and what flotsam is left behind.

As for *After Degas* (no. 44), as gorgeous a painting as Hodgkin has ever conjured, or *After Samuel Palmer* (no. 1), or *After Vuillard* (fig. 33, no. 45), with its cunning glint of blinds and blocked views: what artist other than Hodgkin has derived such profit from the word "after"? It is the most loaded of English prepositions: we speak of taking after our parents, and of living on after they have gone; "after you," we say (or used to say), ushering someone through a door, although we may equally be after his money, or his job; and the artist who comes after Degas, and who thereby knows so much that Degas could never have known, may still indicate homage and deference by titling a painting "*After Degas*," as if there were an ideal to which even his own delicious greens and golds, feathered and fire-red, can but hope to aspire. That is Hodgkin to a tee: summoning a gesture of inimitable splendor, while having the grace to imply that the inspiration belongs to someone else.

One wonders, likewise, what it means for an artist to call a painting *Old Sky* as he nears the middle of his sixties. That work, dated 1996–97 (fig. 34, no. 28), begins with a thick-

33. Howard Hodgkin, After Vuillard, detail of no. 45.

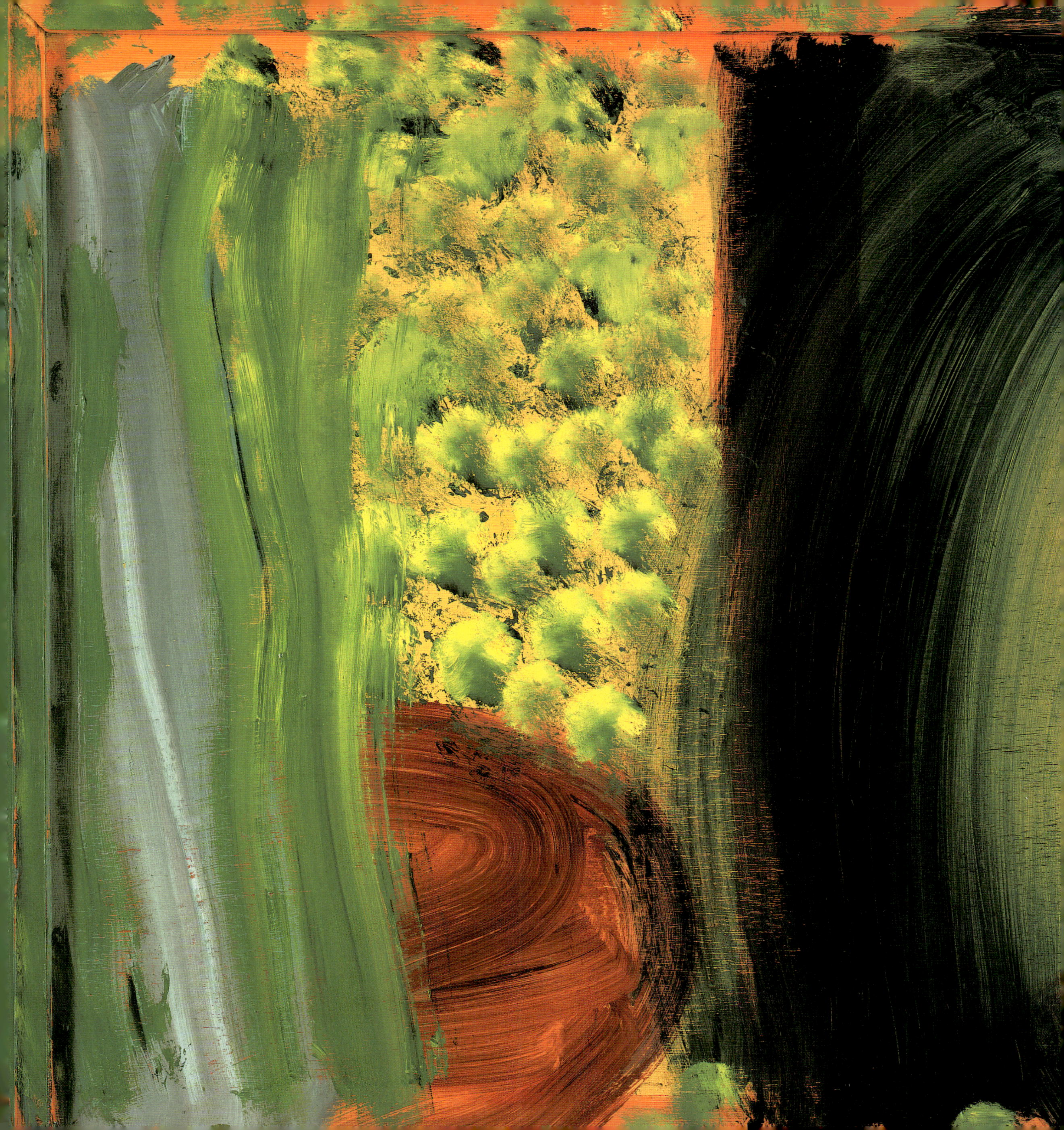

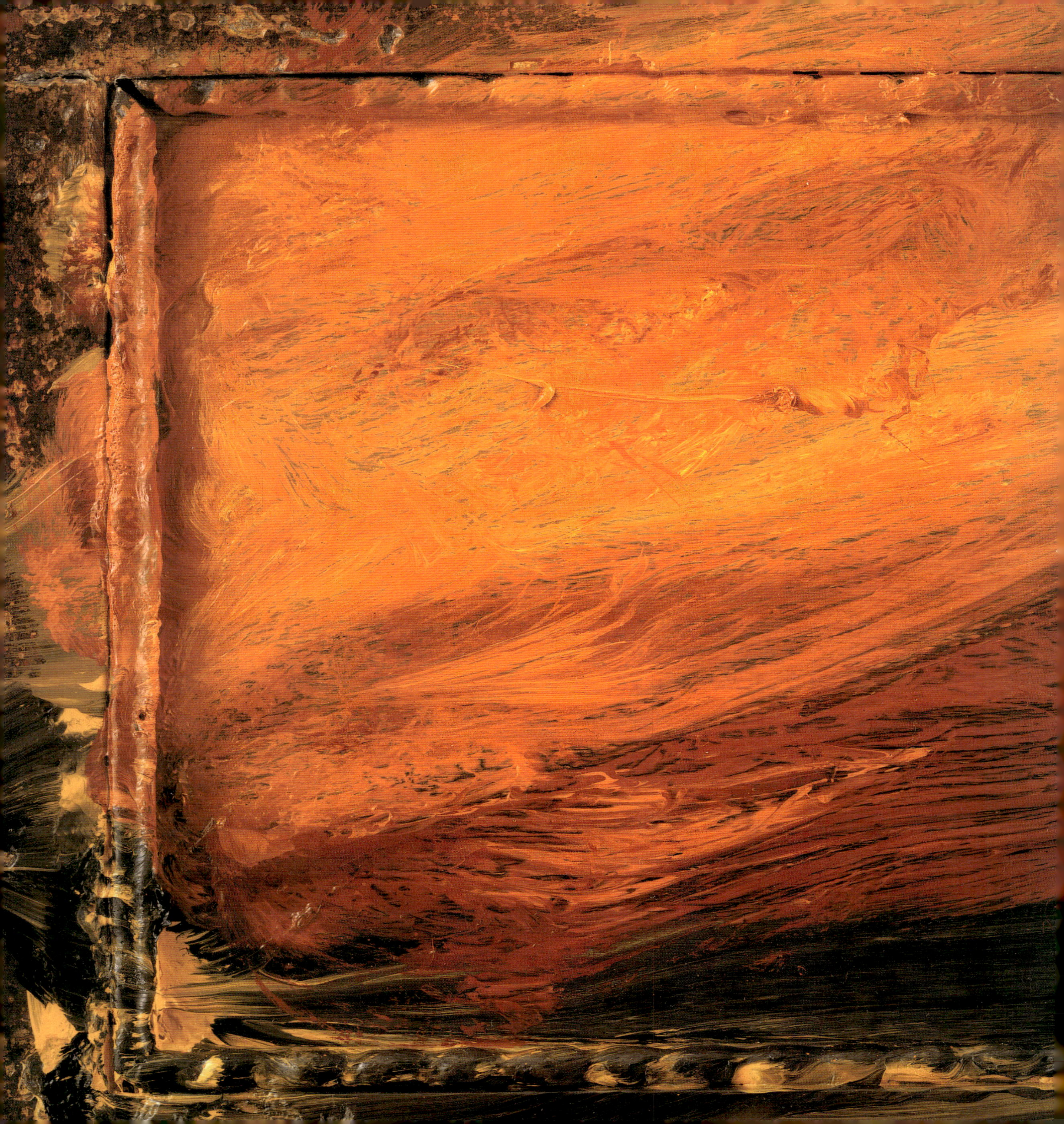

rimmed frame, dotted and stippled with gold. The sense of the precious and rare spreads into the core of the image; one thinks of Henry James's wry observation, "I can stand a great deal of gold"—a bashful confession of luxurious leanings, or a caution that gold is itself so tempting as to constitute a threat?[10] One might as well talk of standing a good deal of pain. And so it is with Hodgkin, who uses the picture to build up a cloudbank of something roaring: a cozy fire in a hearth, or the mouth of hell, or, in between the two—take note of the olive strip at the bottom—a sunset in its final conflagration. Yet even that comes to feel like the scariest option of all. For an artist embarking on the third half of his existence, the voice that incites him to rage against the dying of the light can only grow in power. I have no idea, after watching this picture for a long time, like a movie, what doses of protest and acceptance are stirred into its incandescent pigment; whether, indeed, it might merely commemorate a wonderful evening, spent on a hillside with friends. The last word on it must go to another man: less of a voluptuary, more sparing, and capable of more viciousness than Hodgkin, but alive like him to all the deaths we go through, day on day, like the deaths of small feelings and grand plans. Samuel Beckett was seventy when he wrote "Old Earth,"[11] (quoted in full below), not much older than the Hodgkin of *Old Sky*, and painting and poem are now entwined in my mind as one unimprovable demonstration of human yearning—of longings that are no less golden for being thwarted, or stricken, or lost to the clutches of time:

34. Howard Hodgkin, Old Sky, detail of no. 28.

Old earth, no more lies, I've seen you, it was me, with my other's ravening eyes, too late. You'll be on me, it will be you, it will be me, it will be us, it was never us. It won't be long now, perhaps not tomorrow, nor the day after, but too late. Not long now, how I gaze on you, and what refusal, how you refuse me, you so refused. It's a cockchafer year, next year there won't be any, nor the year after, gaze your fill. I come home at nightfall, they take to wing, rise from my little oaktree and whirr away, glutted, into the shadows. I reach up, grasp the bough, pull myself up and go in. Three years in the earth, those the moles don't get, then guzzle guzzle, ten days long, a fortnight, and always the flight at nightfall. To the river perhaps, they head for the river. I turn on the light, then off, ashamed, stand at gaze before the window, the windows, going from one to another, leaning on the furniture. For an instant I see the sky, the different skies, then they turn to faces, agonies, loves, the different loves, happiness too, yes, there was that too, unhappily. Moments of life, of mine too, among others, no denying, all said and done. Happiness, what happiness, but what deaths, what loves, I knew at the time, it was too late then. Ah to love at your last and see them at theirs, the last minute loved ones, and be happy, why ah, uncalled for. No but now, now, simply stay still, standing before a window, one hand on the wall, the other clutching your shirt, and see the sky, a long gaze, but no, gasps and spasms, a childhood sea, other skies, another body.

Notes

1. J.M.W. Turner, *Cologne: The Arrival of a Packet-Boat; Evening*, 1826, oil and possibly watercolour on canvas, 66⅜ x 88¼ in. (168.6 x 224.2 cm). The Frick Collection, Henry Clay Frick Bequest, 1914.1.119.
2. Anthony Bailey, *Standing in the Sun: A Life of J. M. W. Turner* (London, 1997), p. 249.
3. "The Old Masters at Burlington House, 1877," unsigned notes, originally published in *The Nation*, I, February 1877, in Henry James, *The Painter's Eye: Notes and Essays on the Pictorial Arts*, ed. John L. Sweeney (London, 1956), p. 128.
4. Graham Reynolds, *The Later Paintings and Drawings of John Constable*, 2 vols. (New Haven and London, 1984), p. 226.
5. Robert Hughes, *Nothing if Not Critical: Selected Essays on Art and Artists* (New York, 1990), p. 282.
6. Hughes, p. 284.
7. Andrew Graham-Dixon, *Howard Hodgkin* (London, 2001), p. 98.
8. Alfred Tennyson, "Tears, Idle Tears," part of "The Princess", in *The Poems of Tennyson*, ed. Christopher Ricks, 3 vols., 2nd edn. (Harlow, 1987), vol. 2, p. 232.
9. Reynolds, *The Later Paintings*, p. 65.
10. Reported by Desmond MacCarthy, and reprinted in *The Legend of the Master: Henry James as Others Saw Him*, ed. Simon Nowell-Smith (Oxford, 1985), p. 50.
11. "Fizzles 1, 2, 3, 4, 5, 6," by Samuel Beckett. Originally written in French (1972–75) as "Foirades," in *Pour finir encore et autres foirades*. Copyright © 1976 by Les Éditions de Minuit. English translation by Samuel Beckett. From *The Complete Short Prose, 1929–1989*, by Samuel Beckett, pp. 238–39. Copyright © 1995 by the Estate of Samuel Beckett (Grove Press, 1995). Reprinted by permission of Georges Borchardt, Inc., for Les Éditions de Minuit.

GALLERY

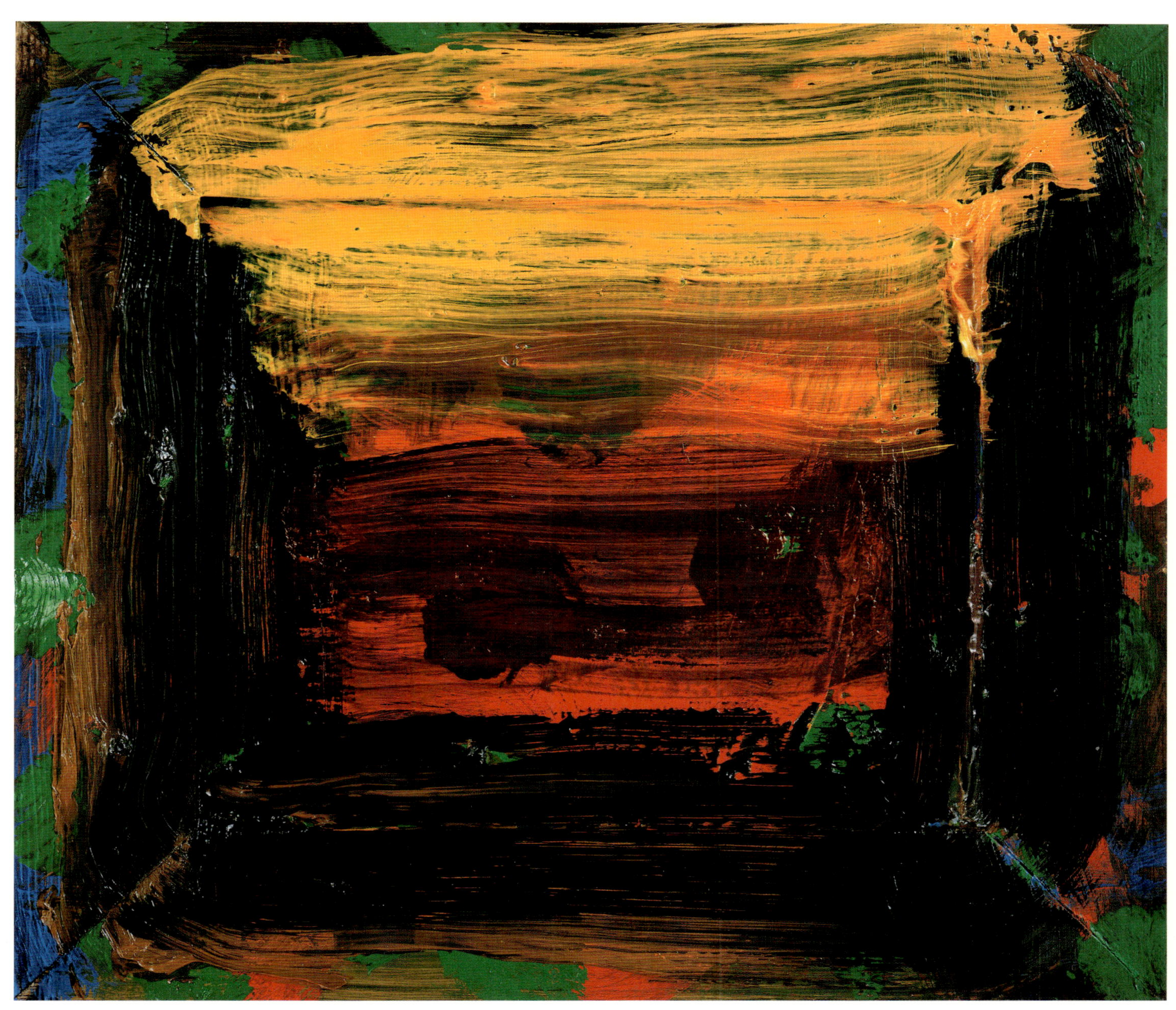

1. After Samuel Palmer, 2003–05

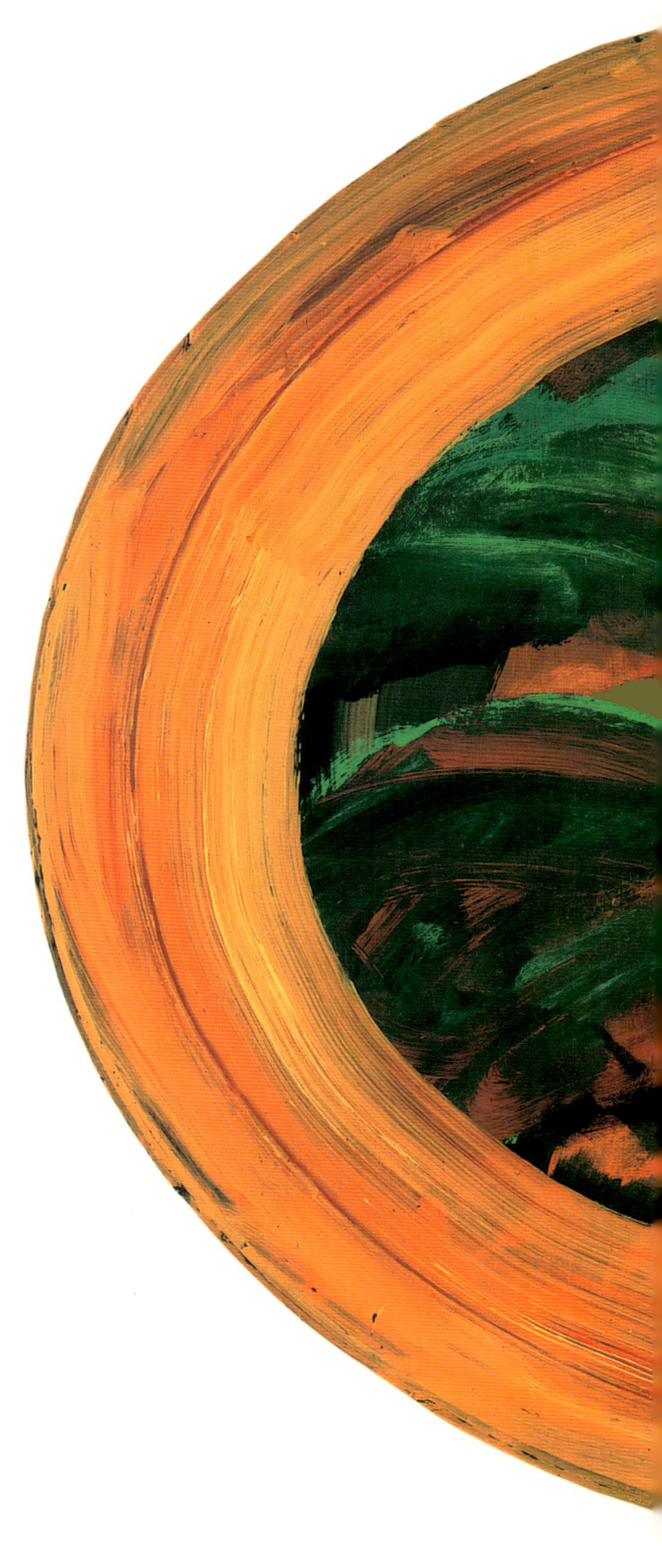

2. Afternoon Flowers, 1989–95

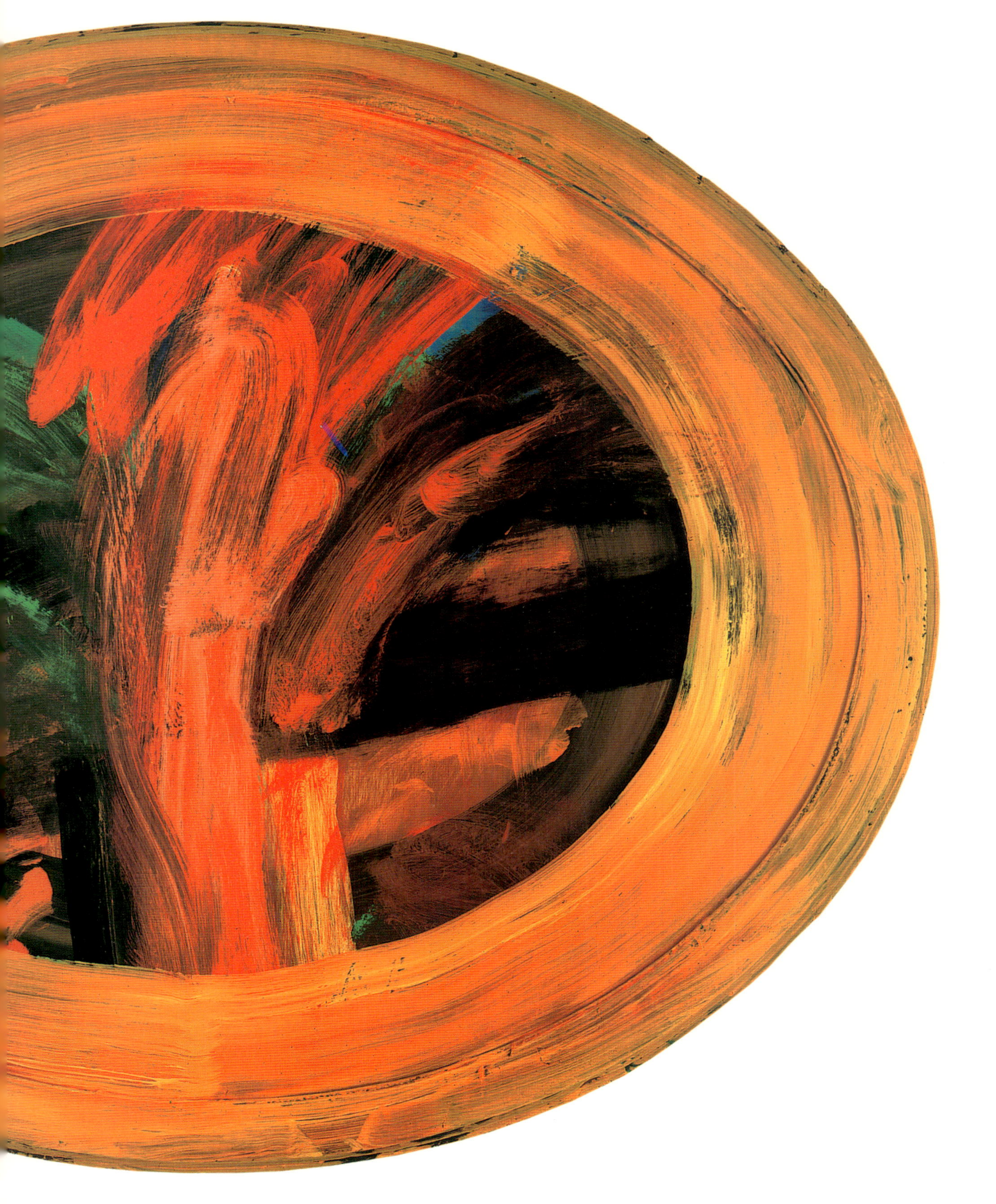

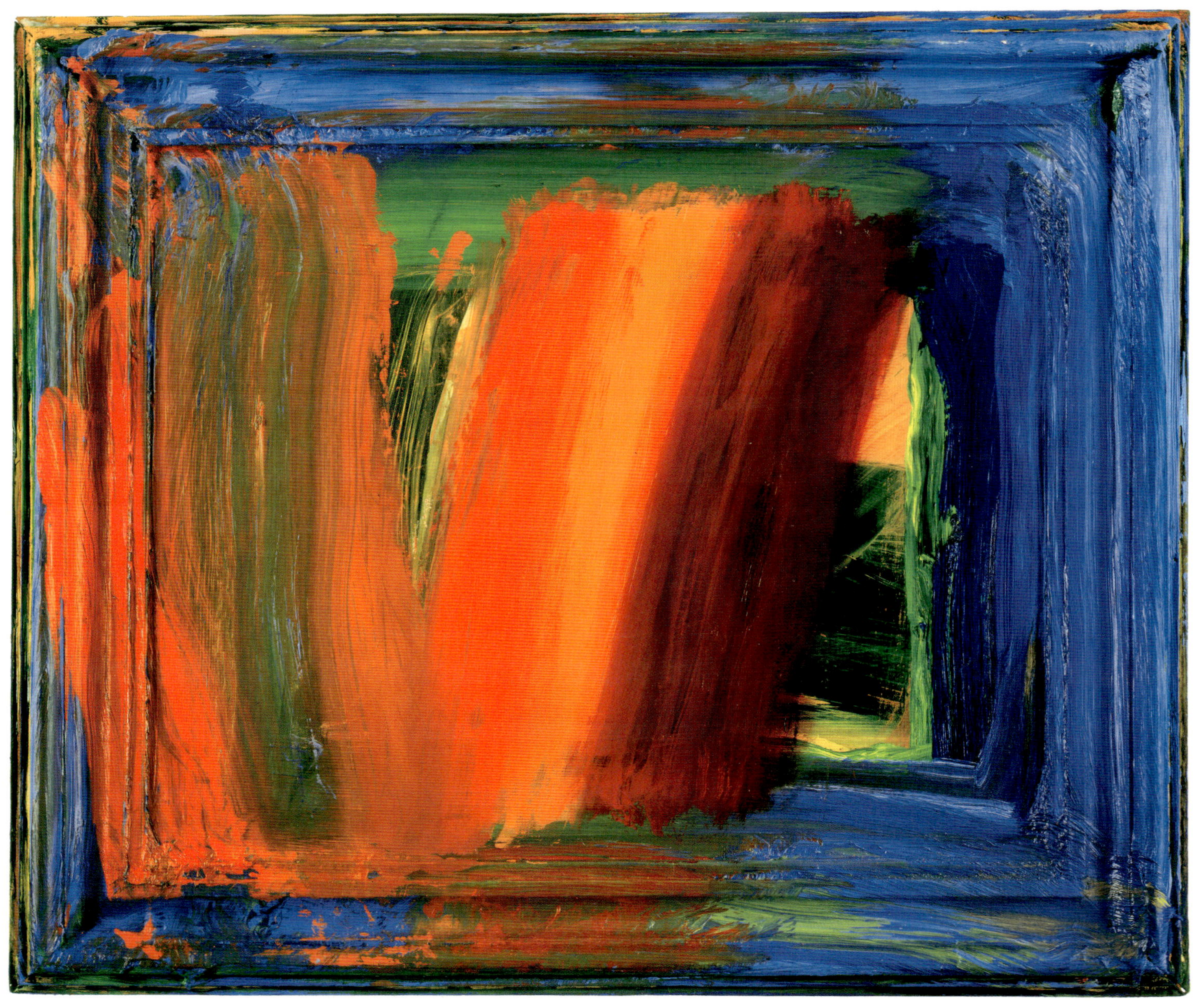

3. Bamboo, 1995–97

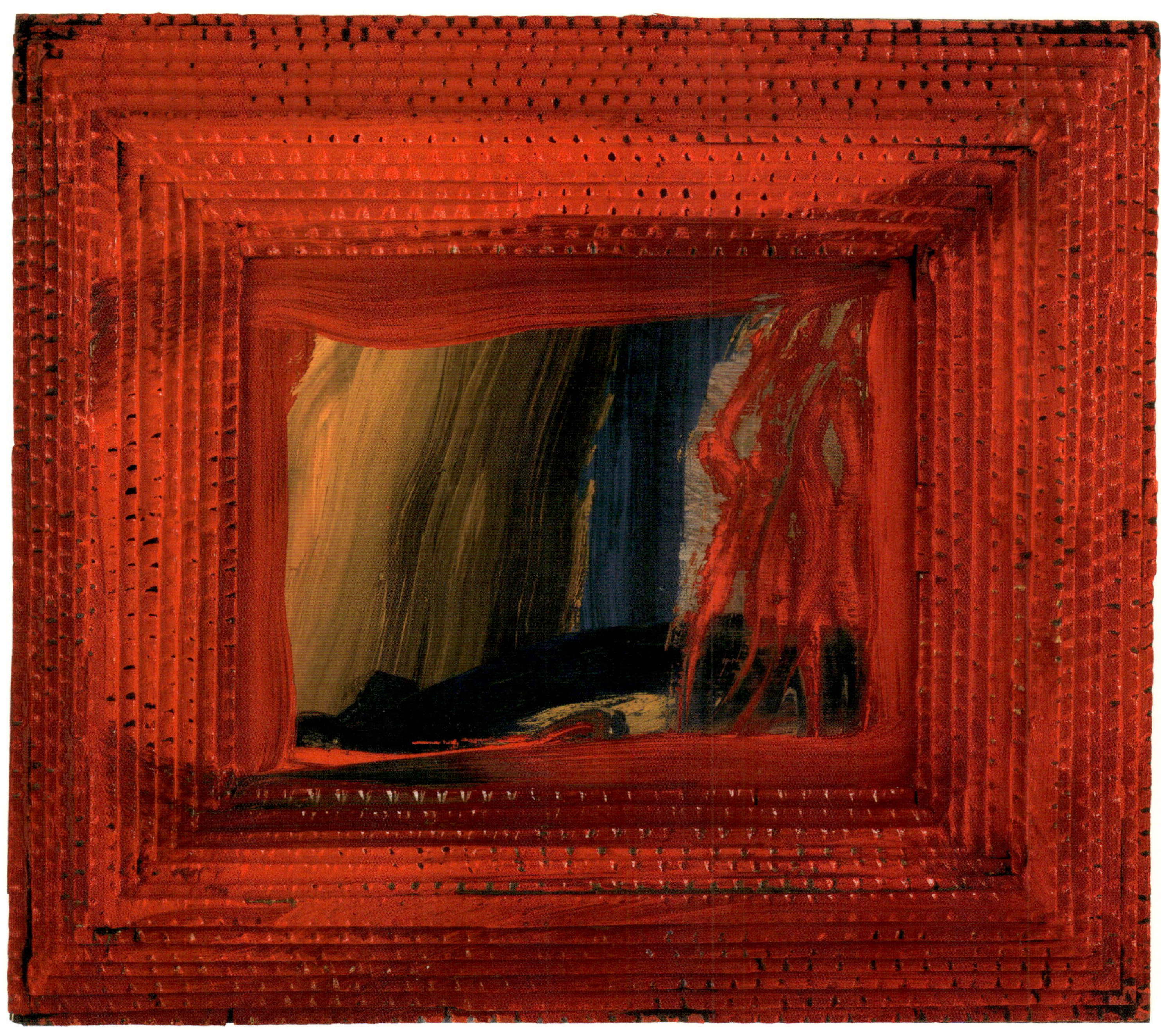

4. Chinoiserie, 1994–97

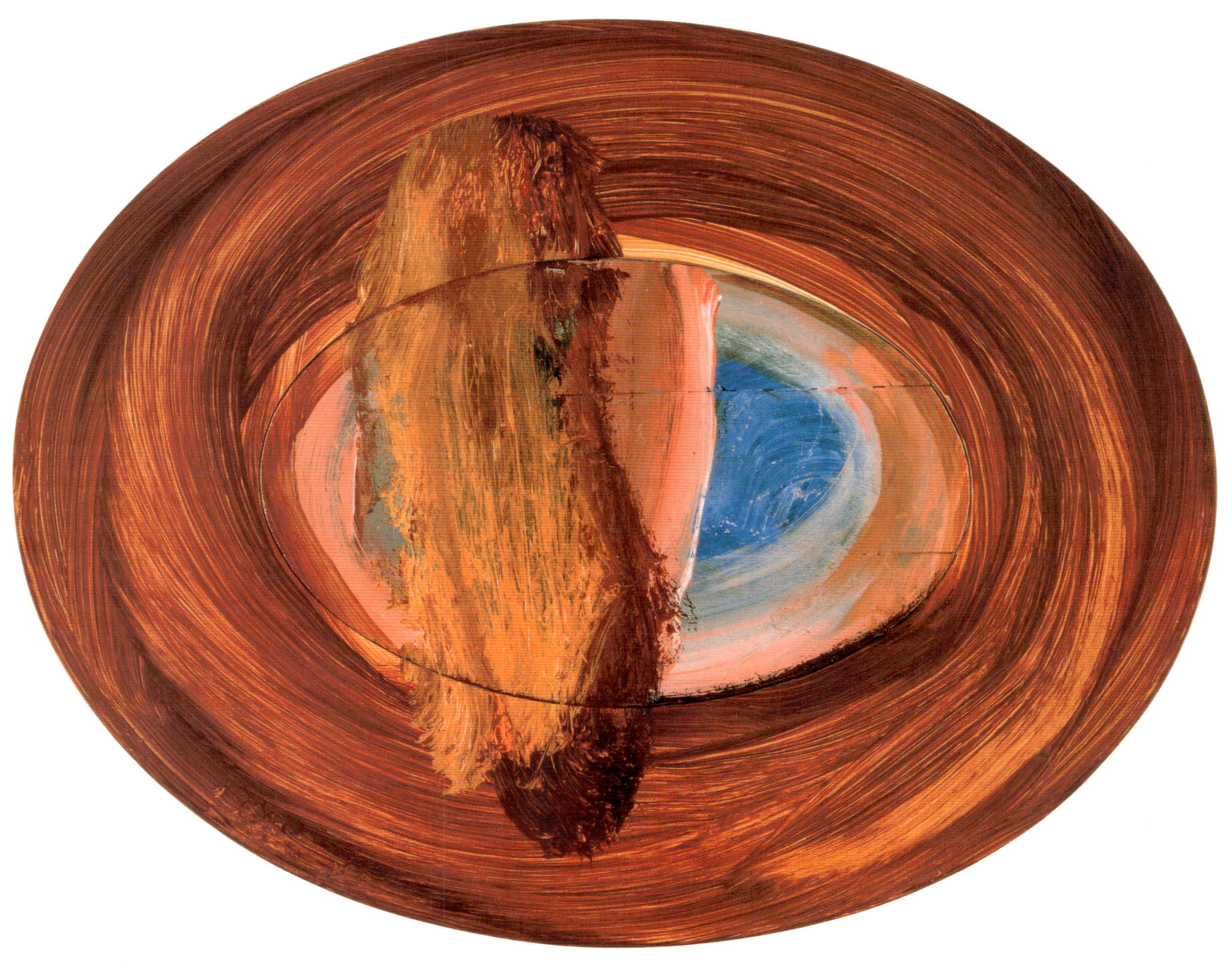

5. When in Rome, 1996–97

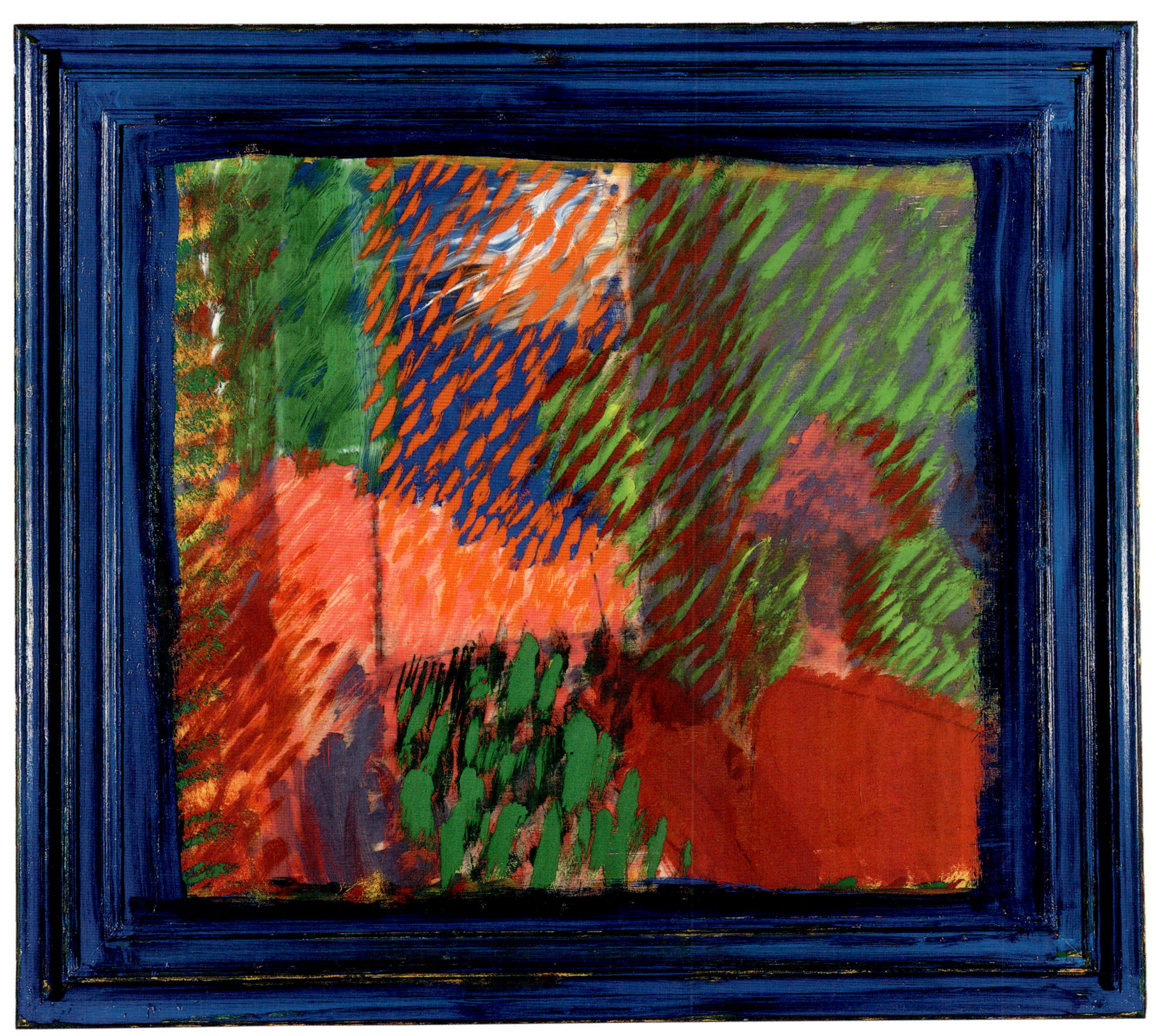

6. A Visit to Paul and Bernard, 1990

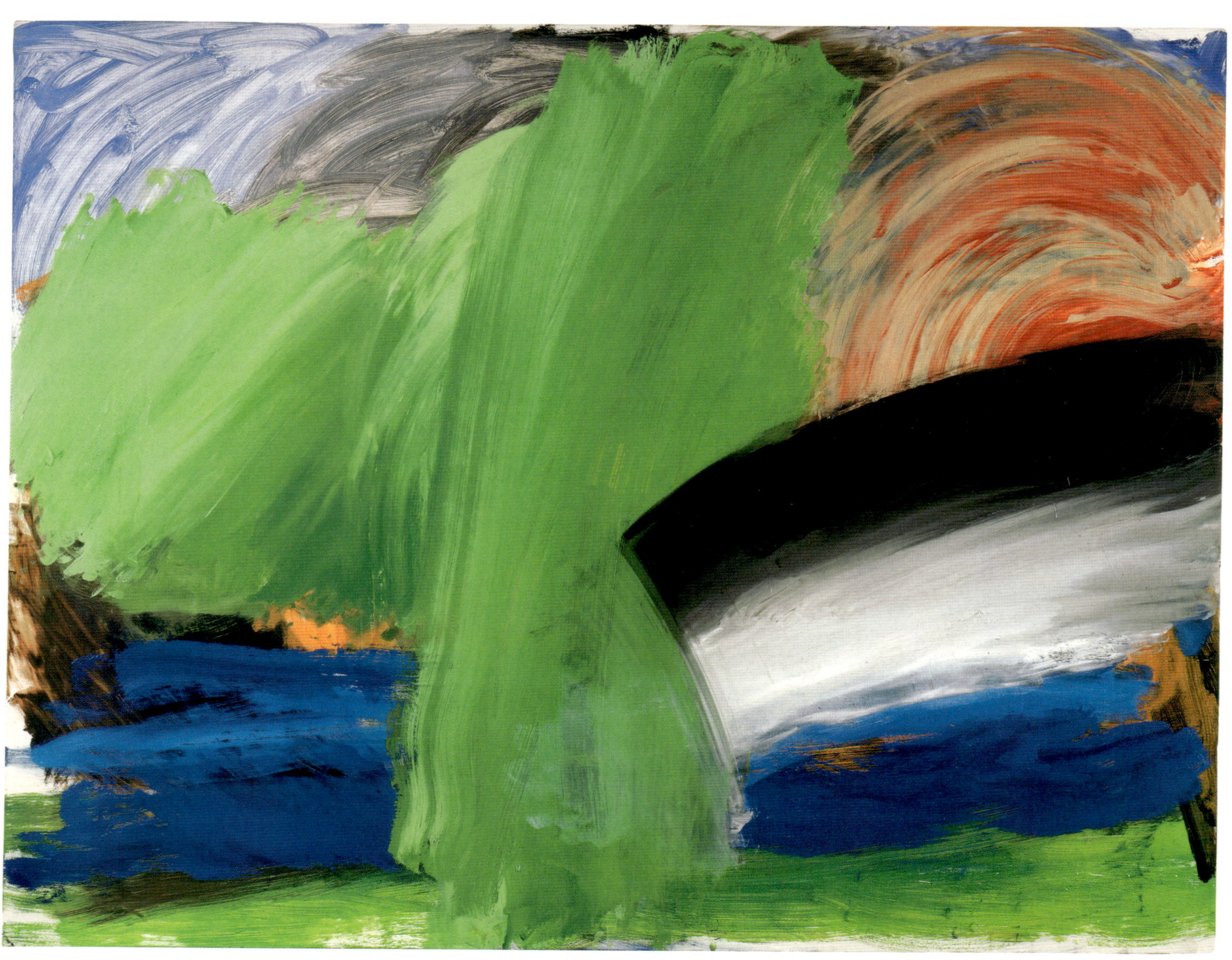

7. Rain at Il Palazzo, 1993–98

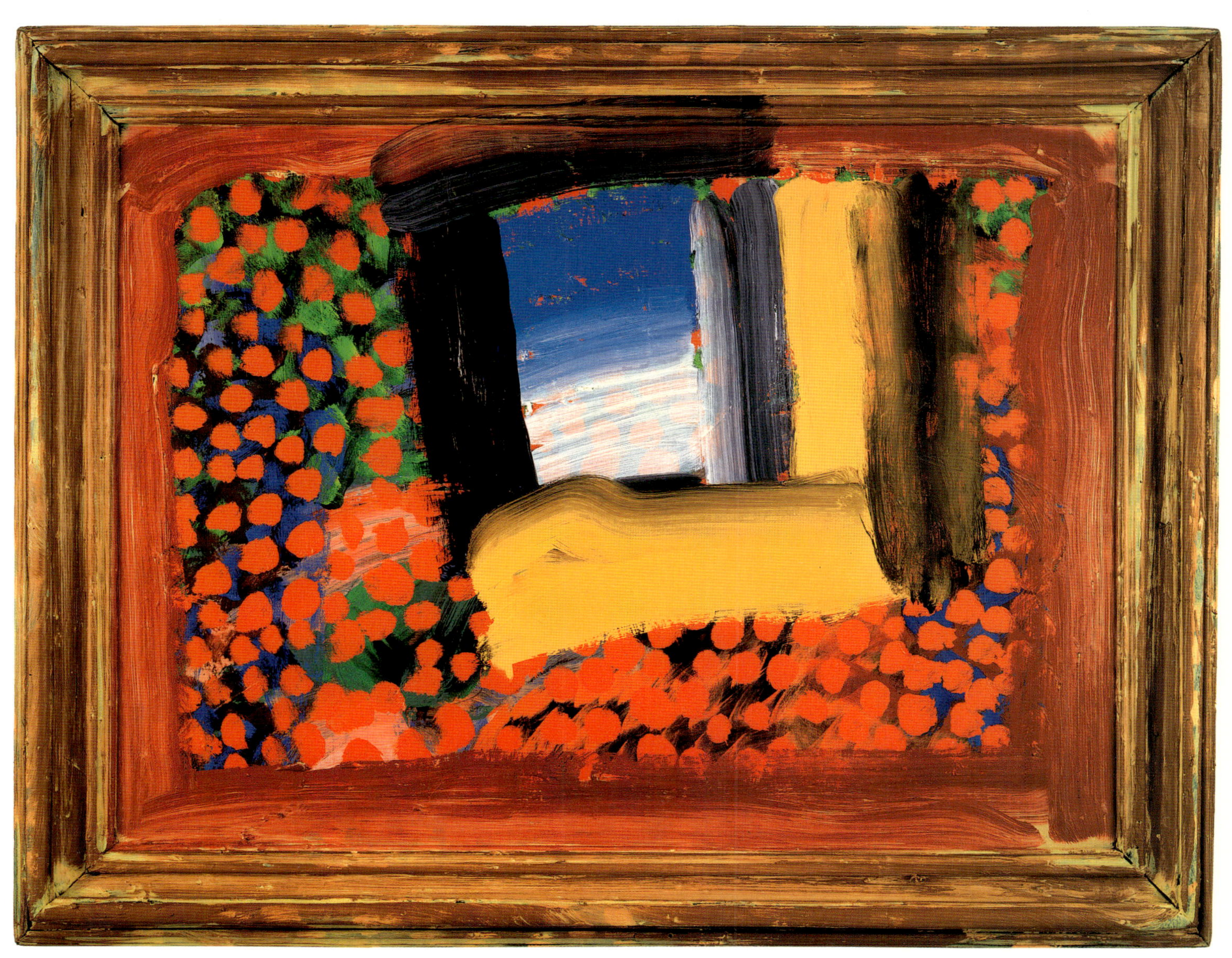

8. **Bedroom Window, 1992–94**

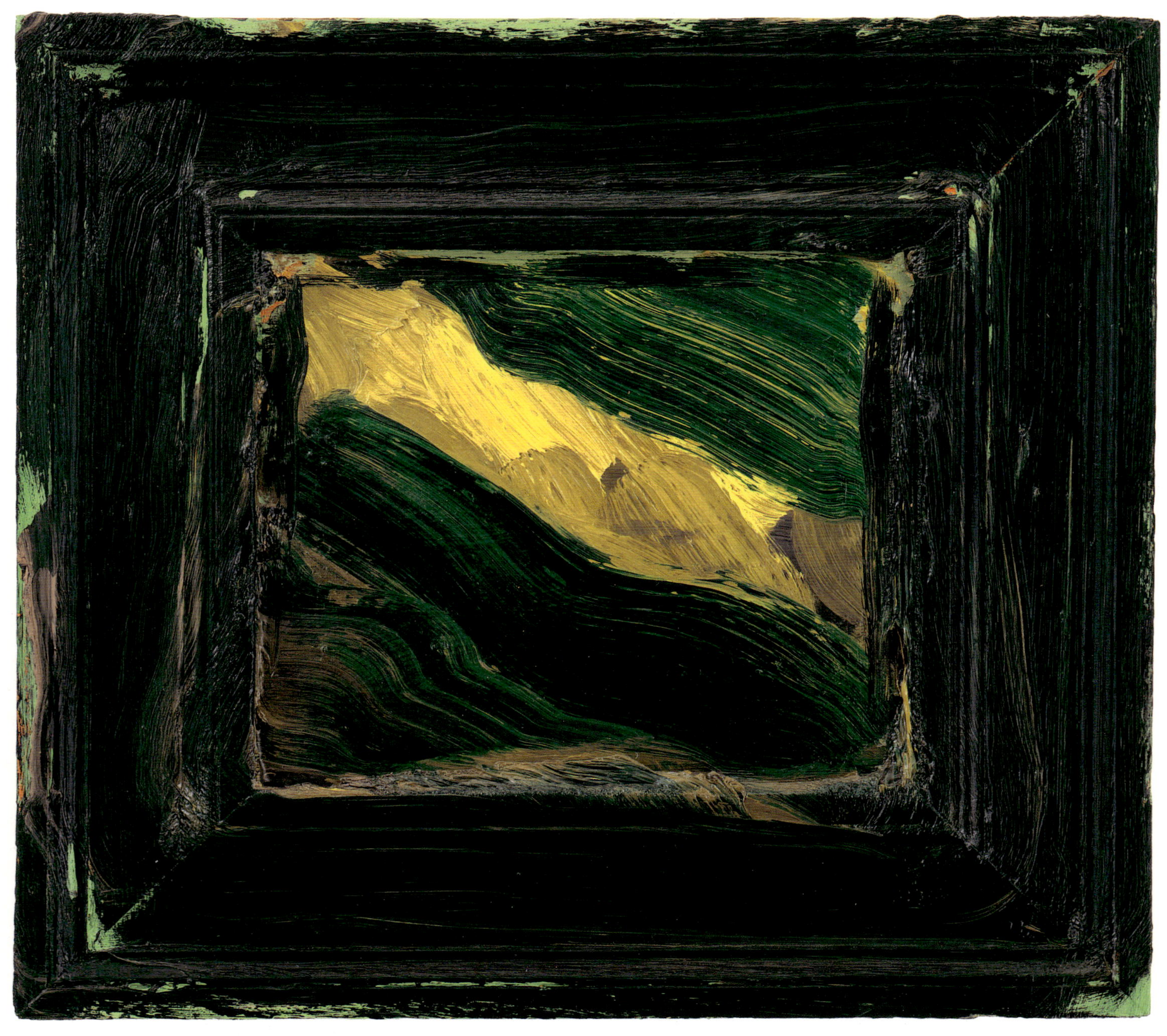

9. Small Rain, 1998–99

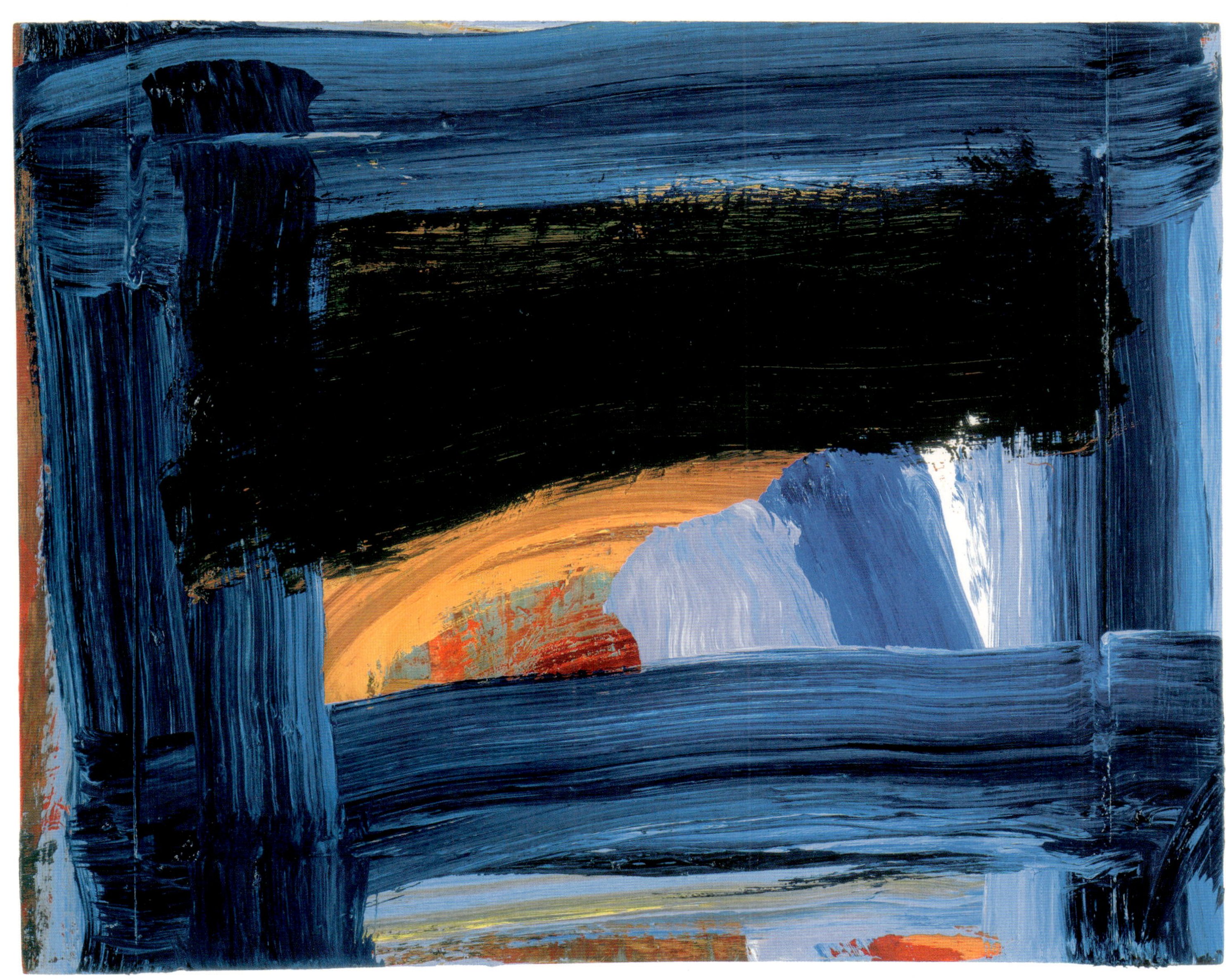

10. Please Explain, 2000

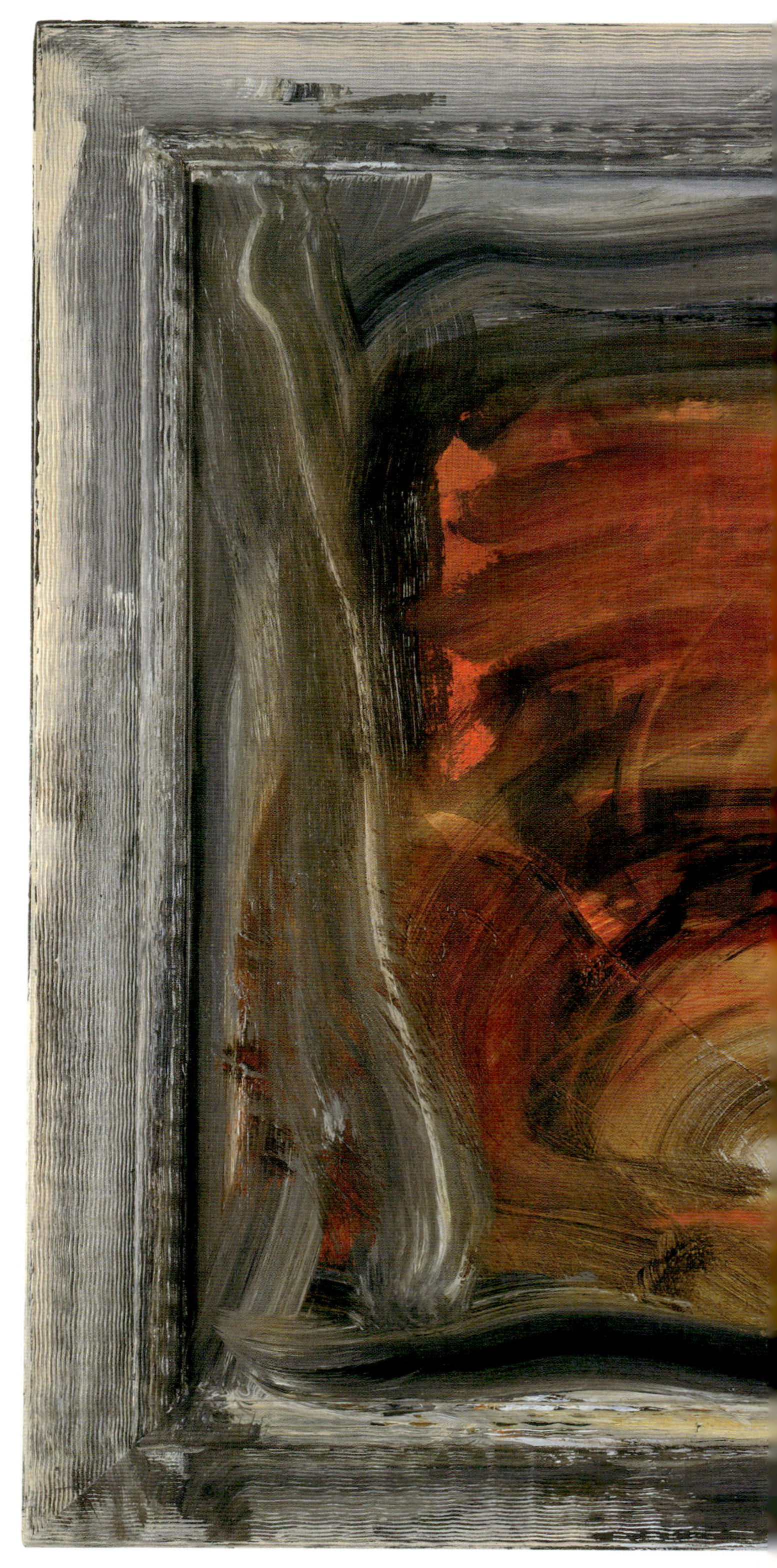

11. Autumn Foliage, 1998–99

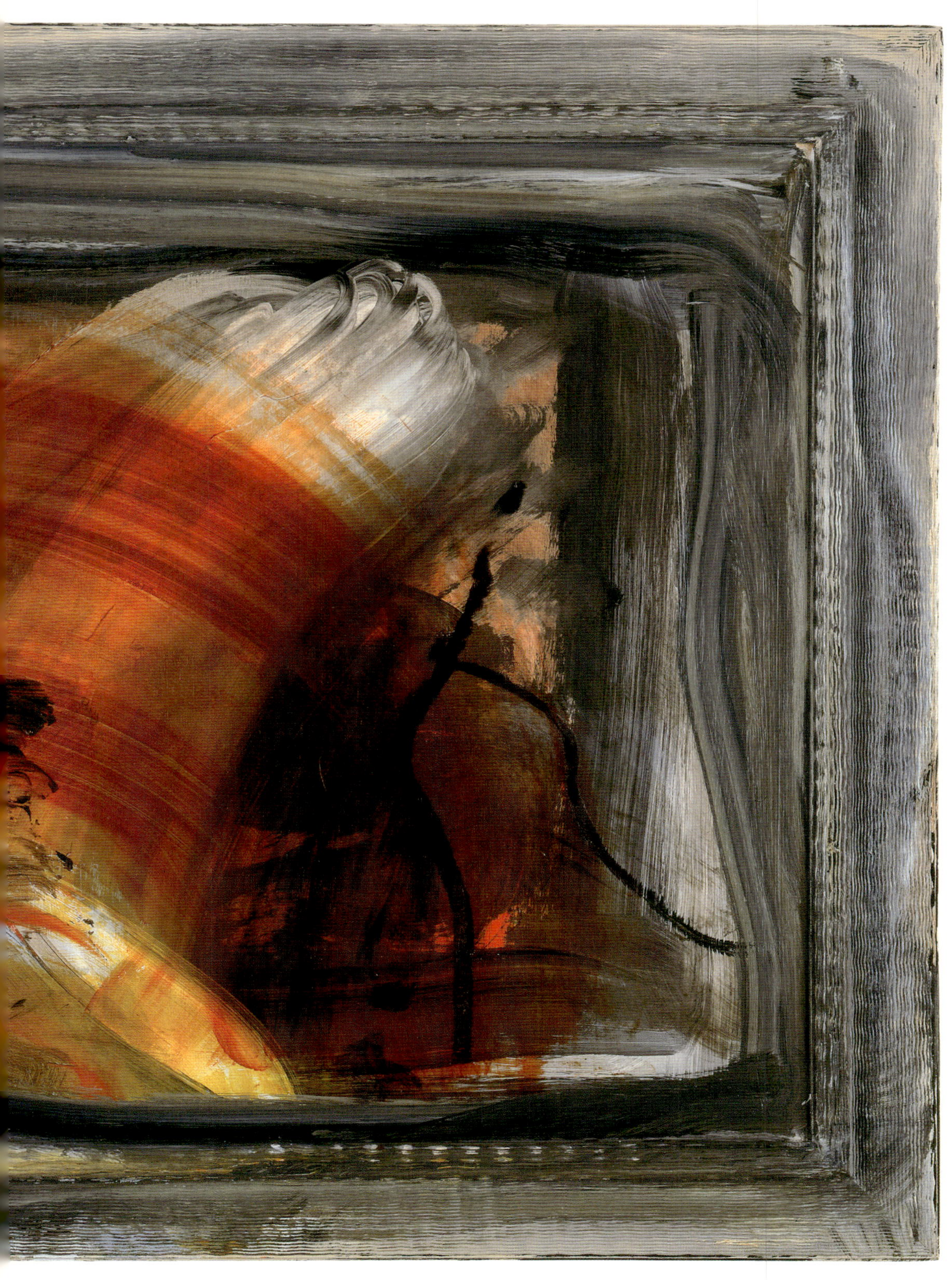

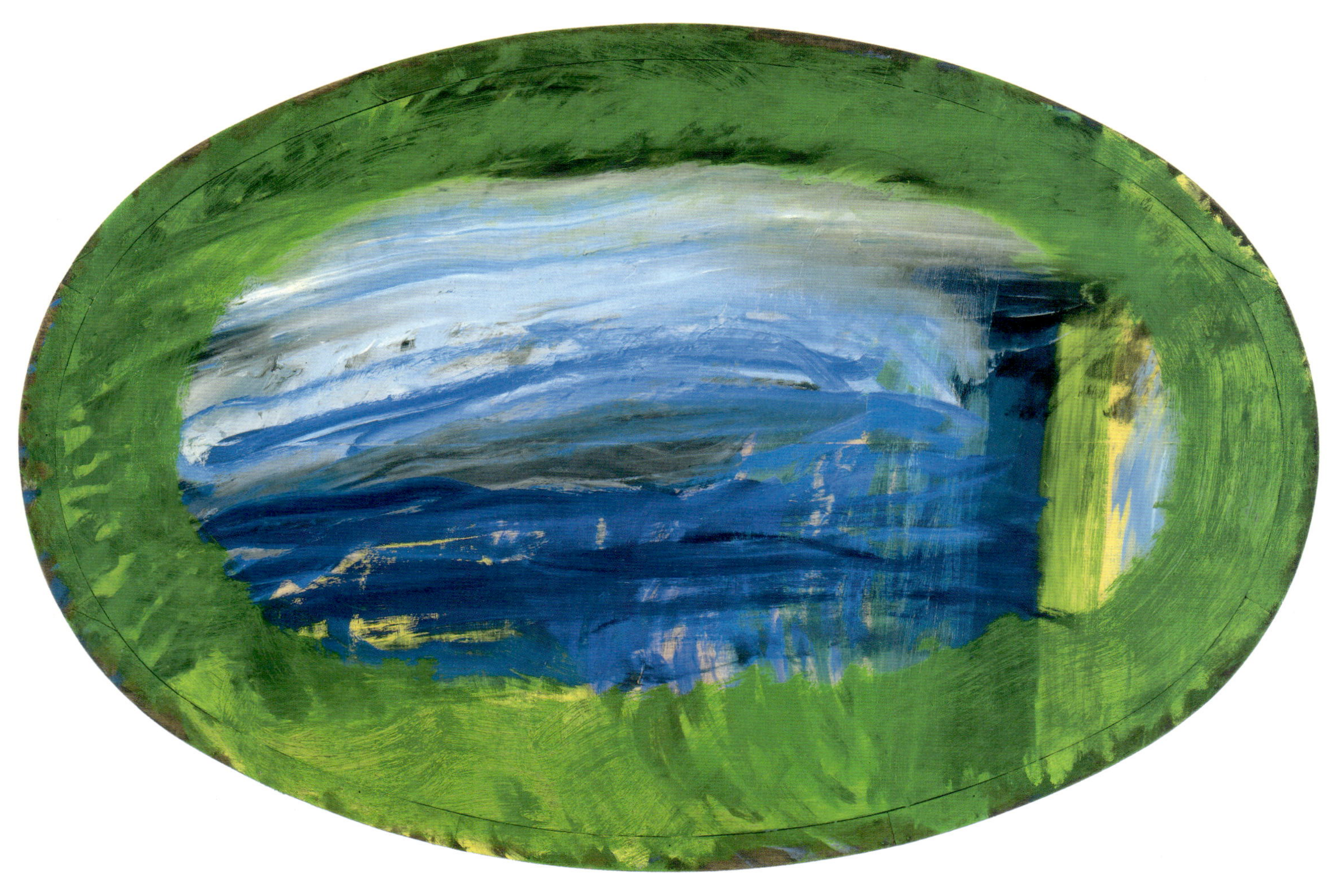

12. Evening Sea, 1998

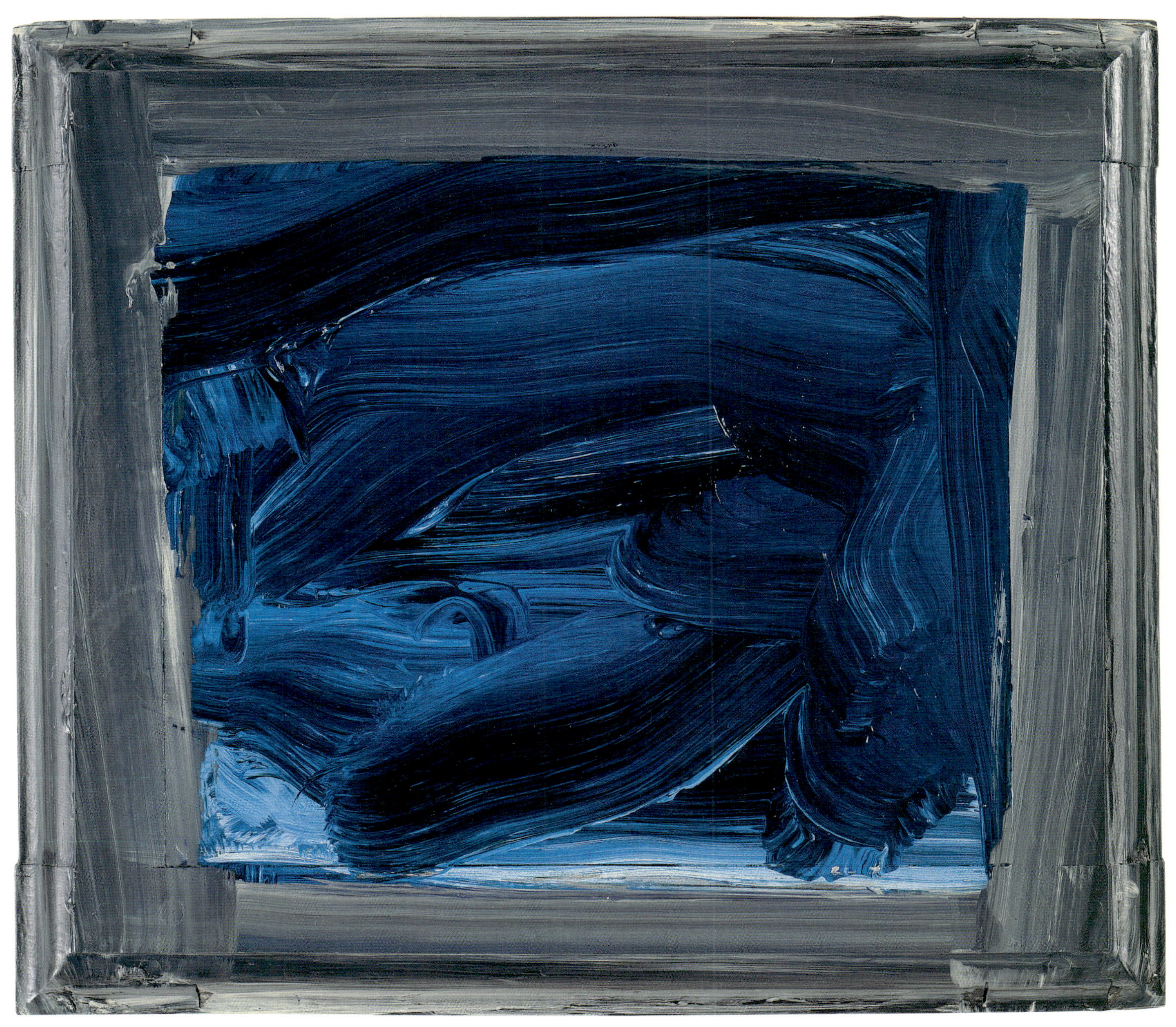

13. Ultramarine, 2000–05

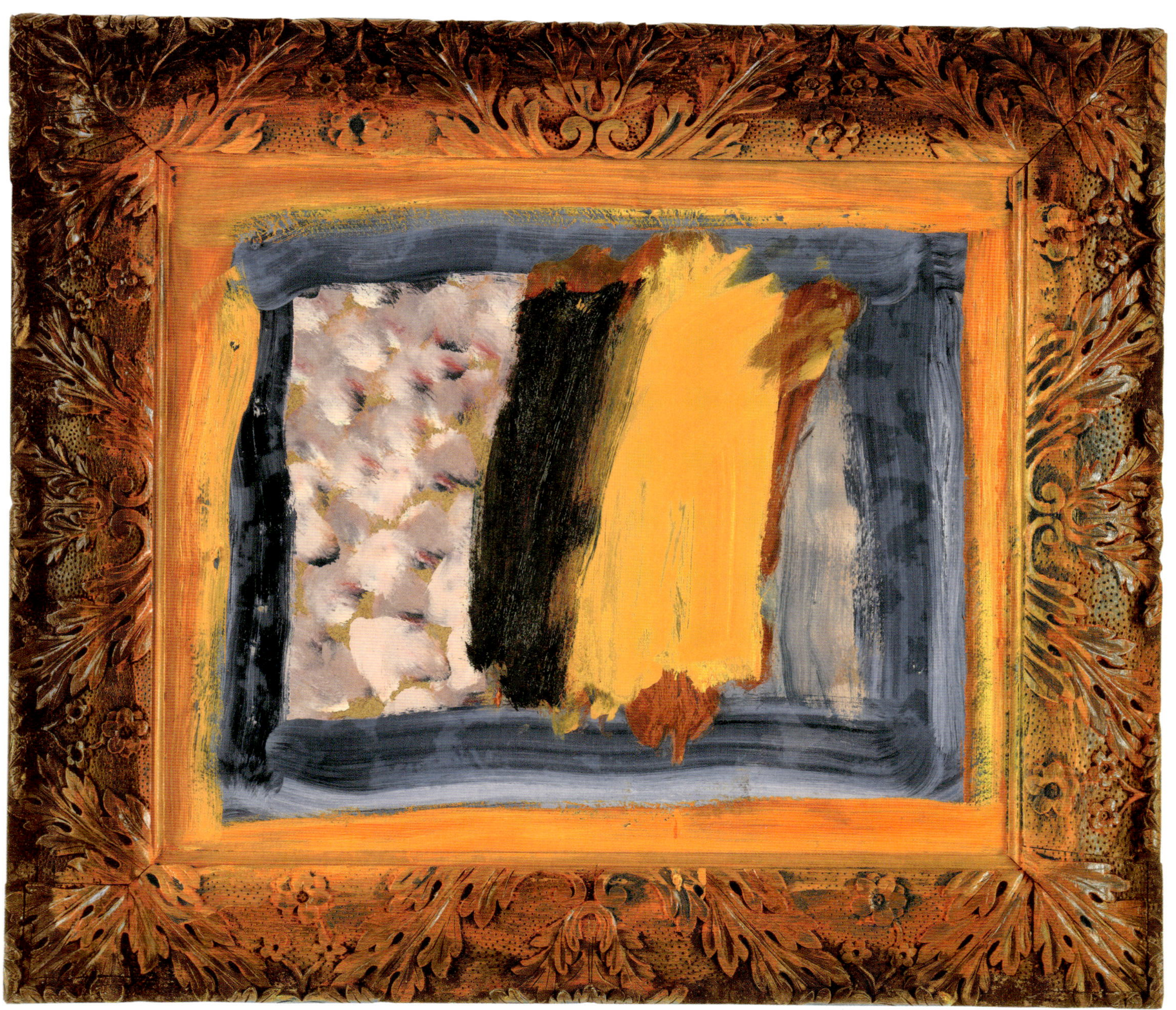

14. Double Portrait, 2000–03

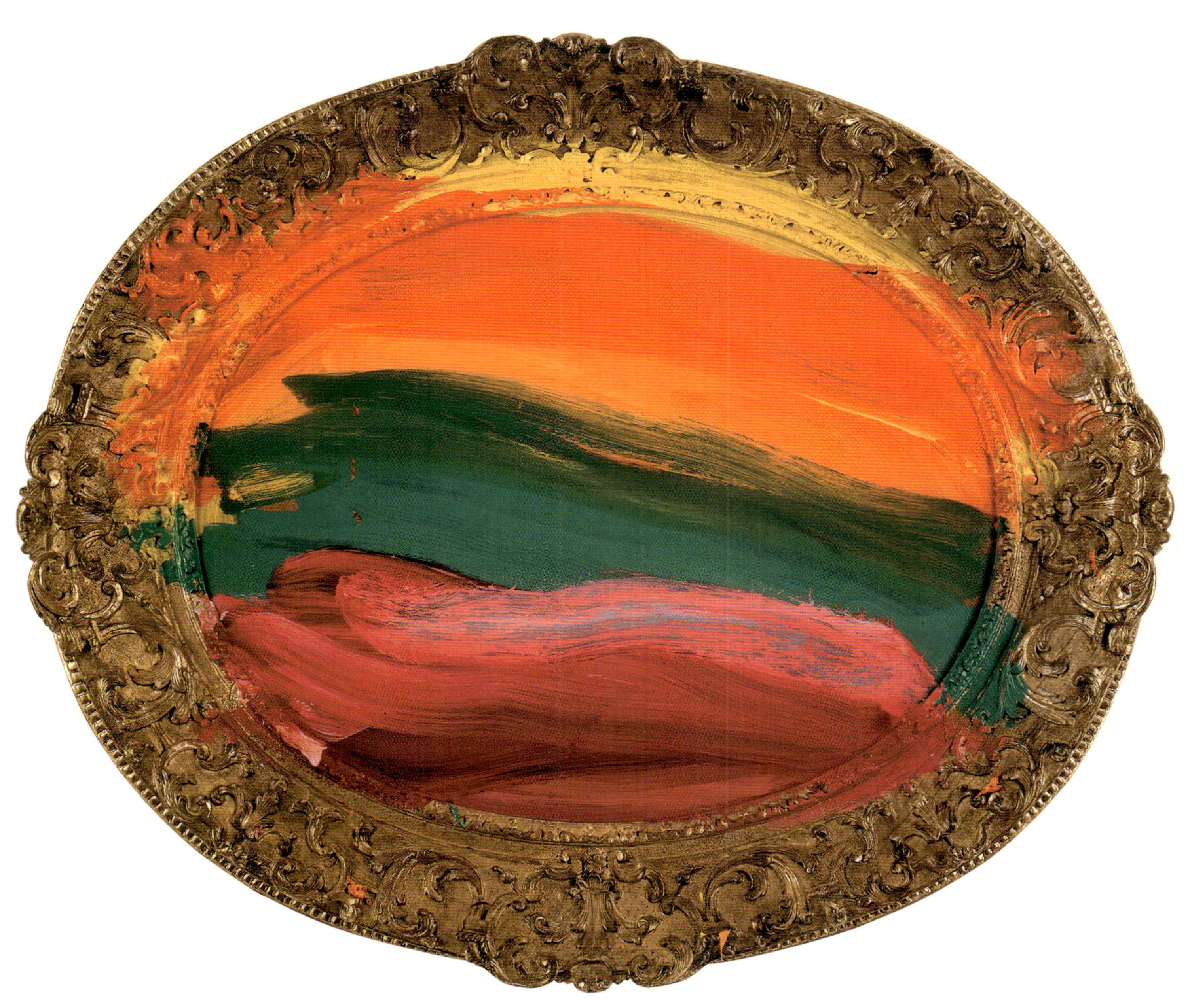

15. Out of the Window, 2000

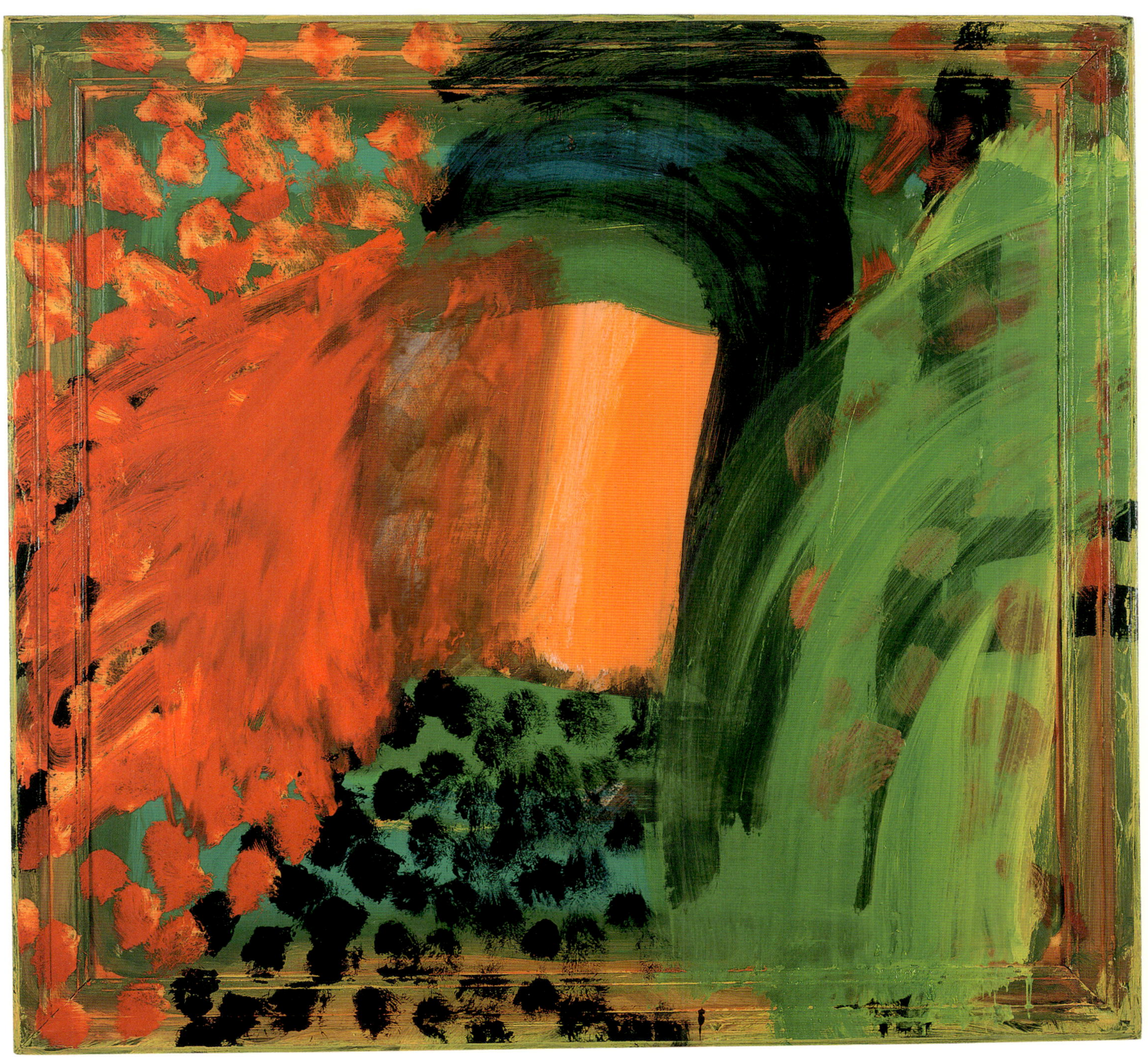

16. Torso, 2000

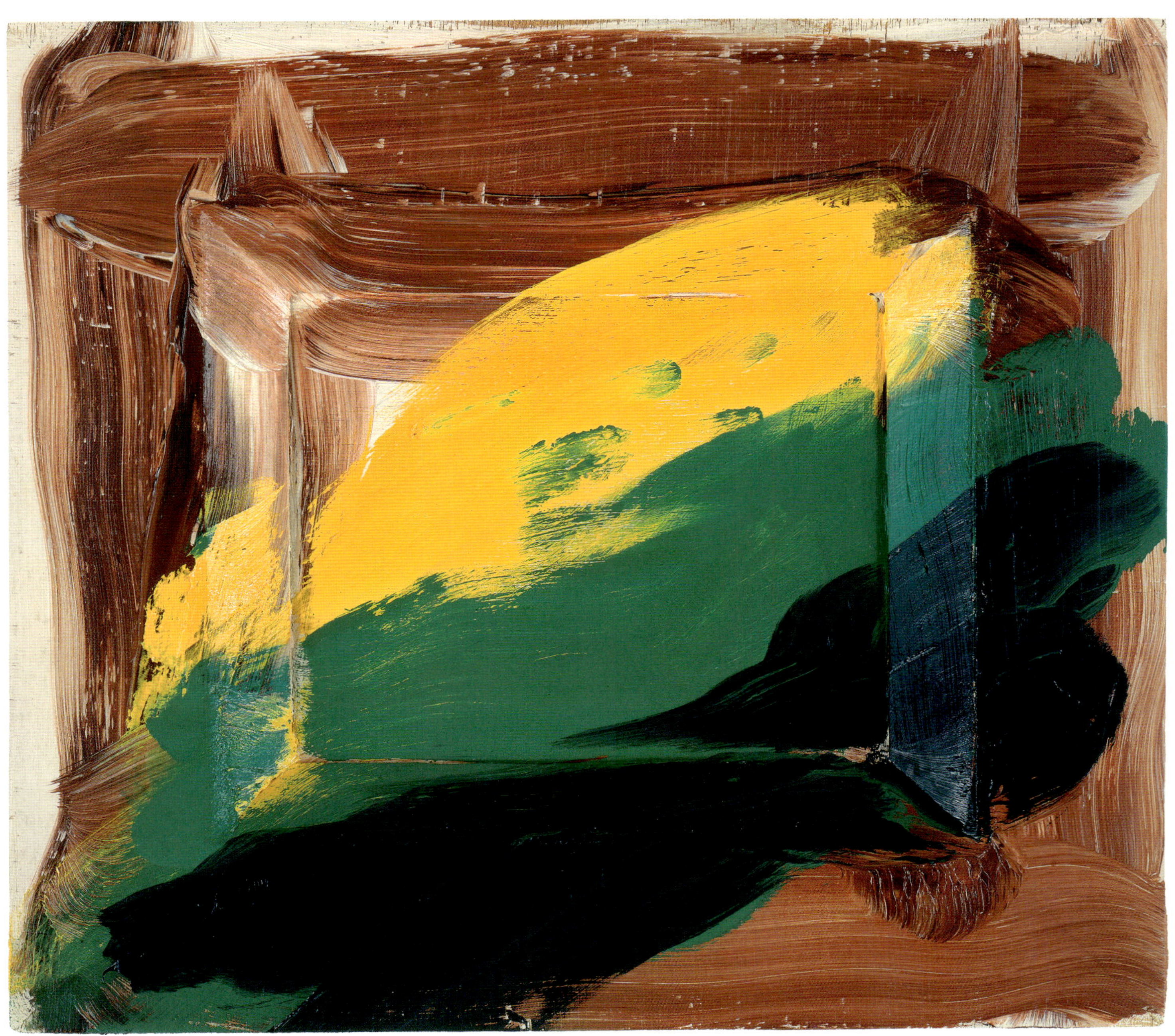

17. Chintz, 2002–03

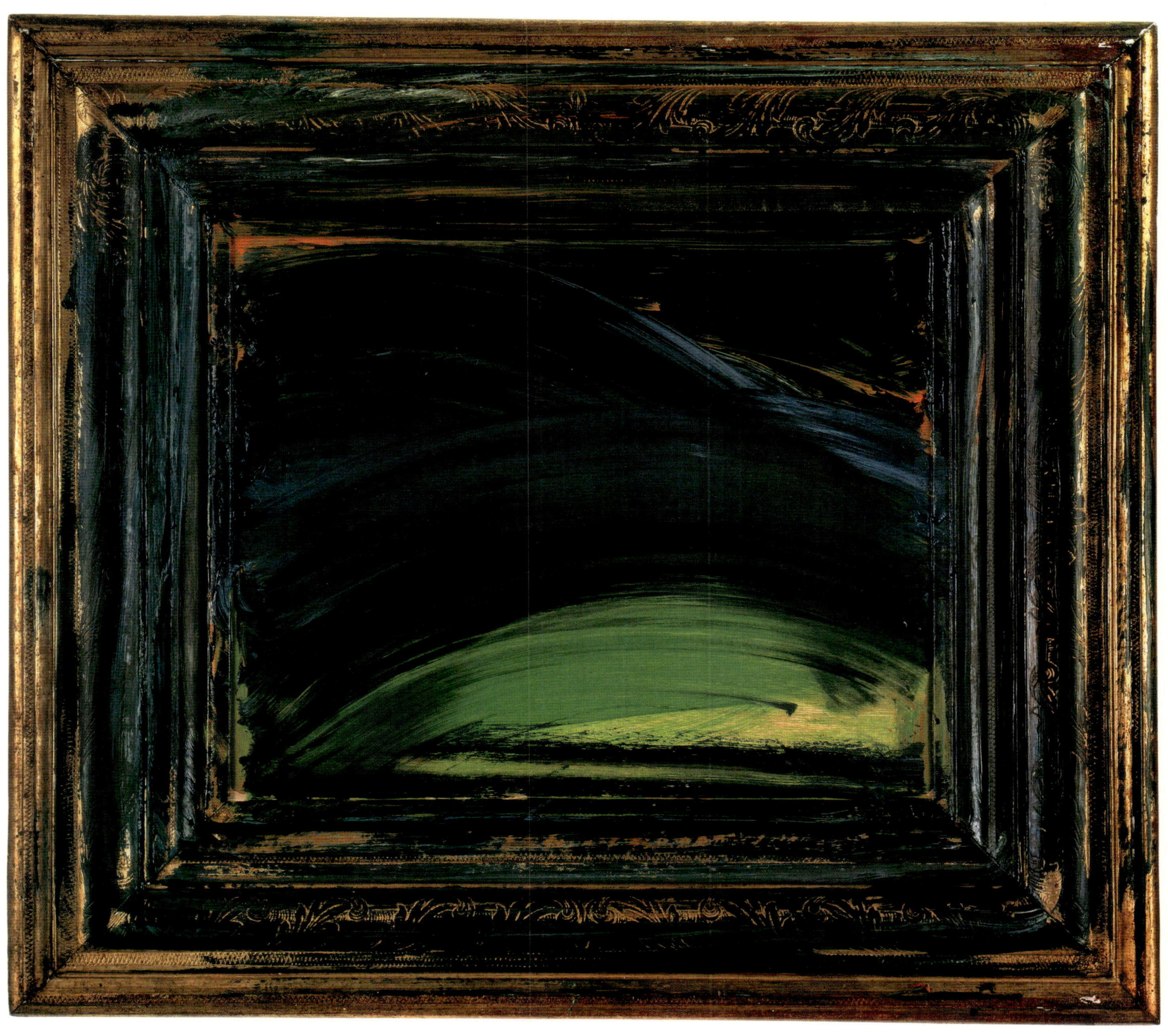

18. After the Storm, 2000

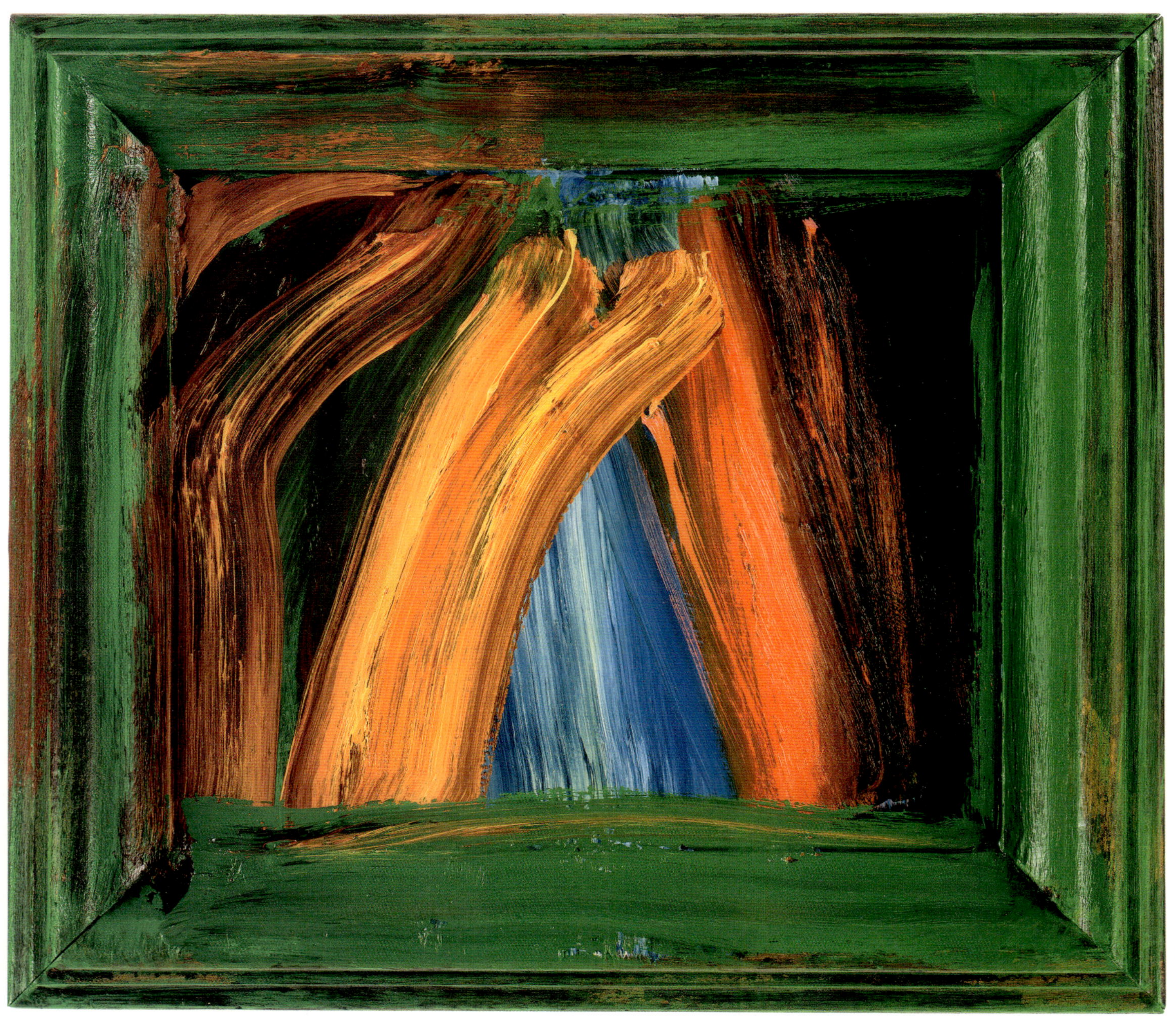

19. Visitors, 2002–05

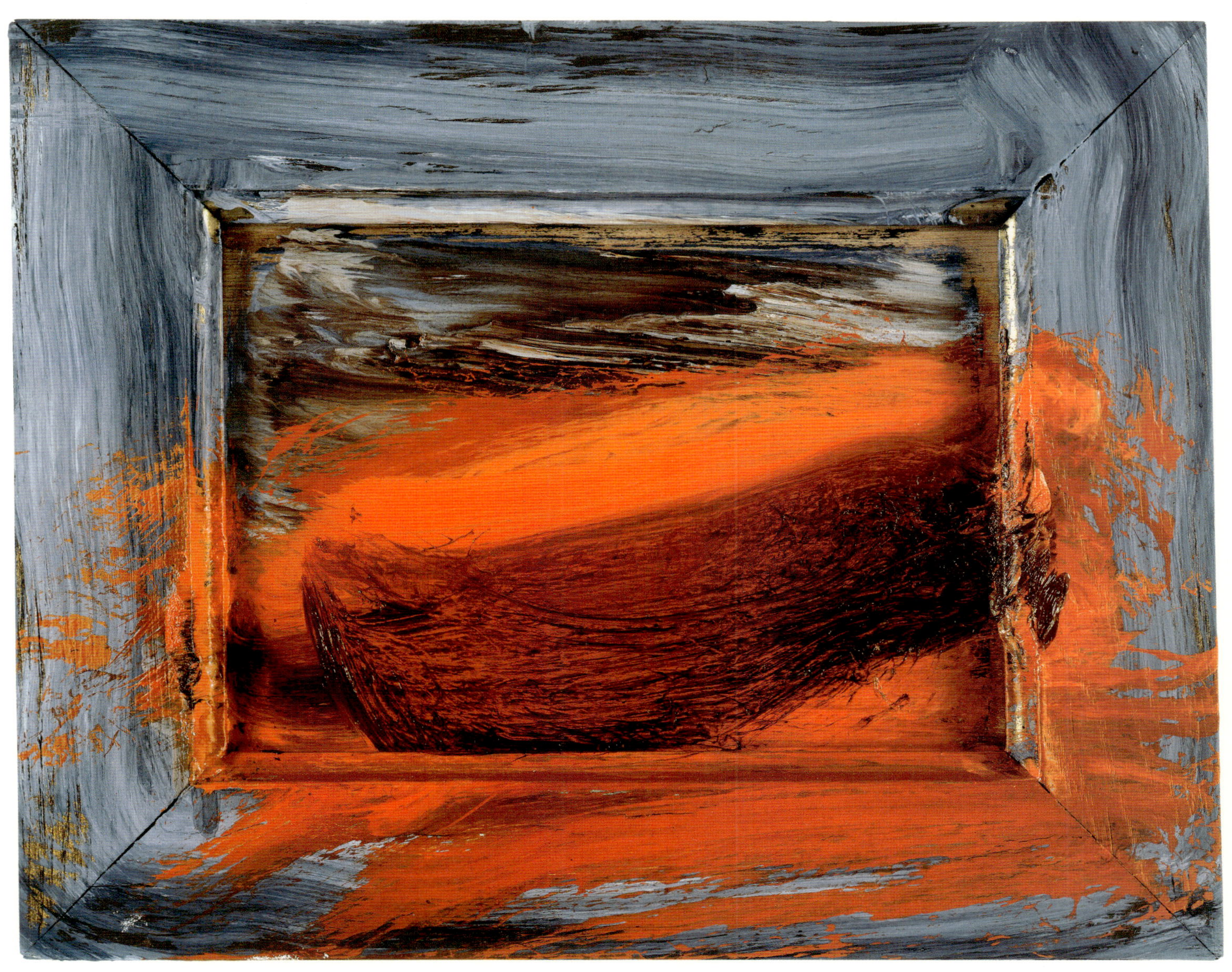

20. Little Venice, 2003

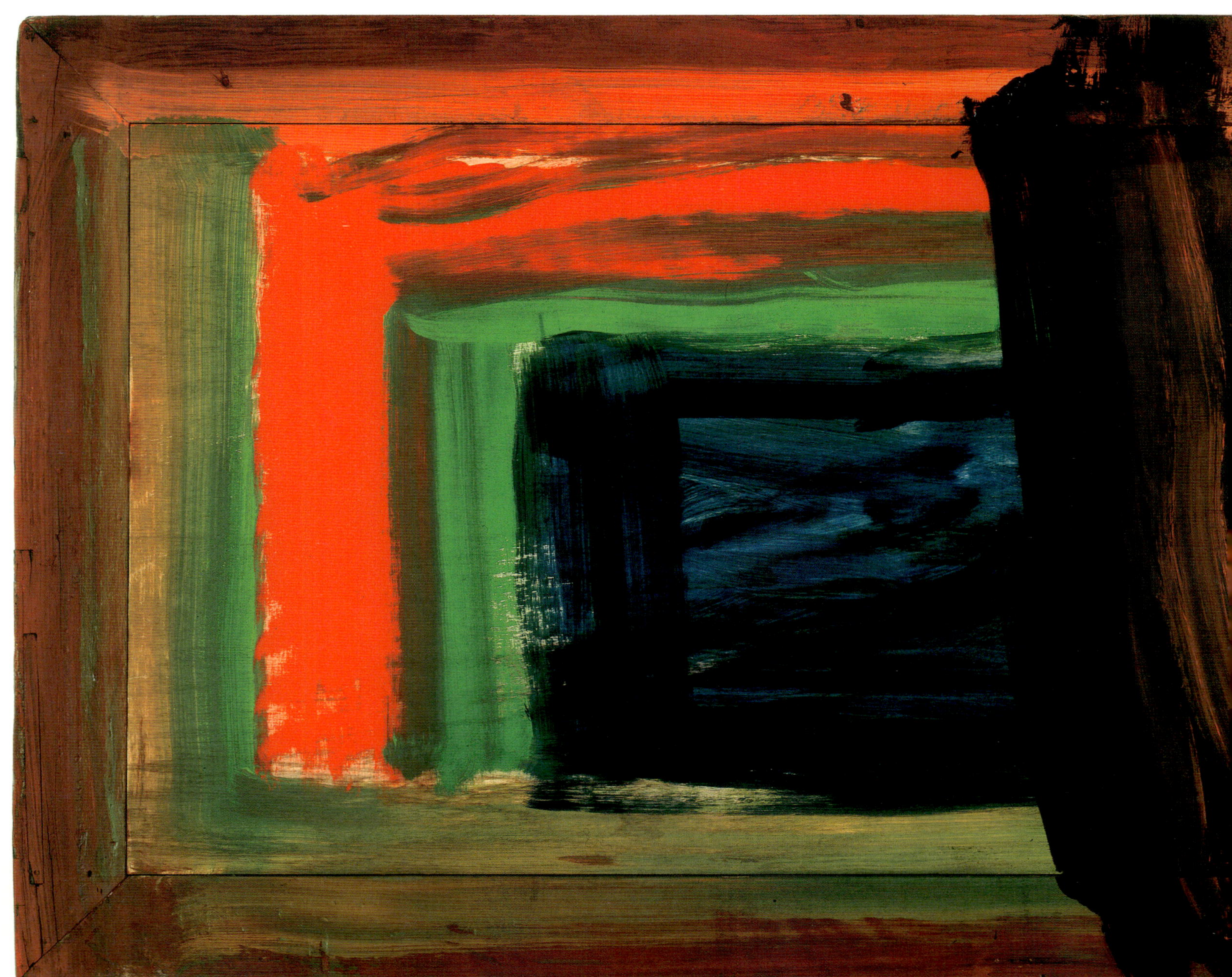

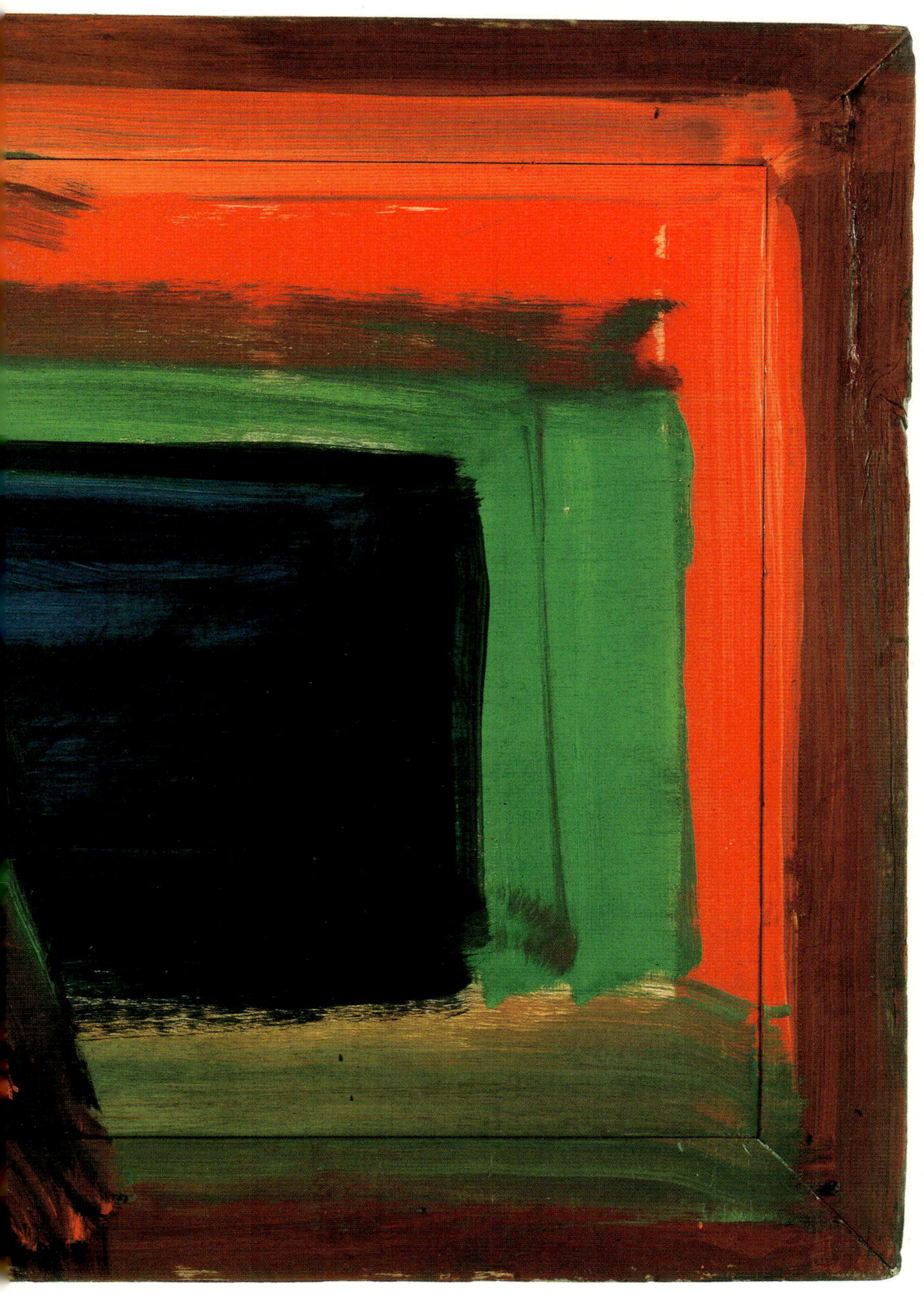

21. Performance Art, 2003–04

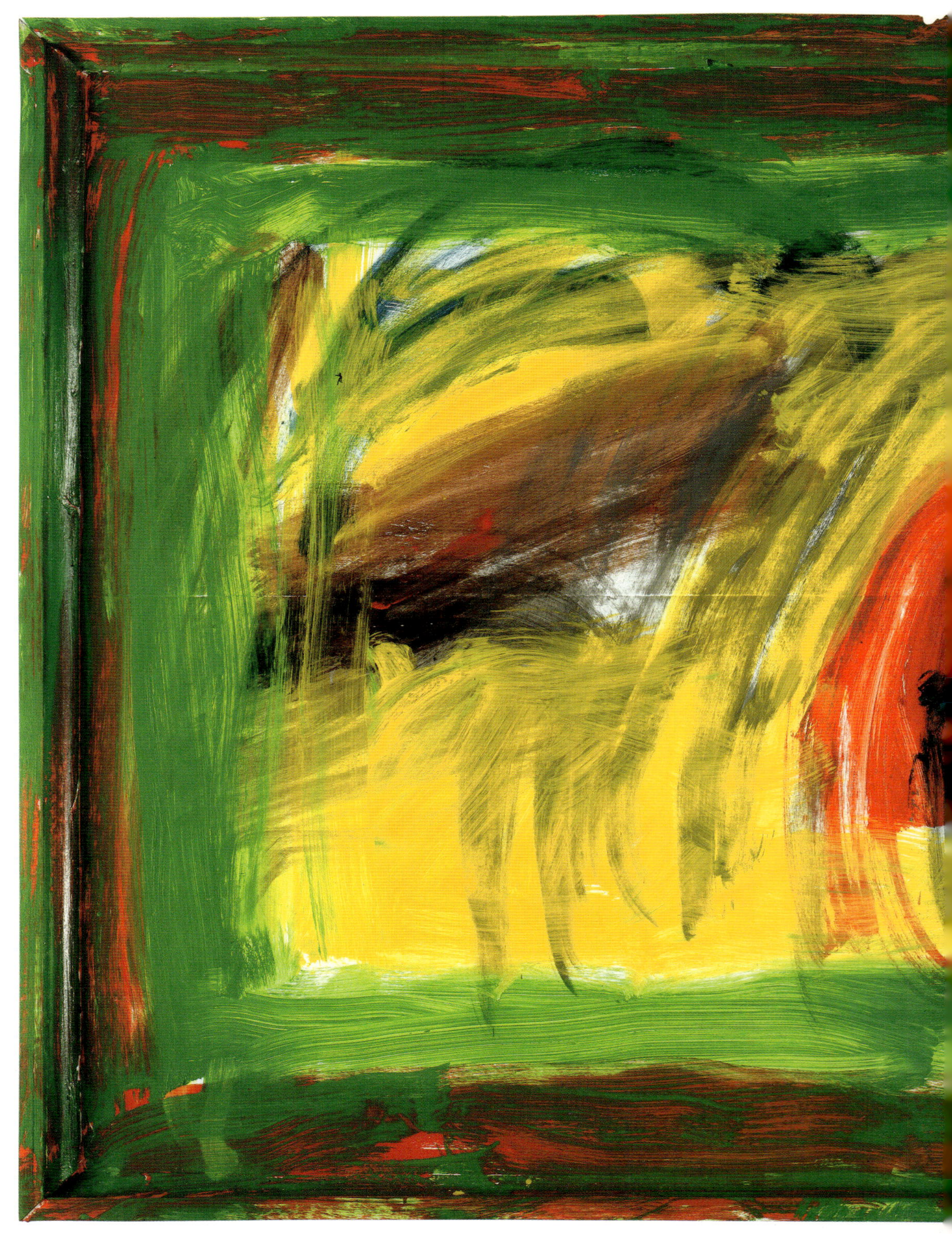

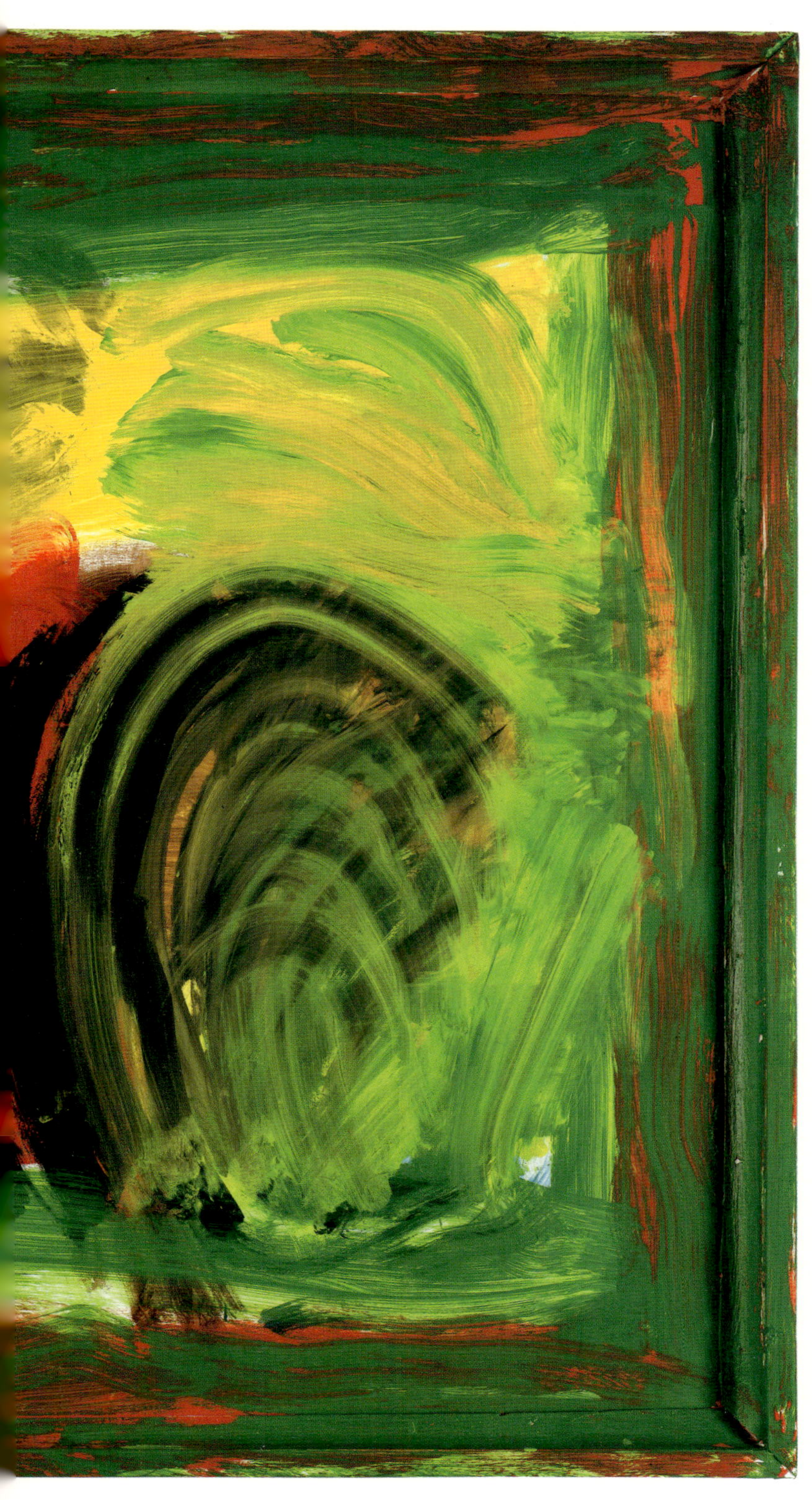

22. Memorial, 2000–03

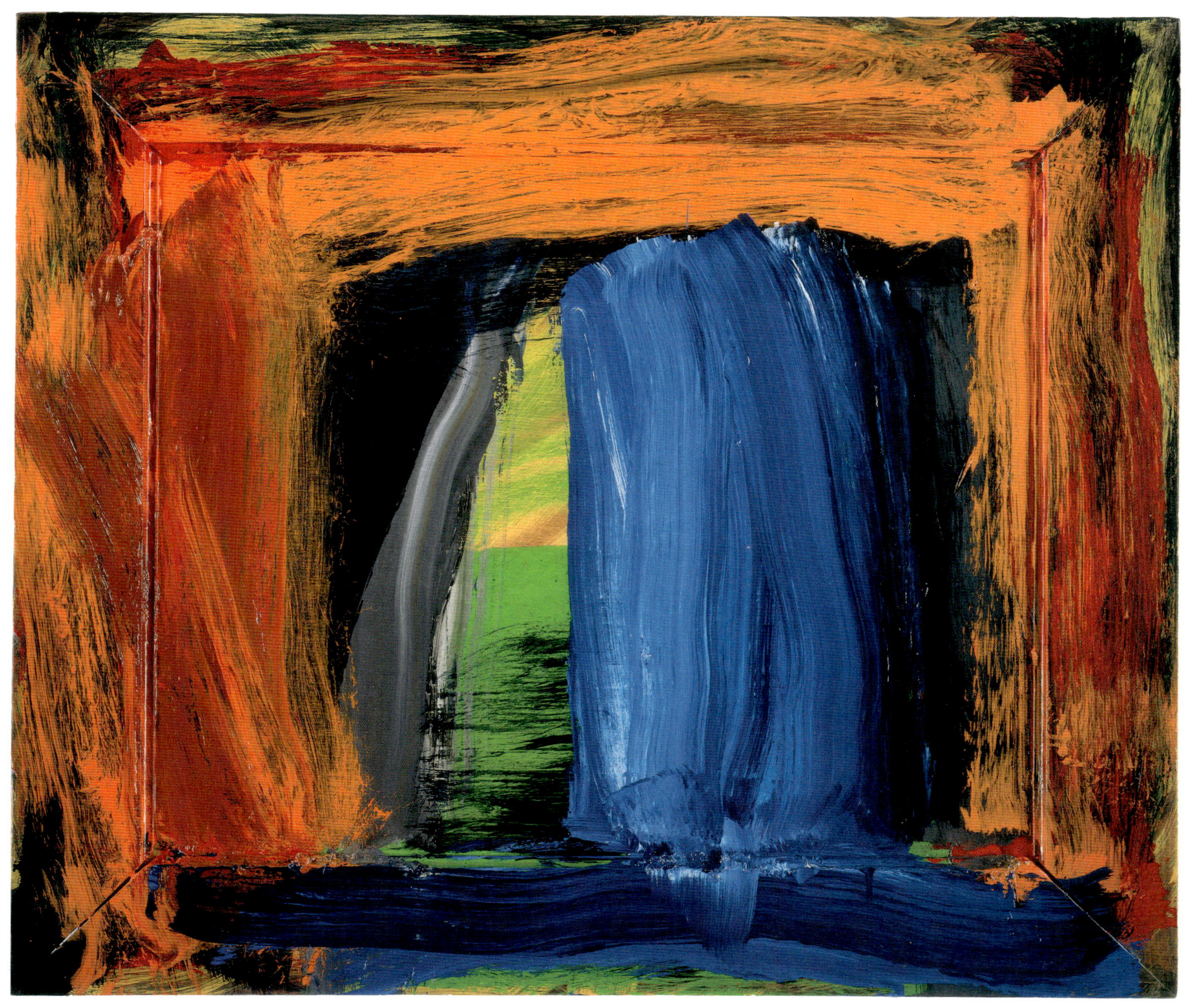

23. Navy Blue, 2002–04

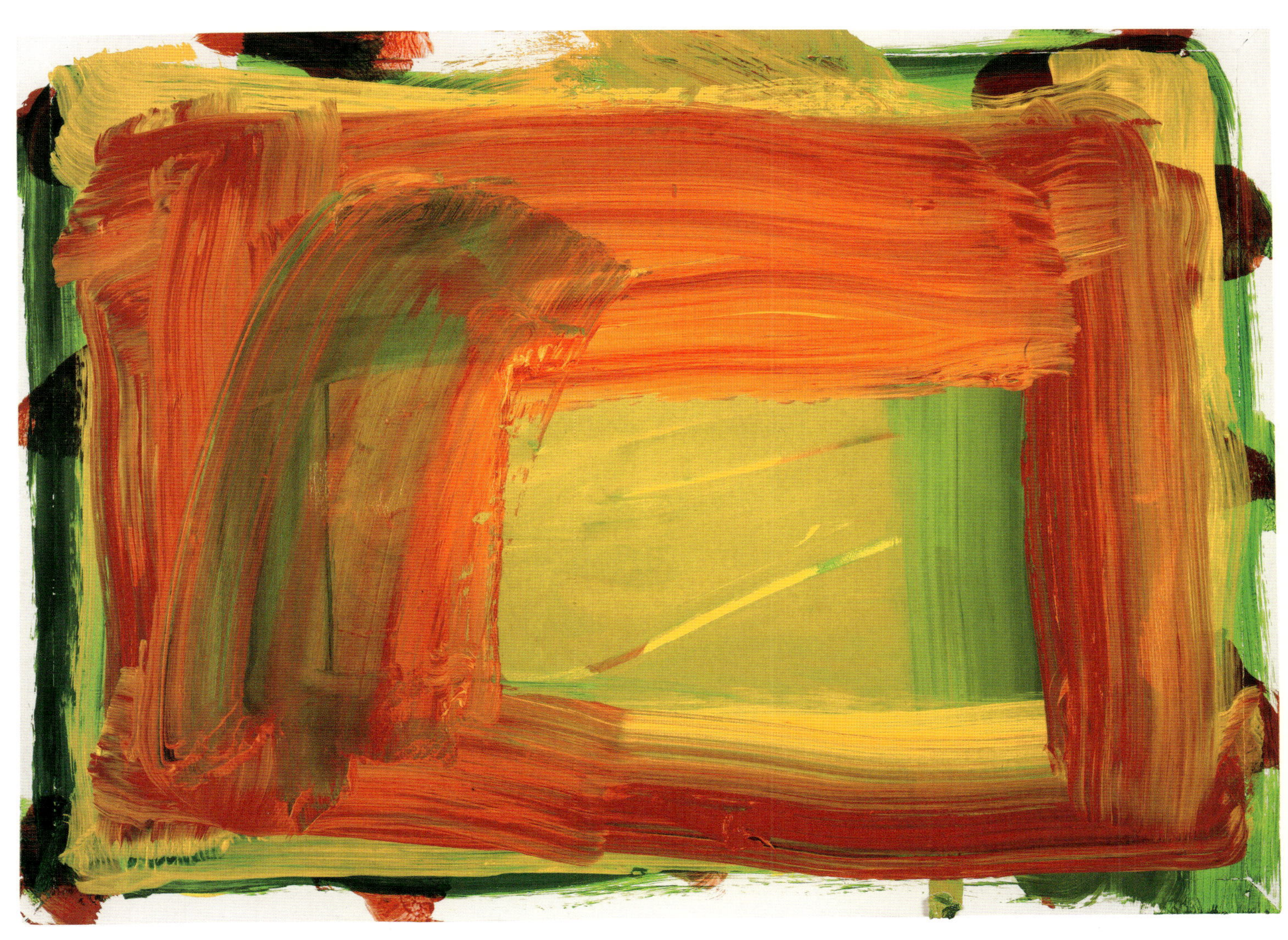

24. Heat, 2003–04

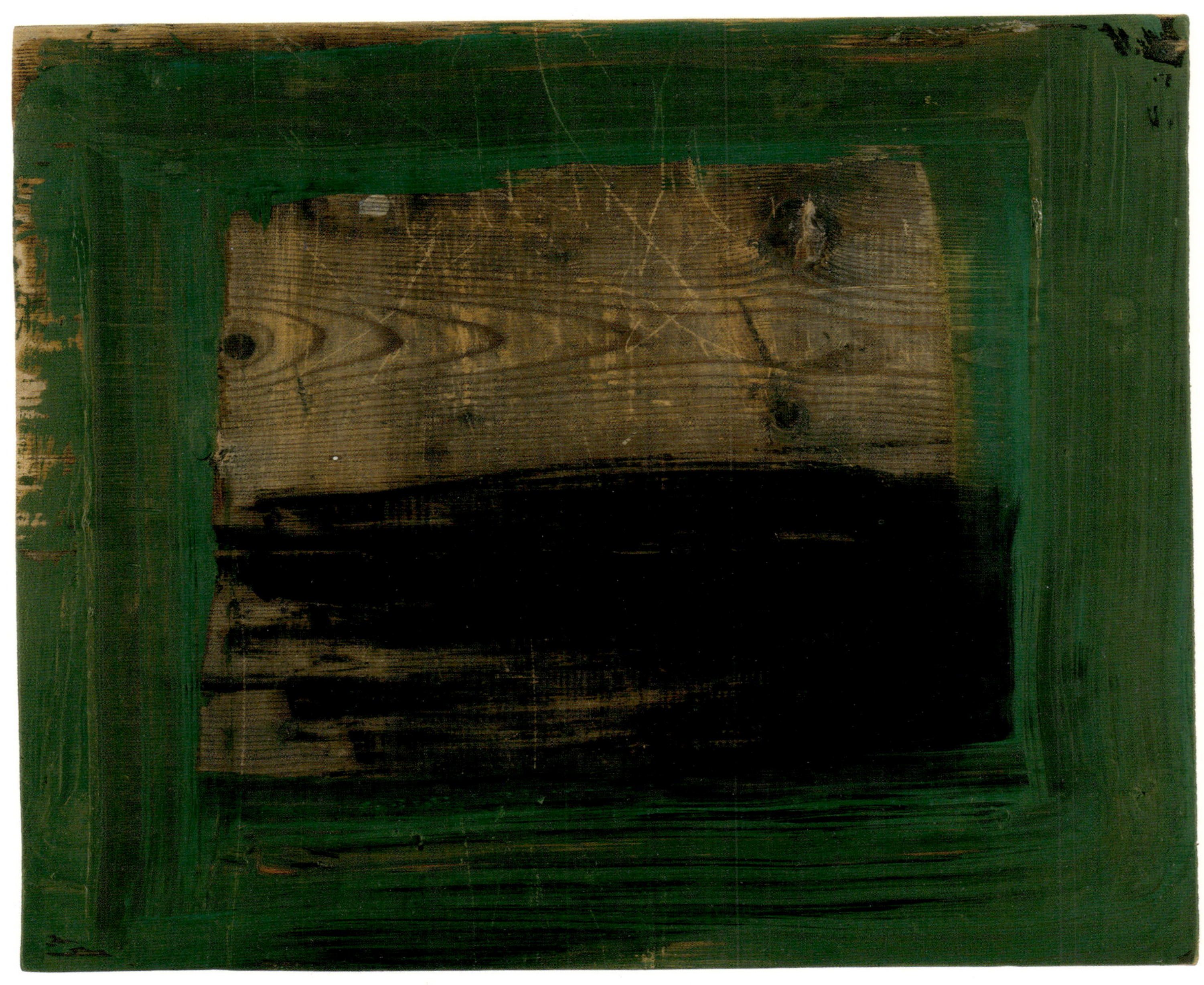

25. Mud, 2002

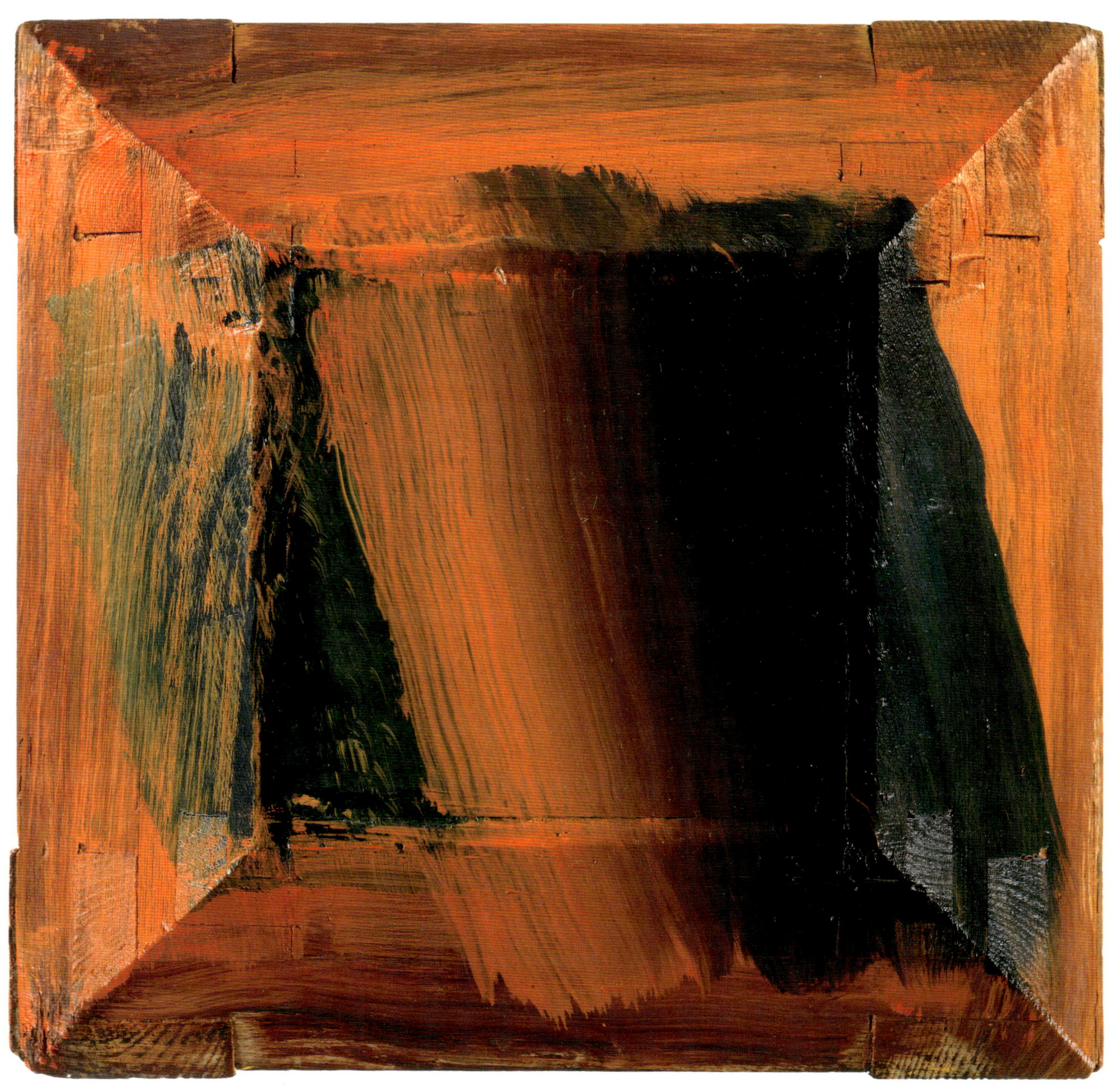

26. Silence, 1997–2004

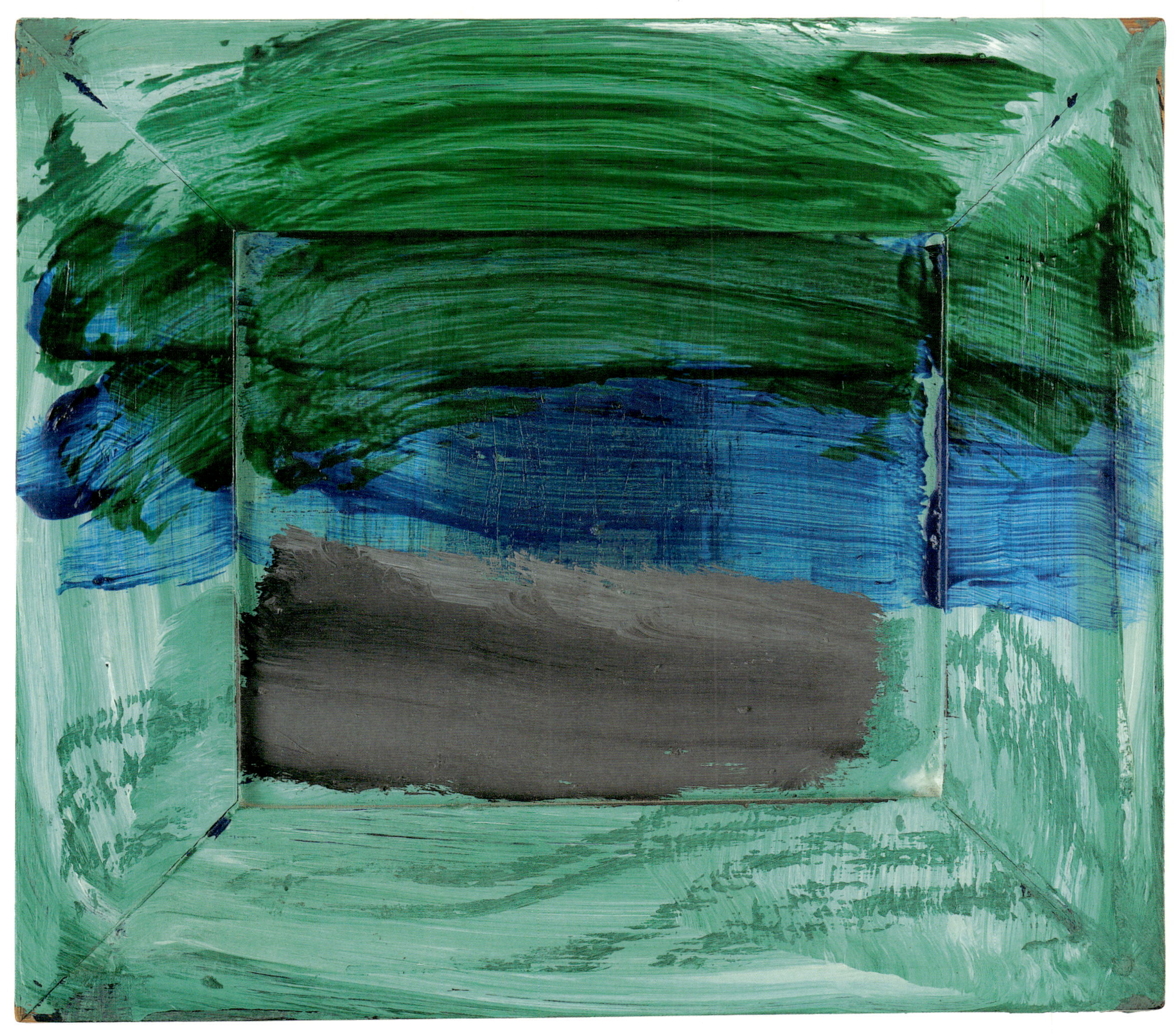

27. Venice Grey Water, 1988–89

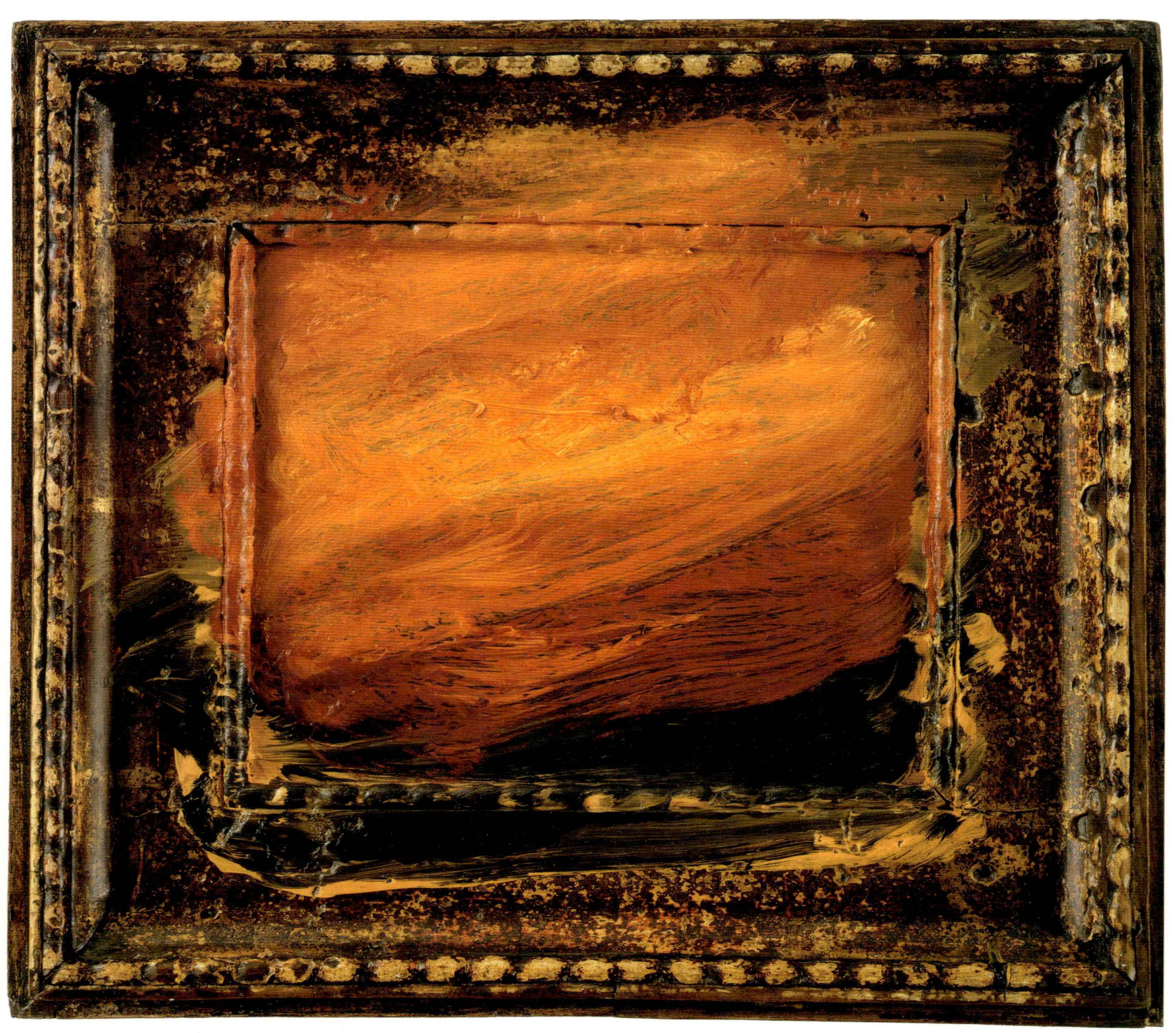

28. Old Sky, 1996–97

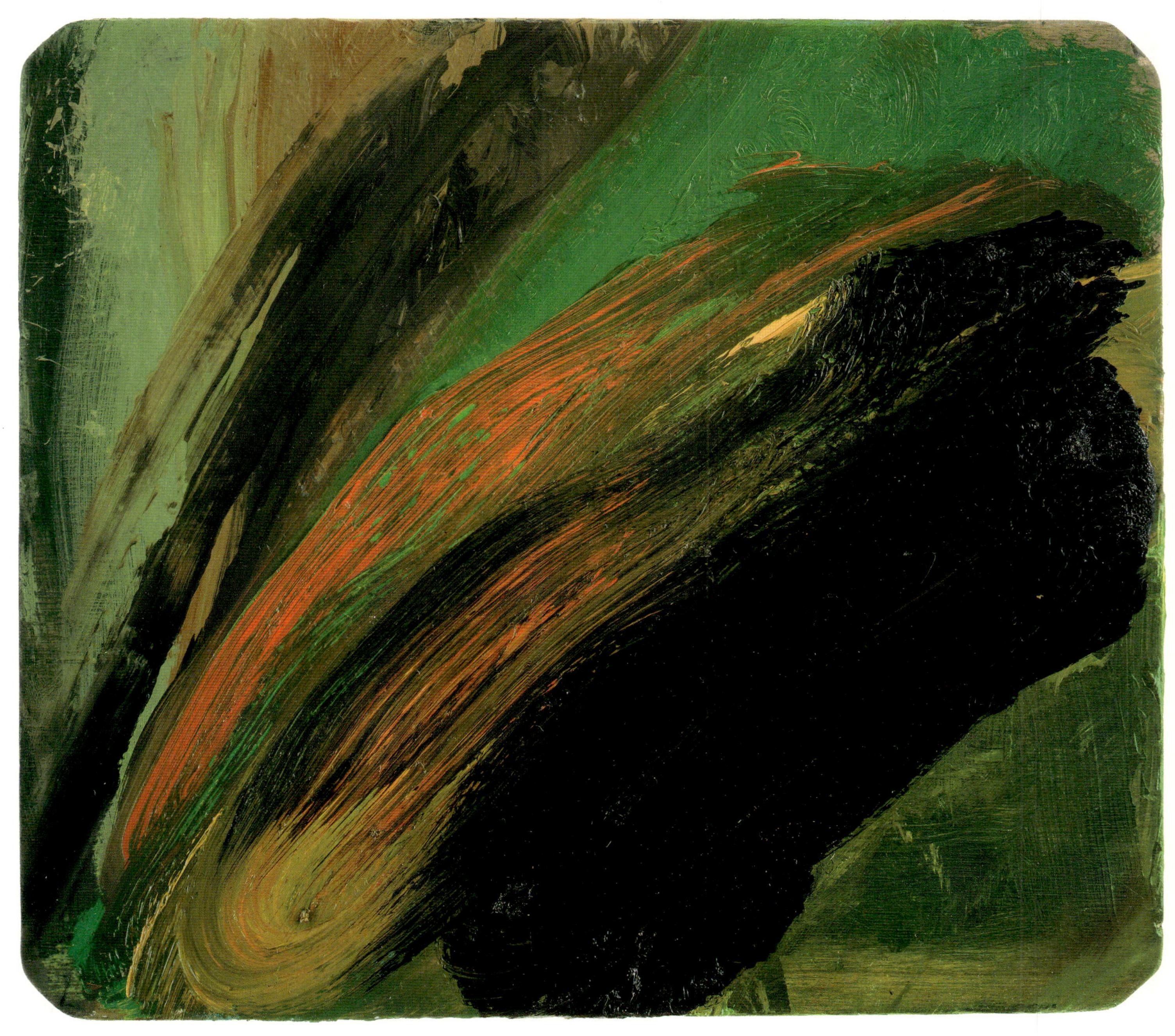

29. An Autumn Leaf, 2000

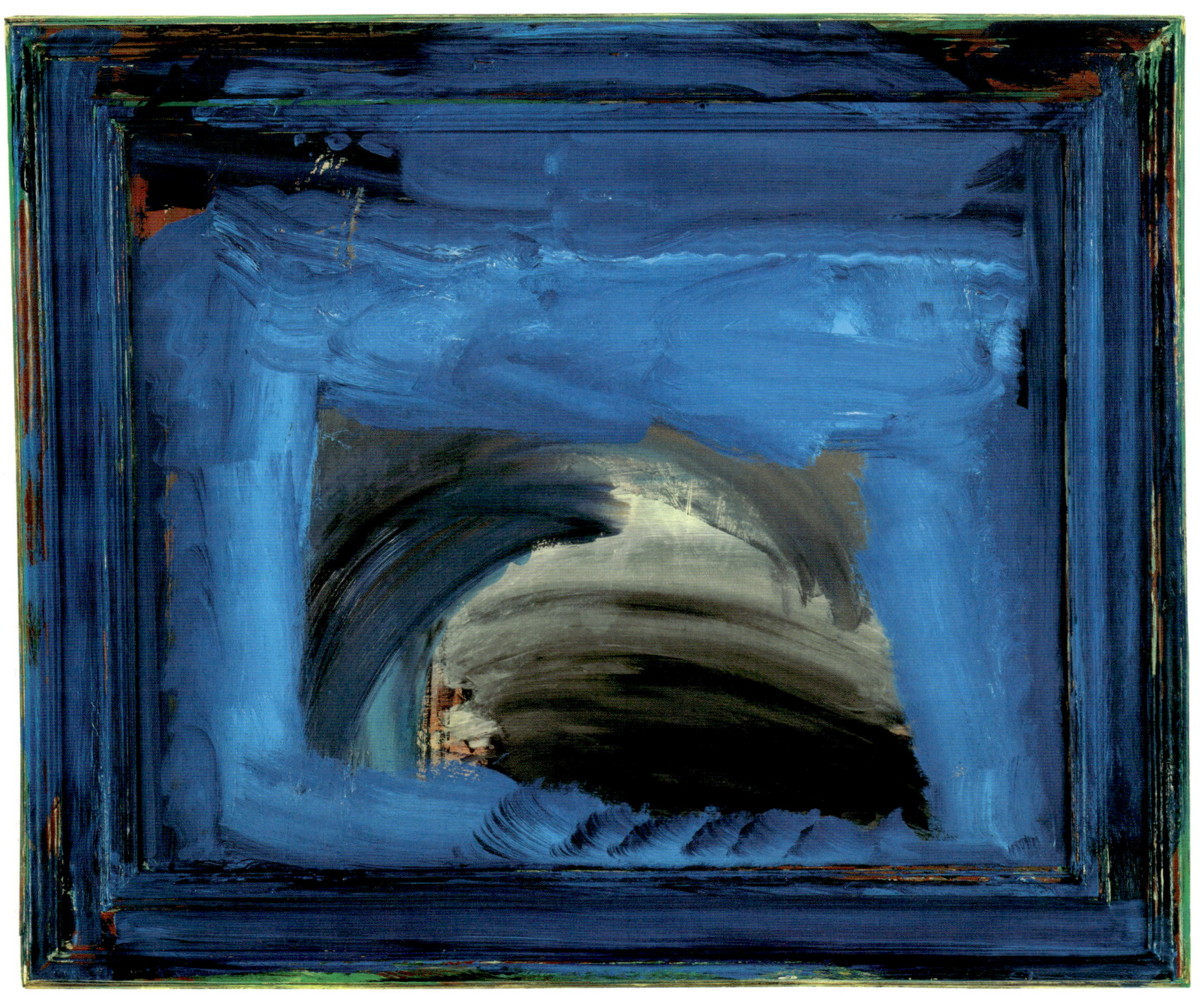

30. Thunder, 1999–2002

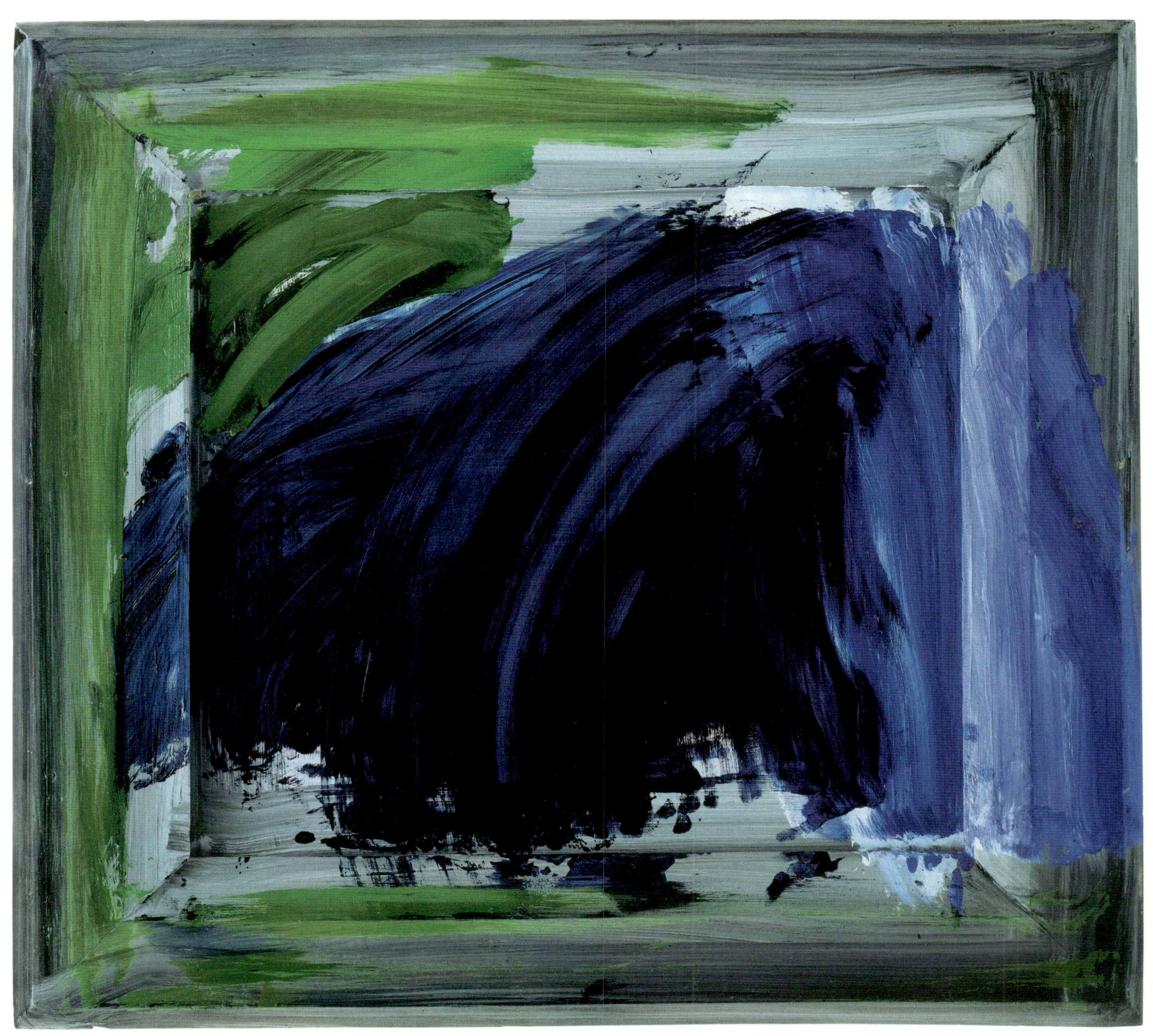

31. **Spring Rain, 2000–02**

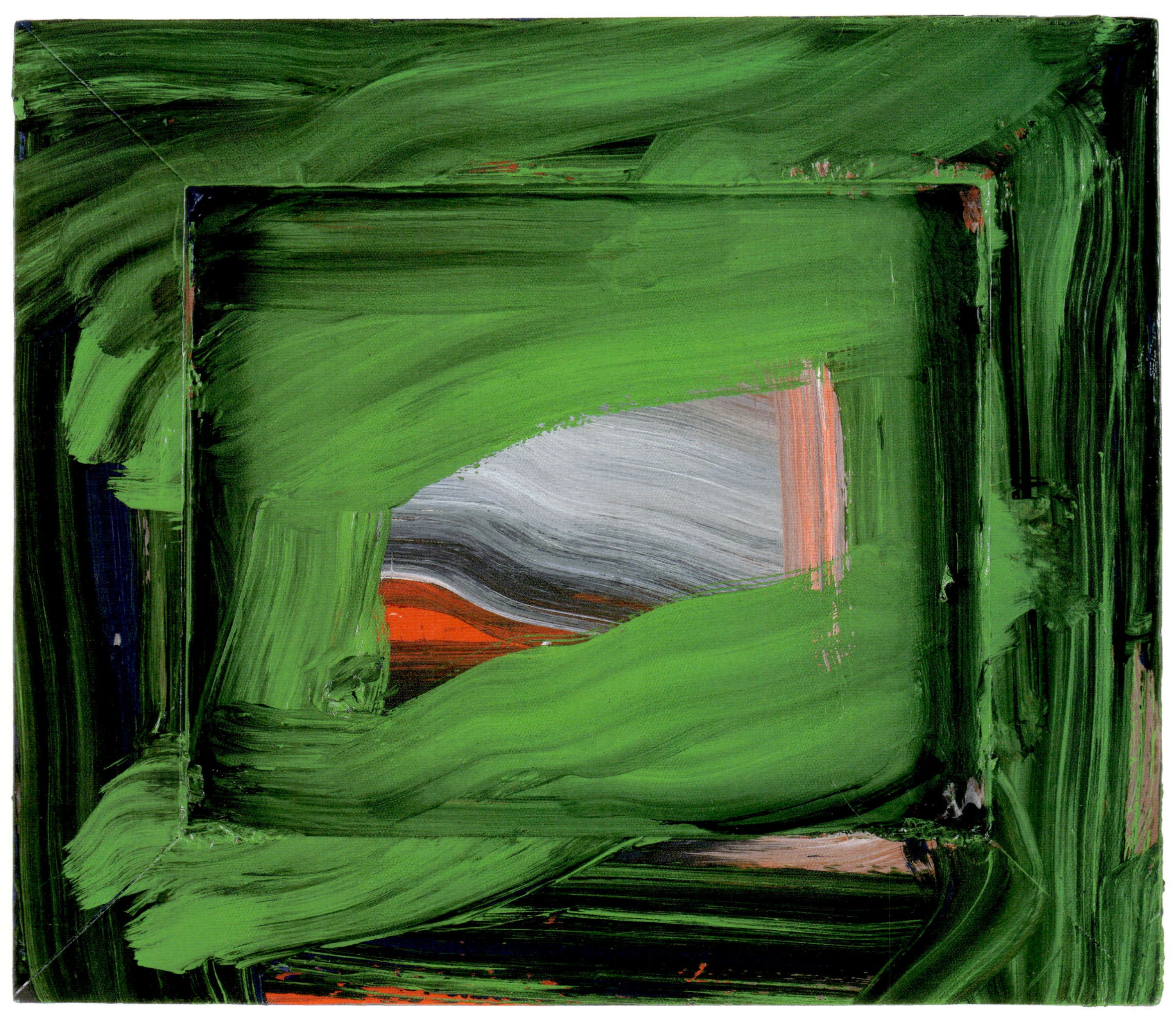

32. Echo, 2000–02

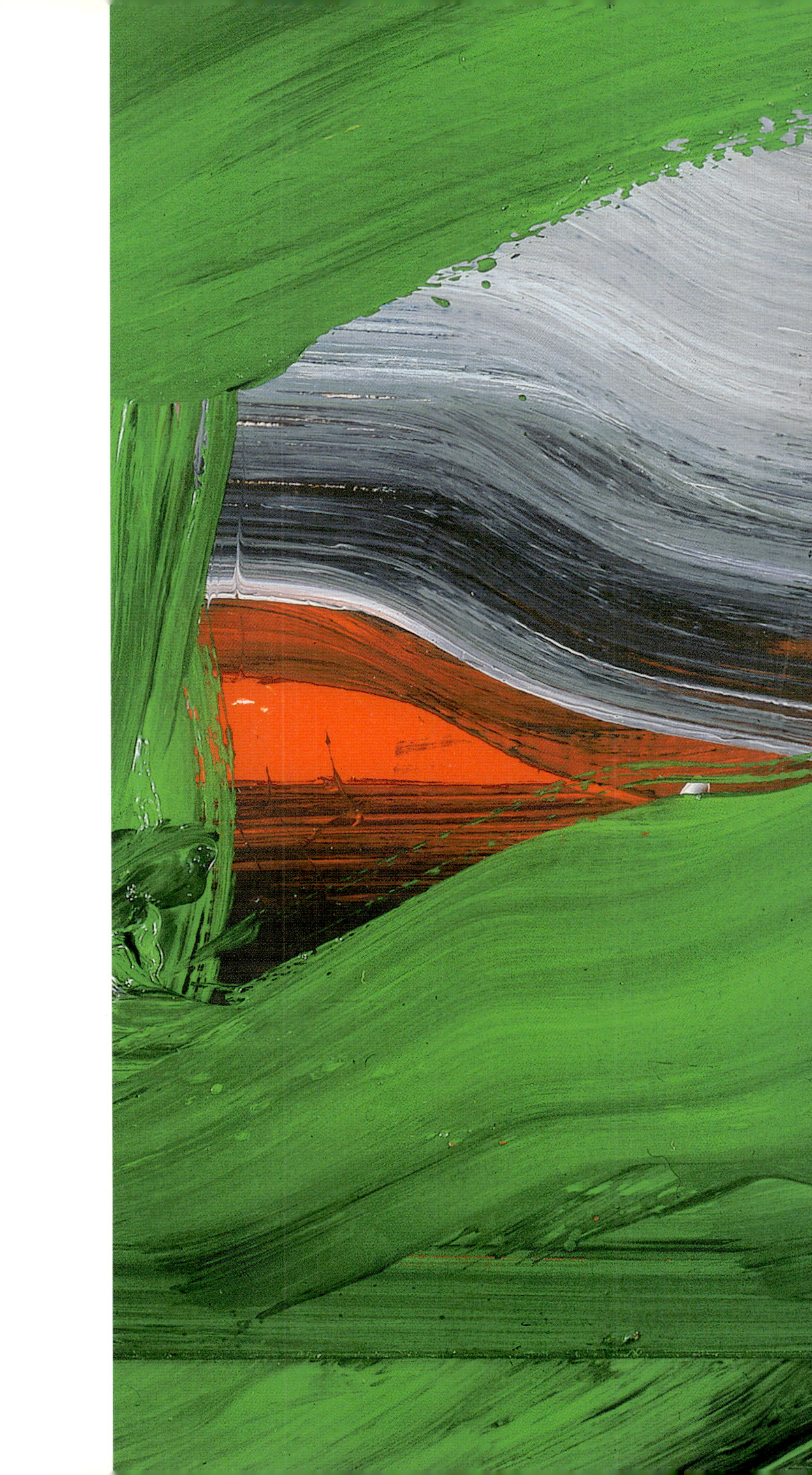

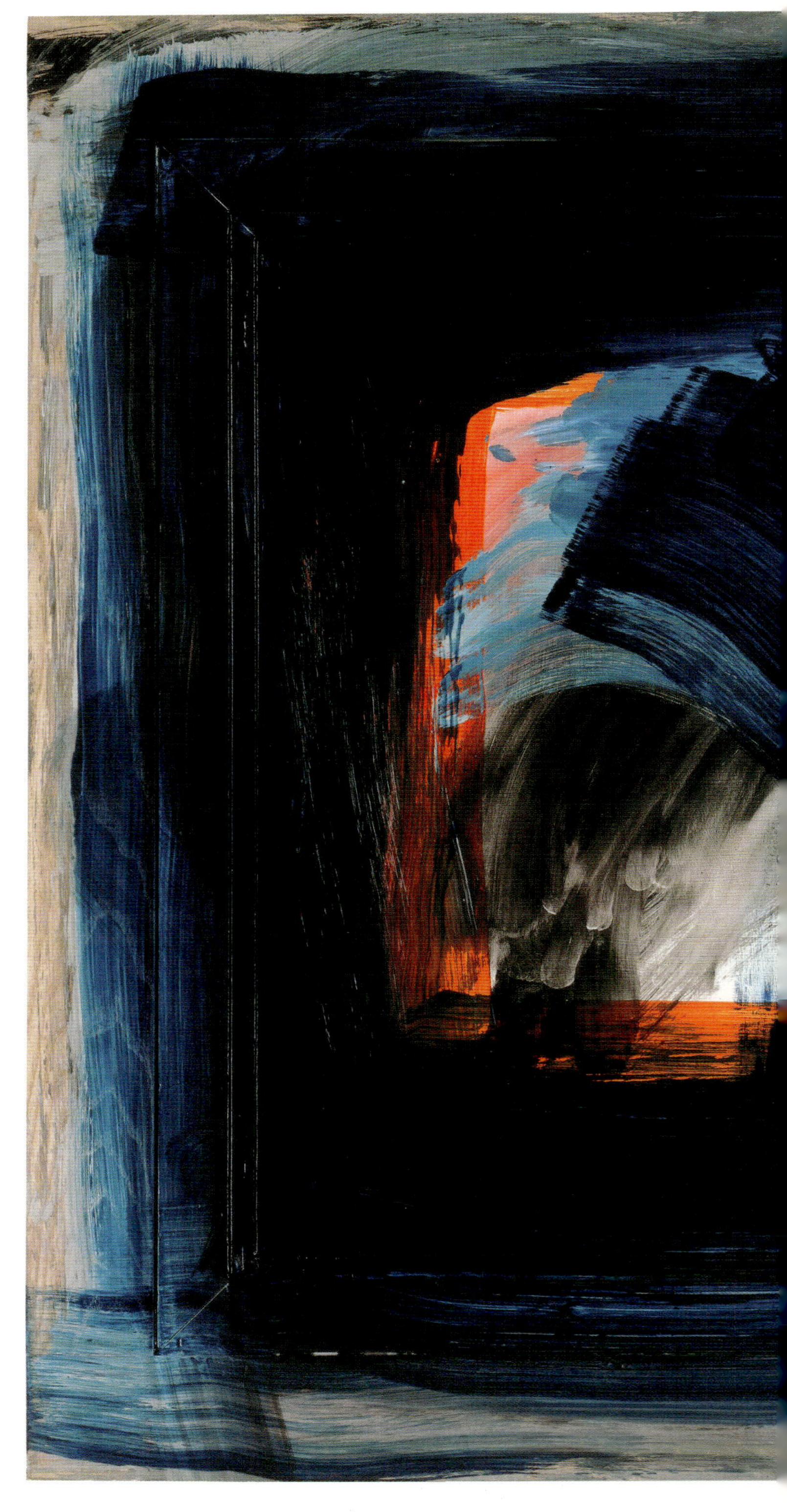

33. Grief, 2002

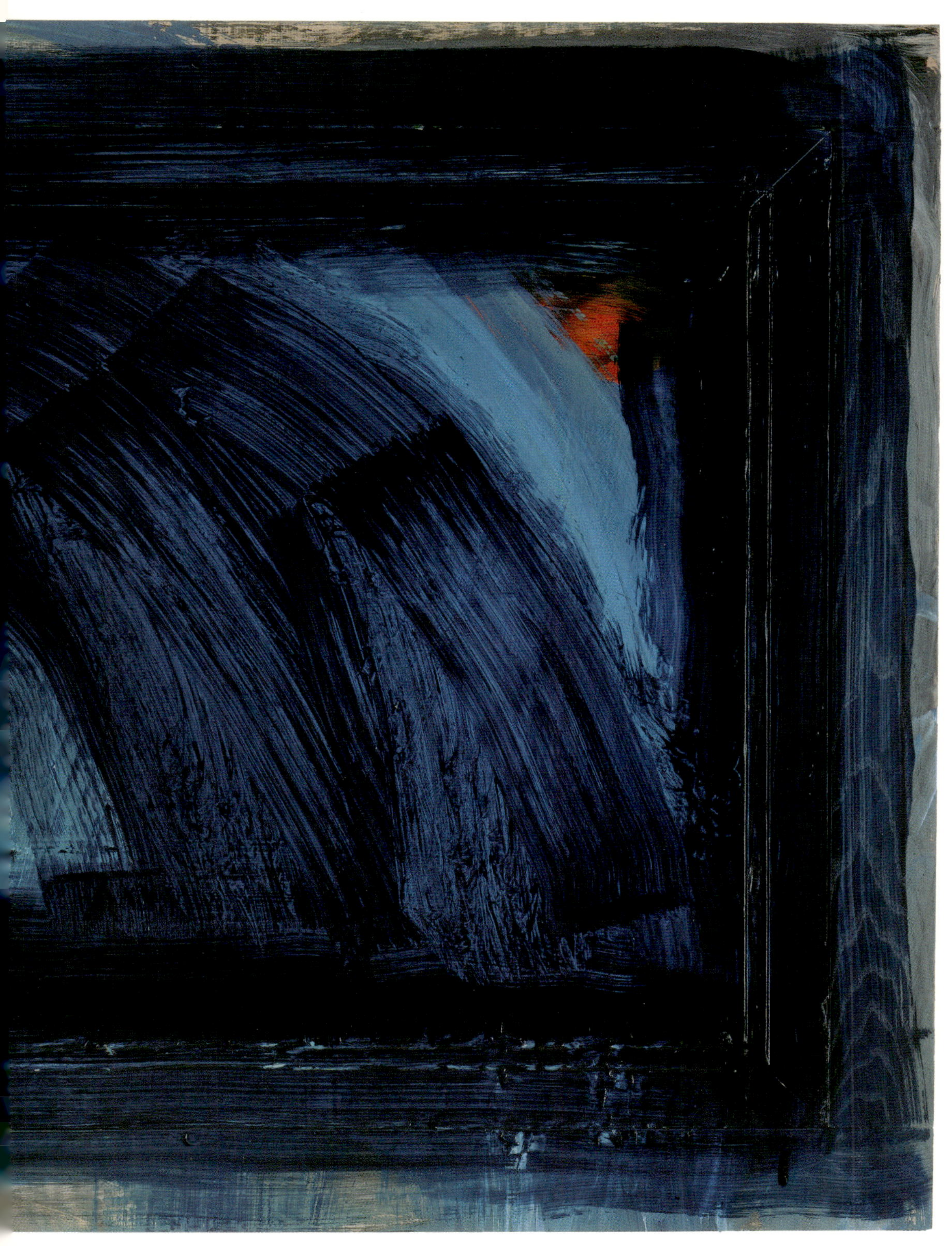

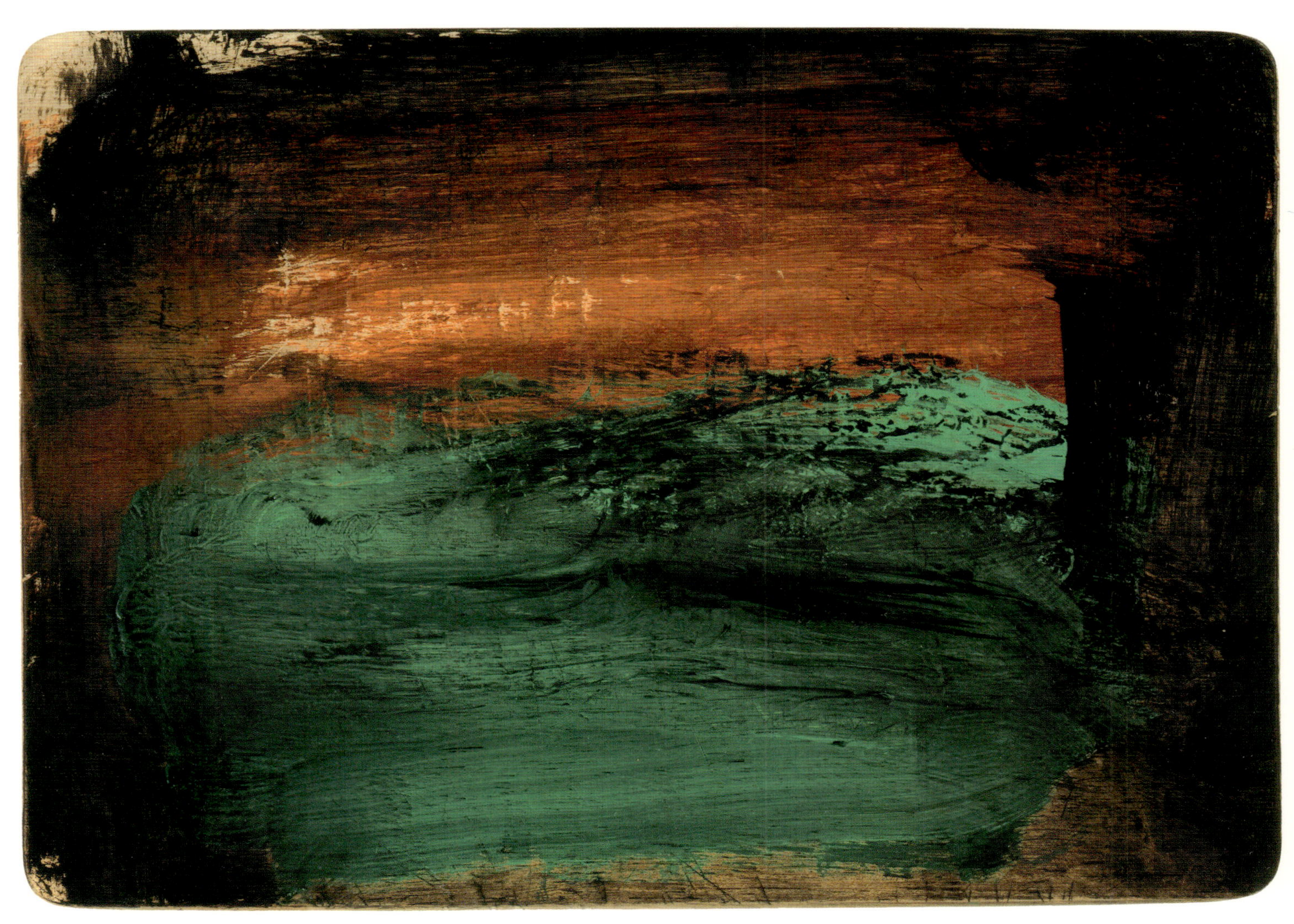

34. Dirty Weather, 2001

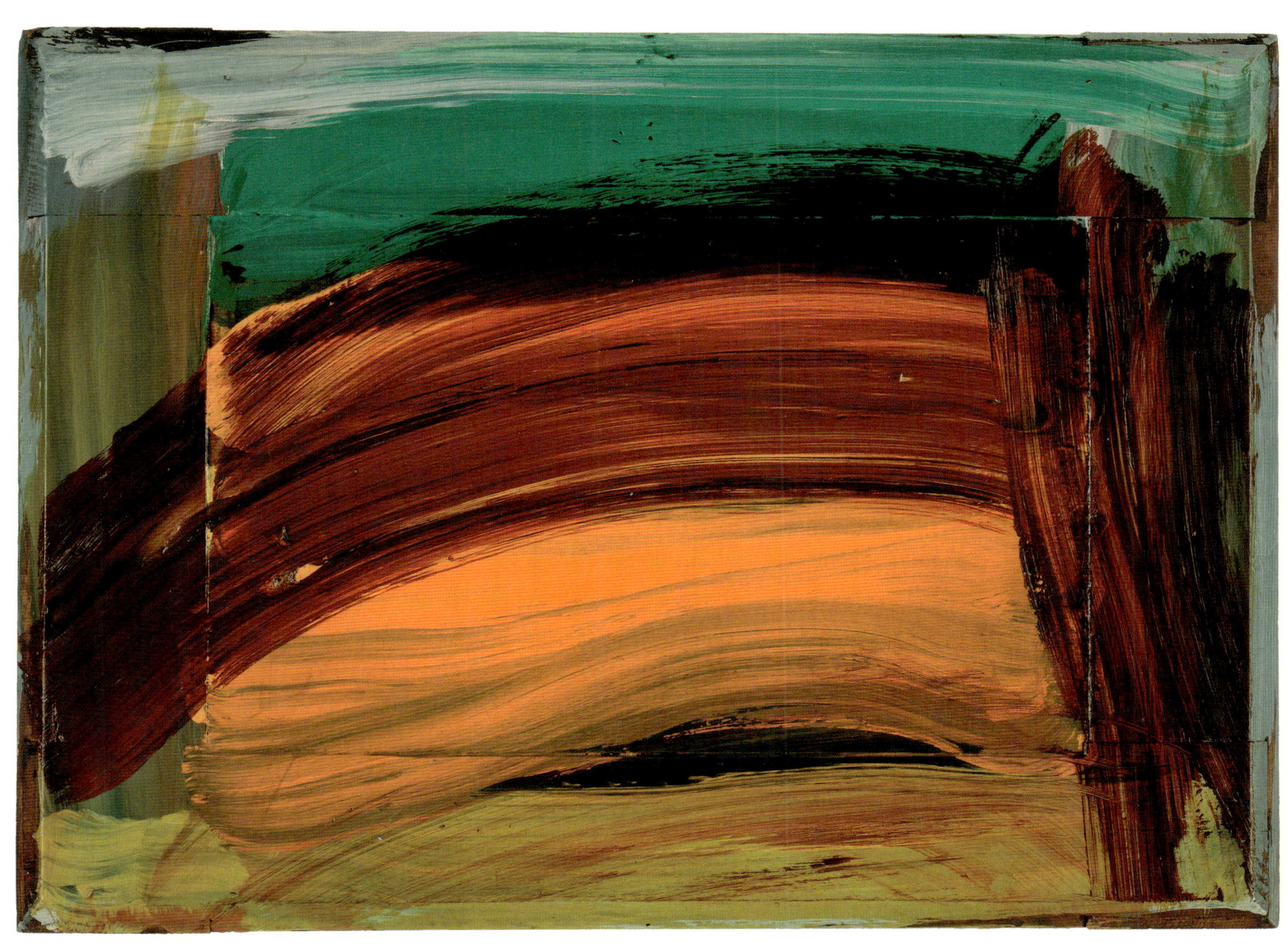

35. First Light, 2005

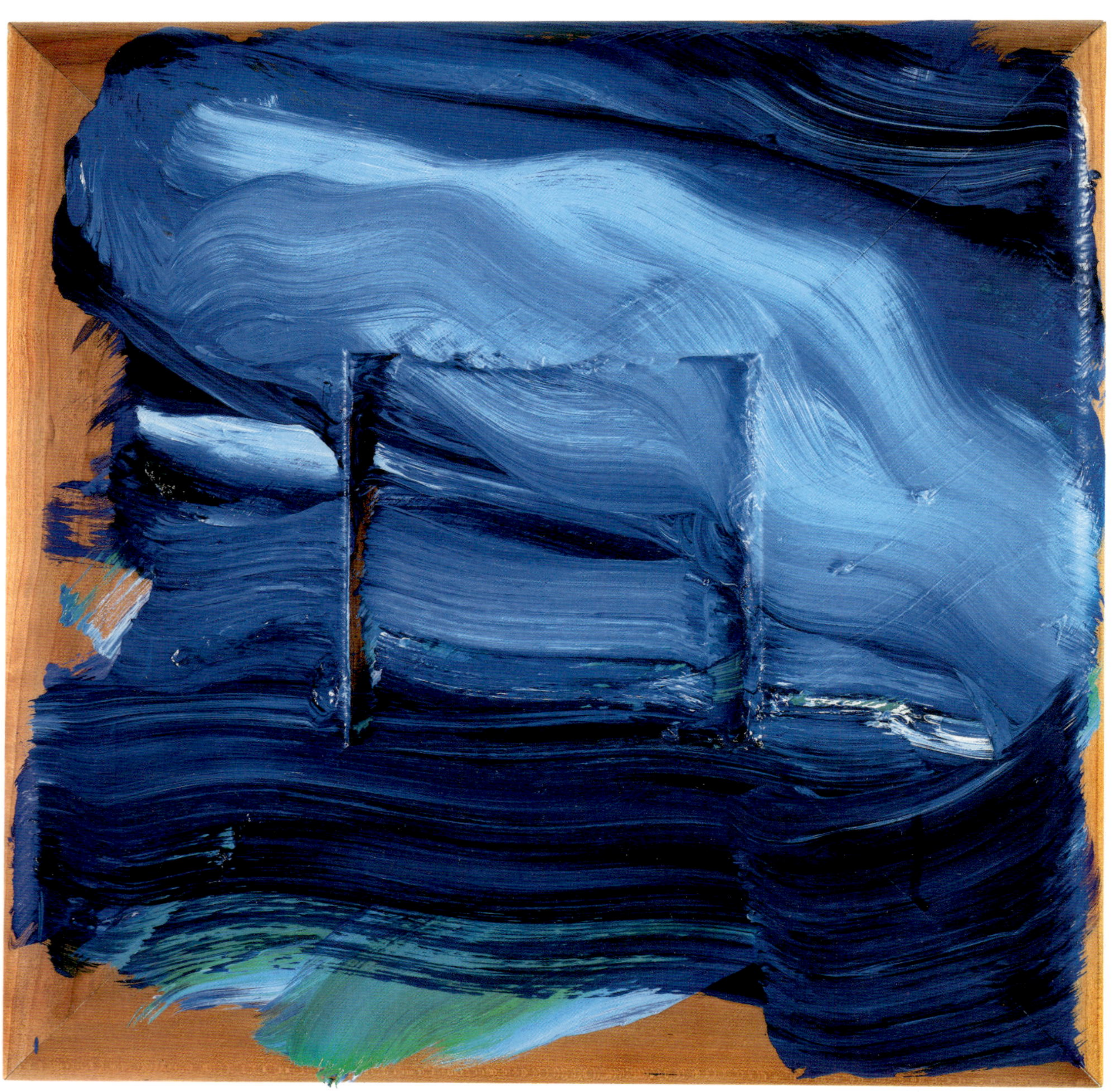

36 Déjà vu, Déjà Blue, 2004

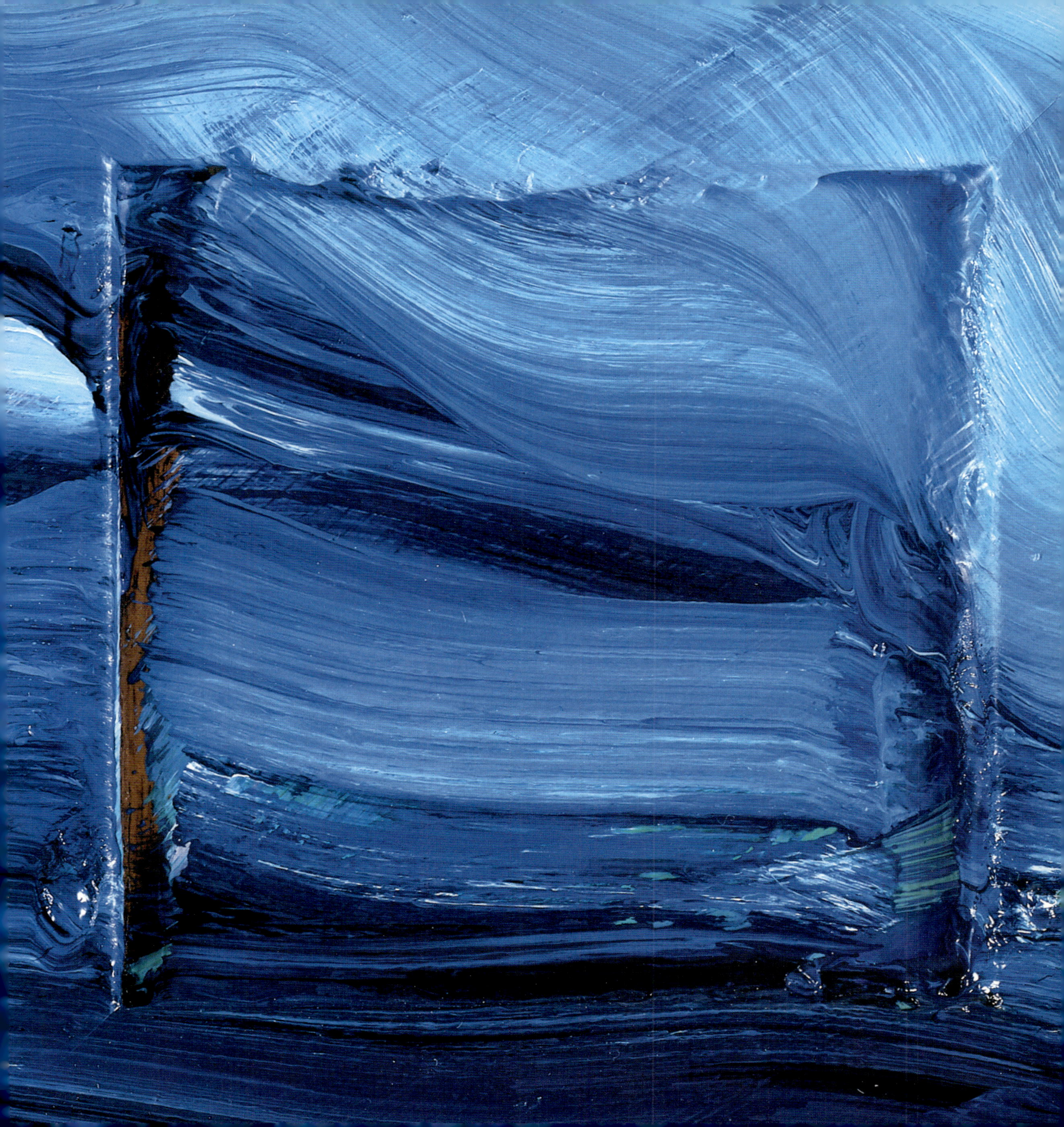

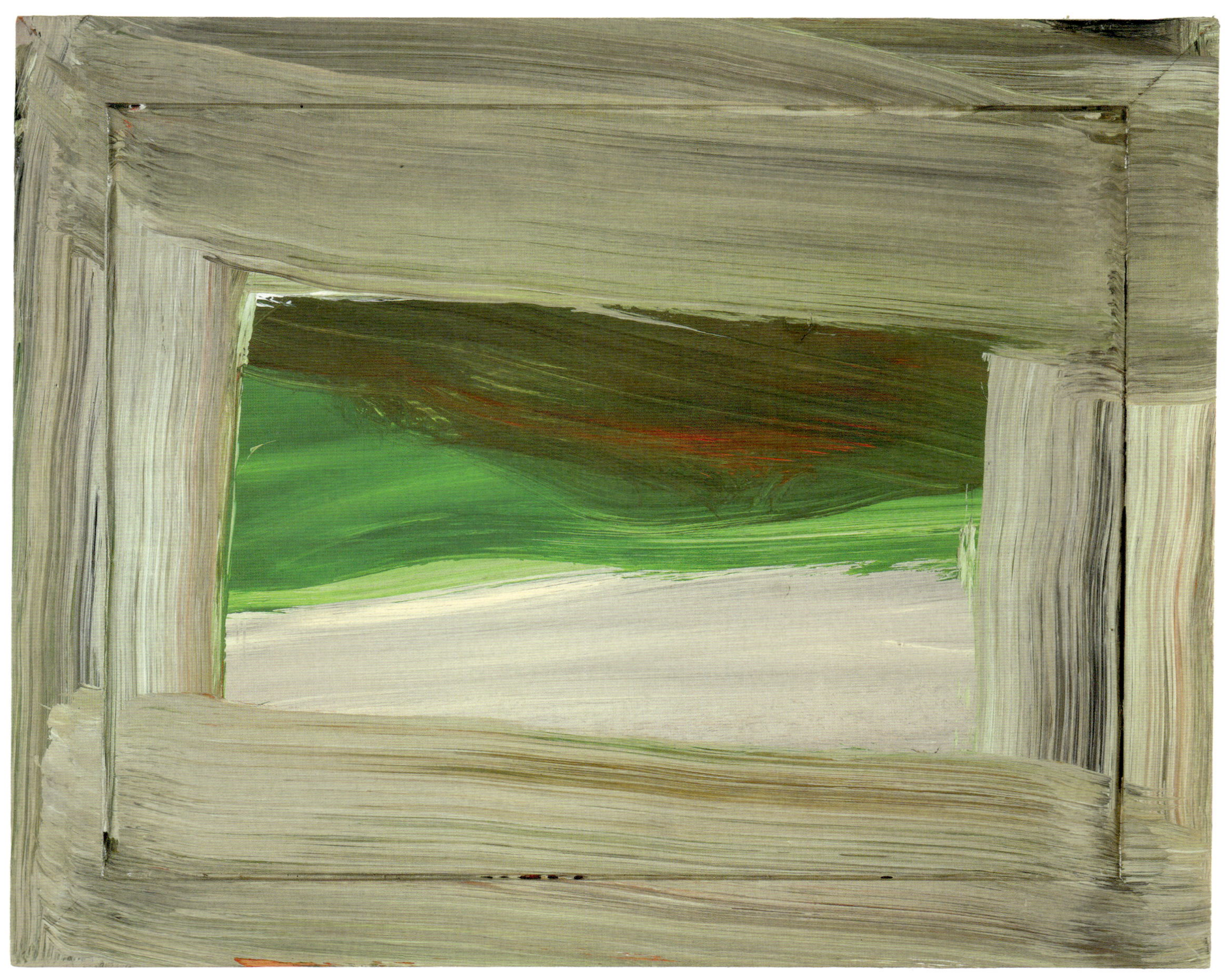

37.   Alone, 2002

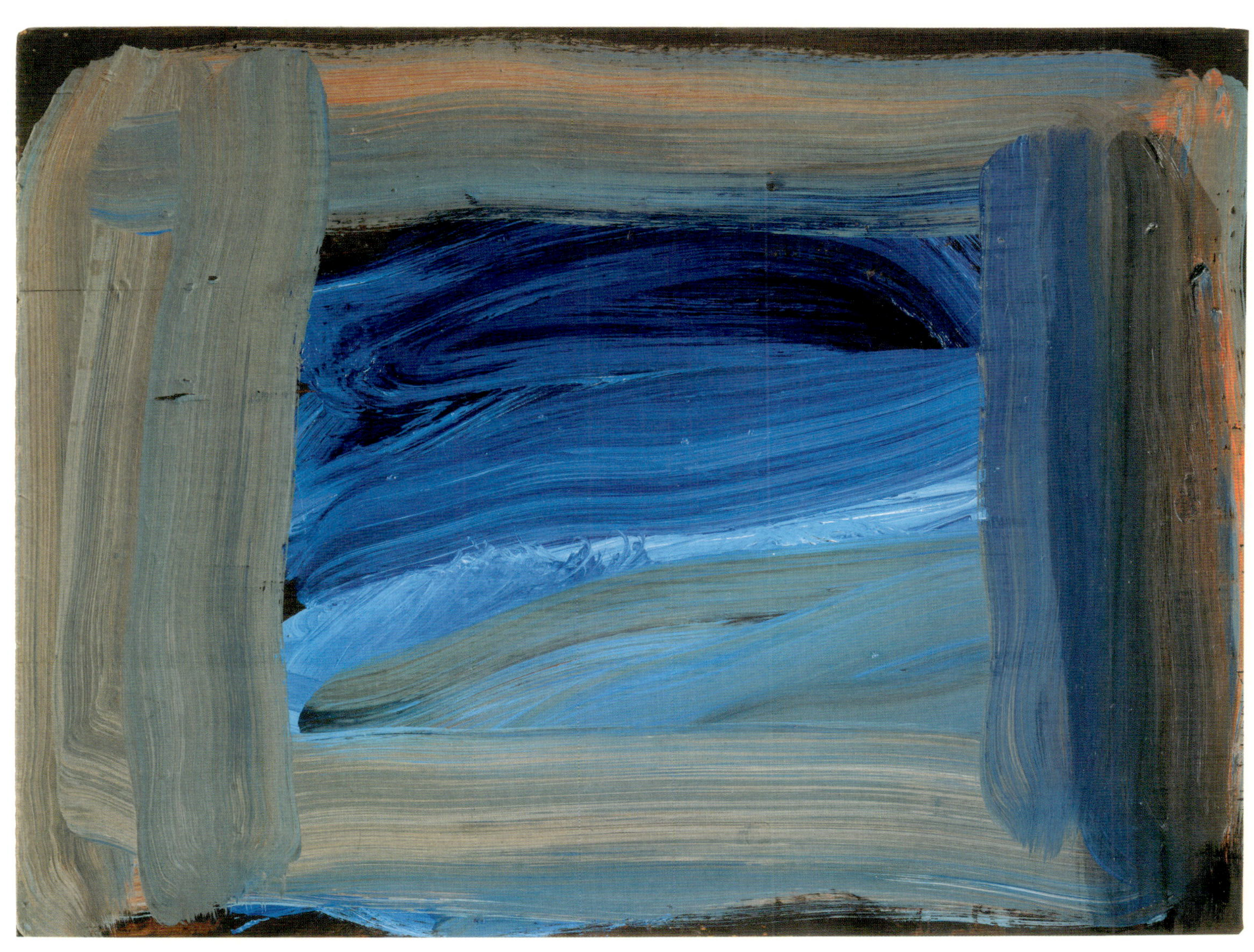

38. On the Rocks, 2002

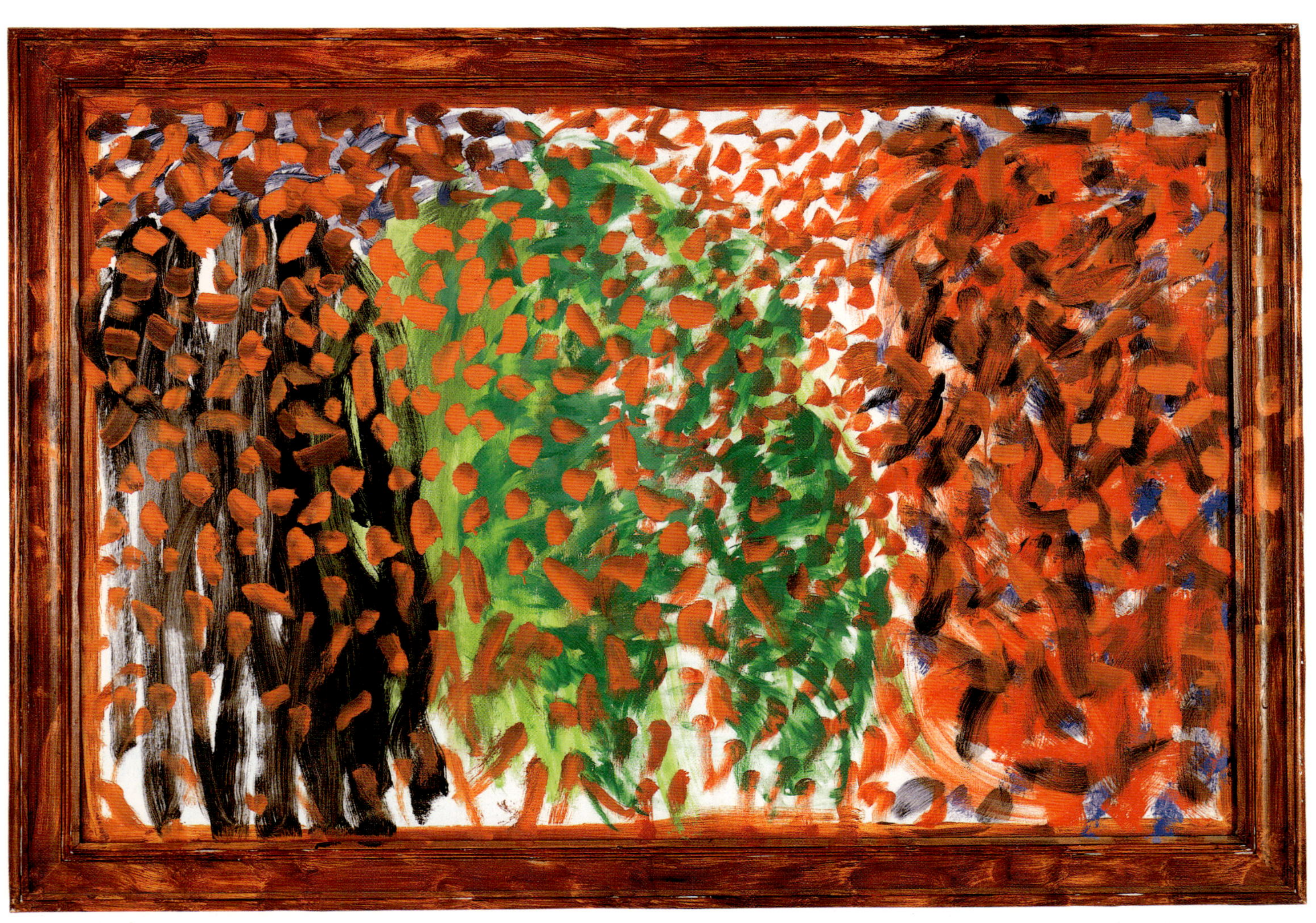

39. Autumn, 1998–2003

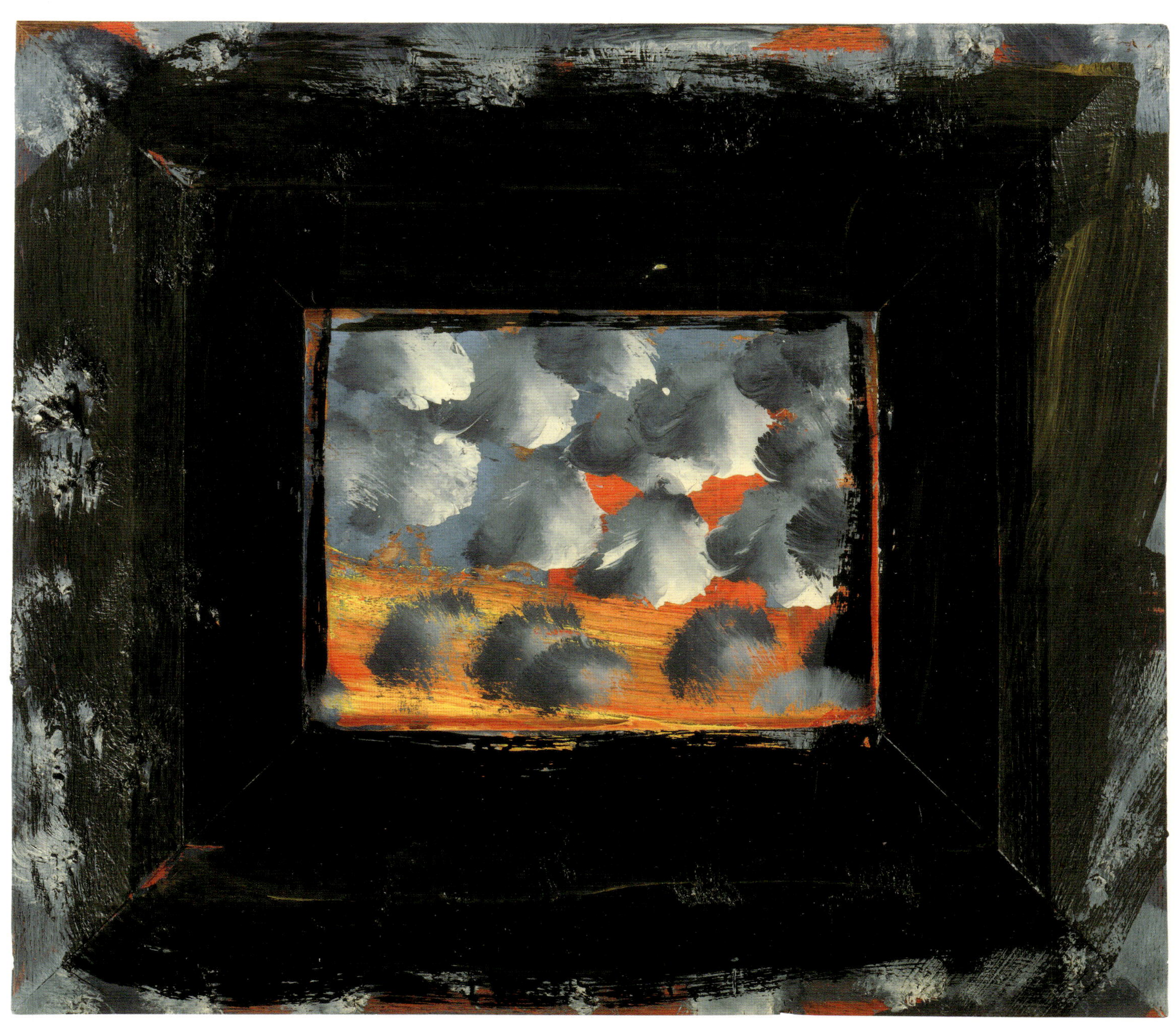

40. Christmas, 2002–03

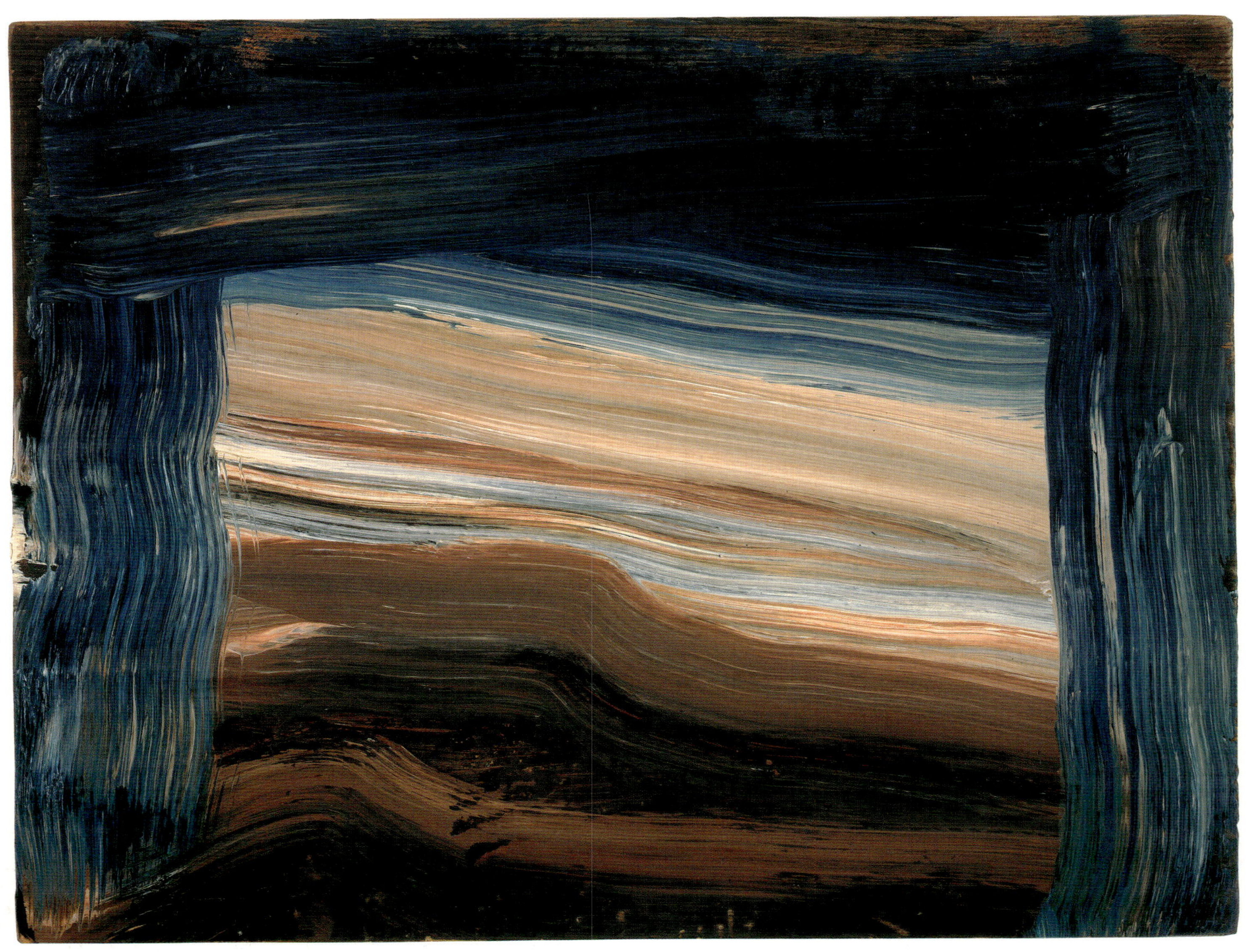

41. Low Tide, 2002

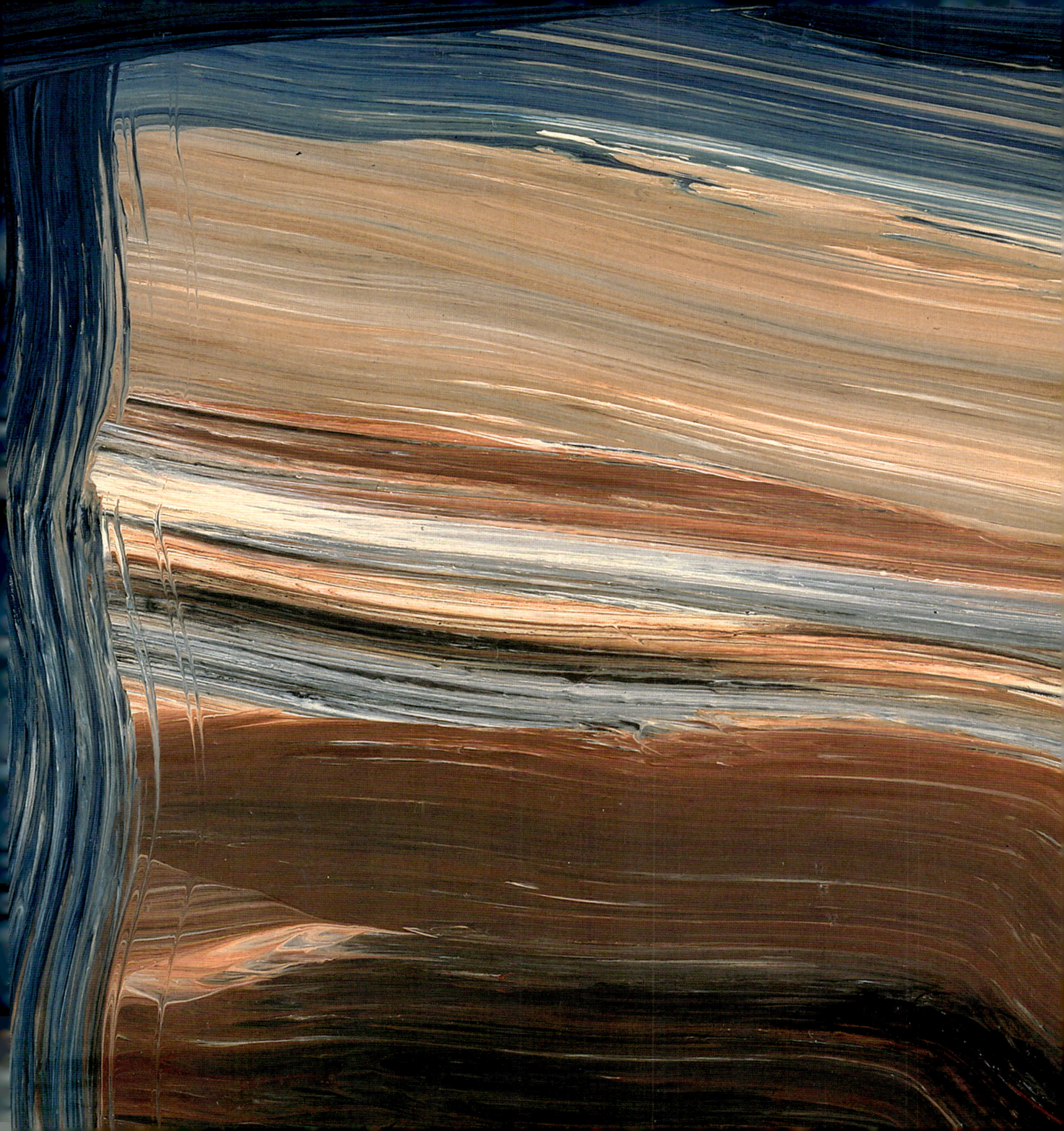

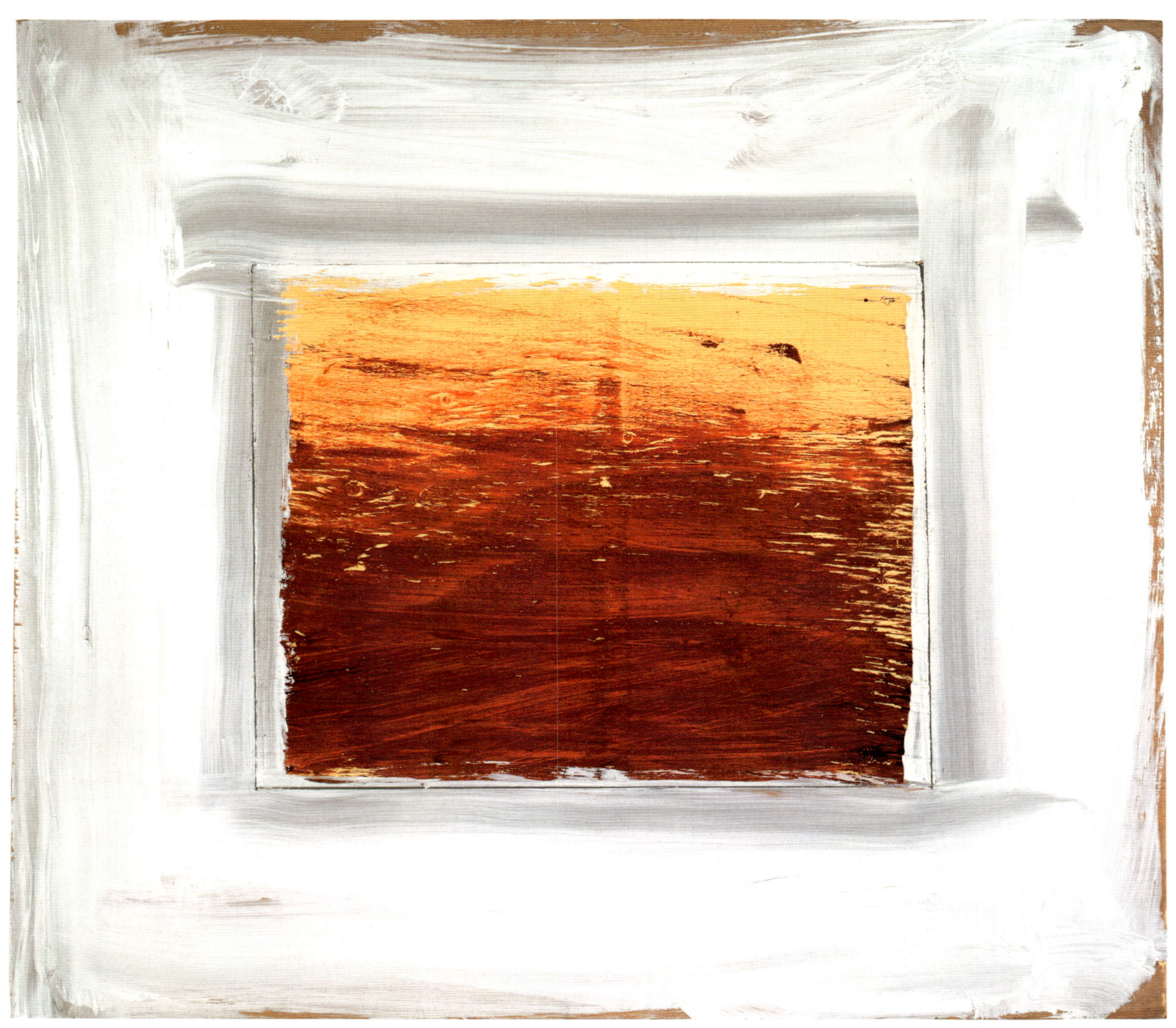

42. Walking on Water, 1999–2001

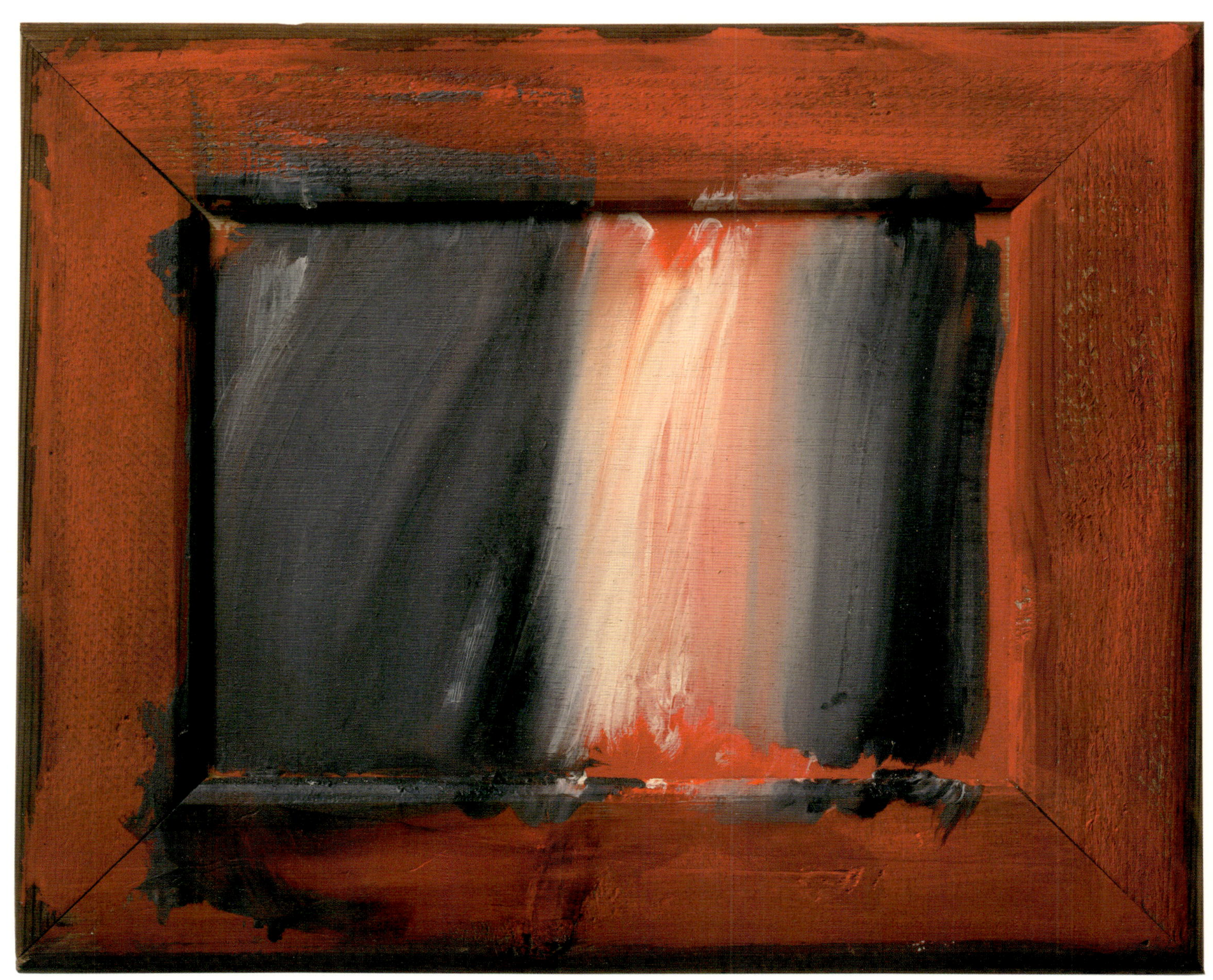

43. Theatre, 1998–99

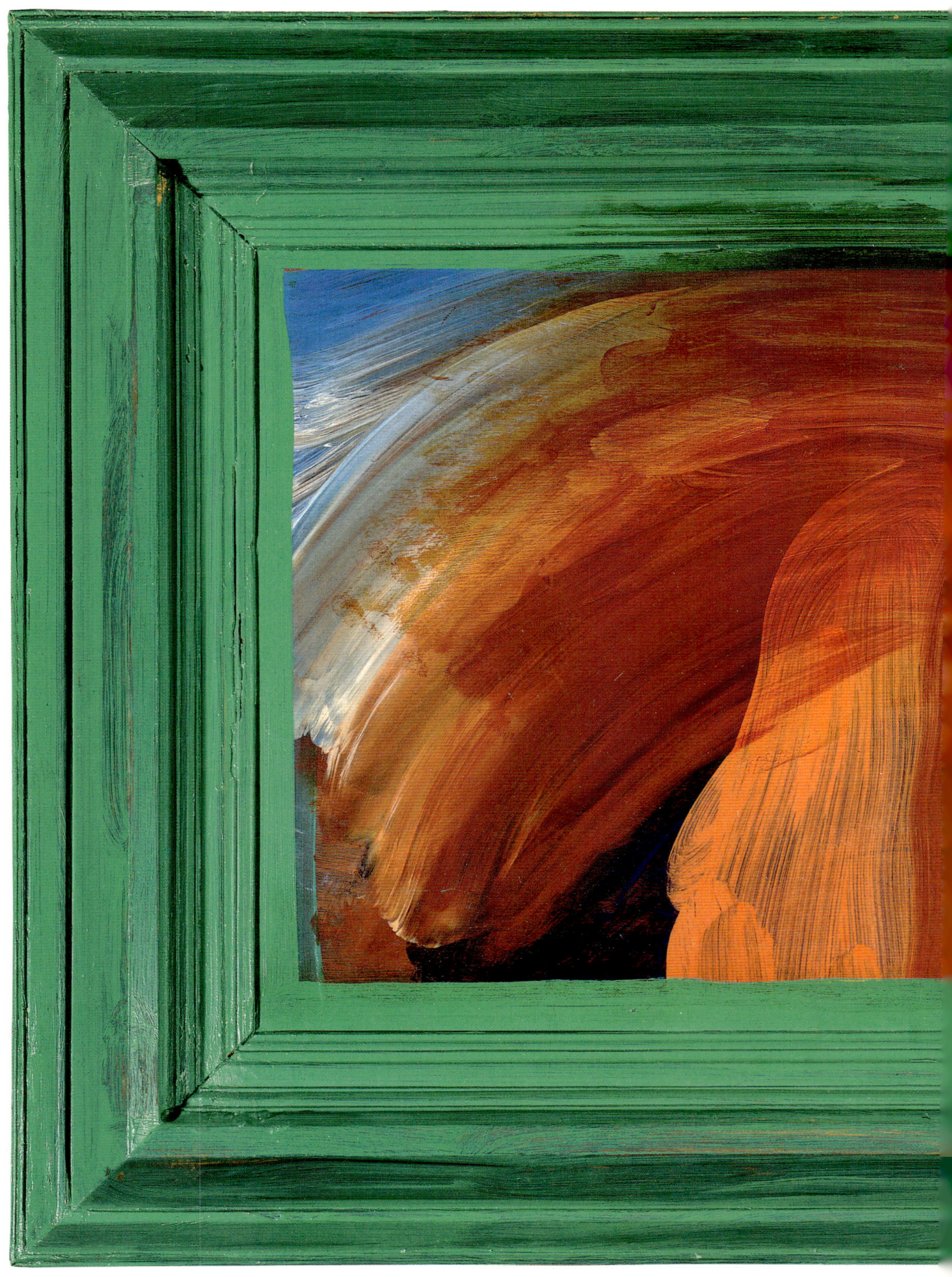

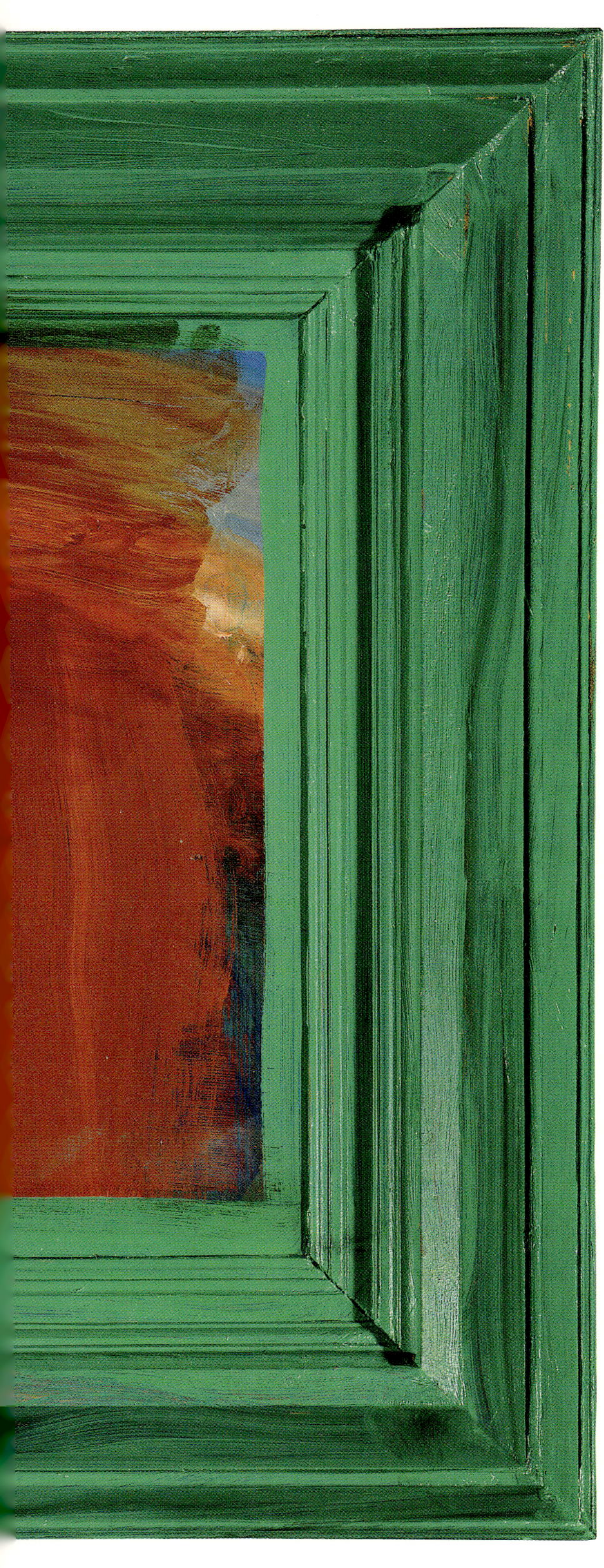

44. After Degas, 1993

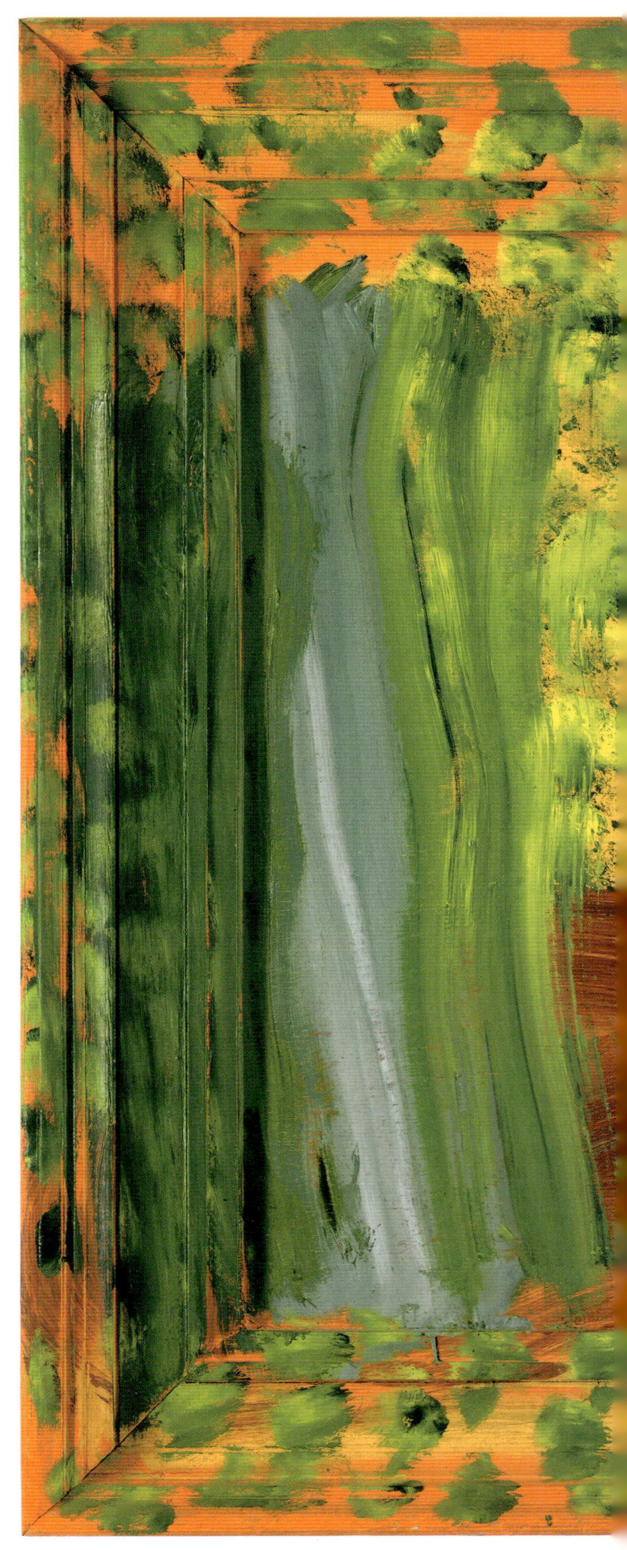

45. After Vuillard, 1996–2002

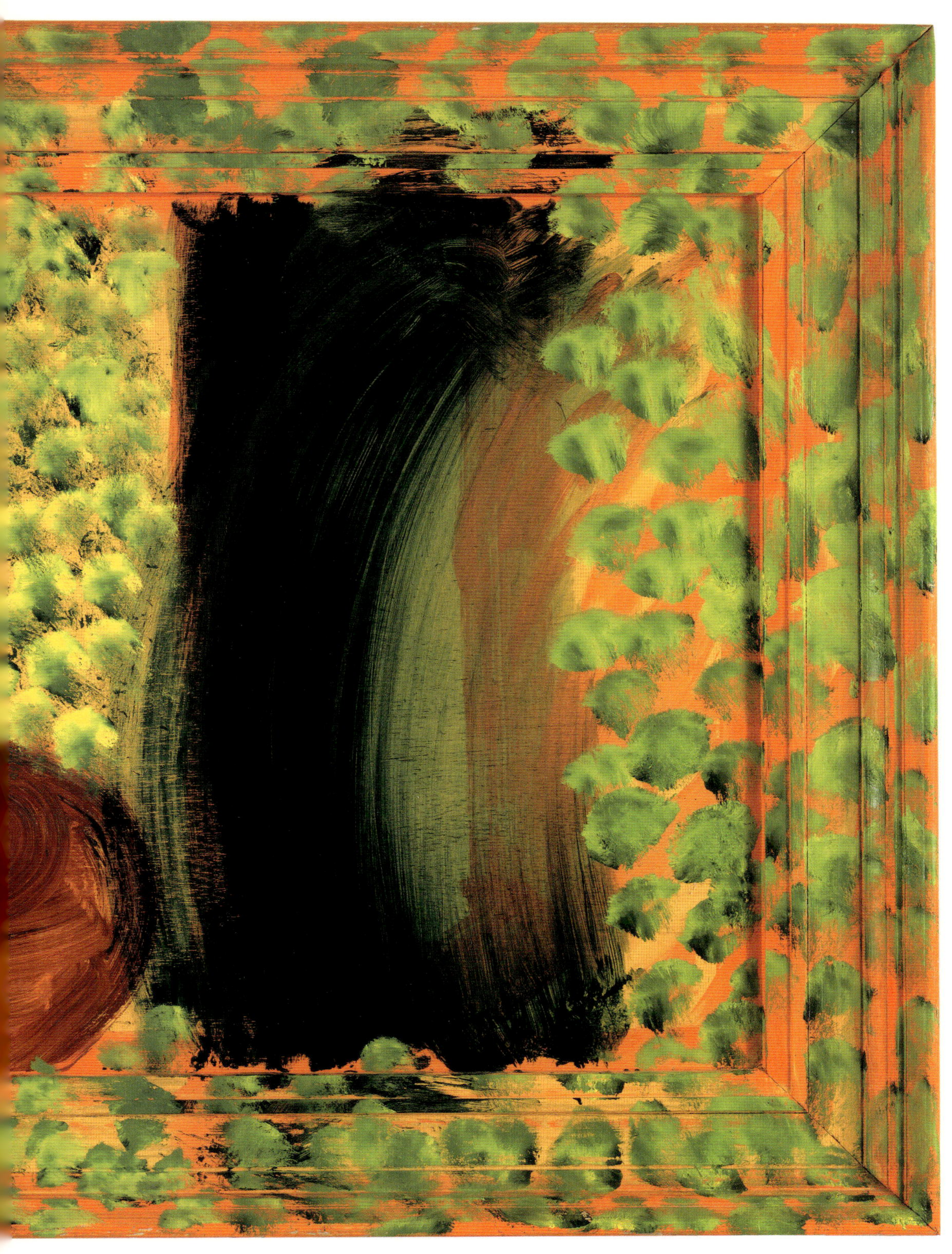

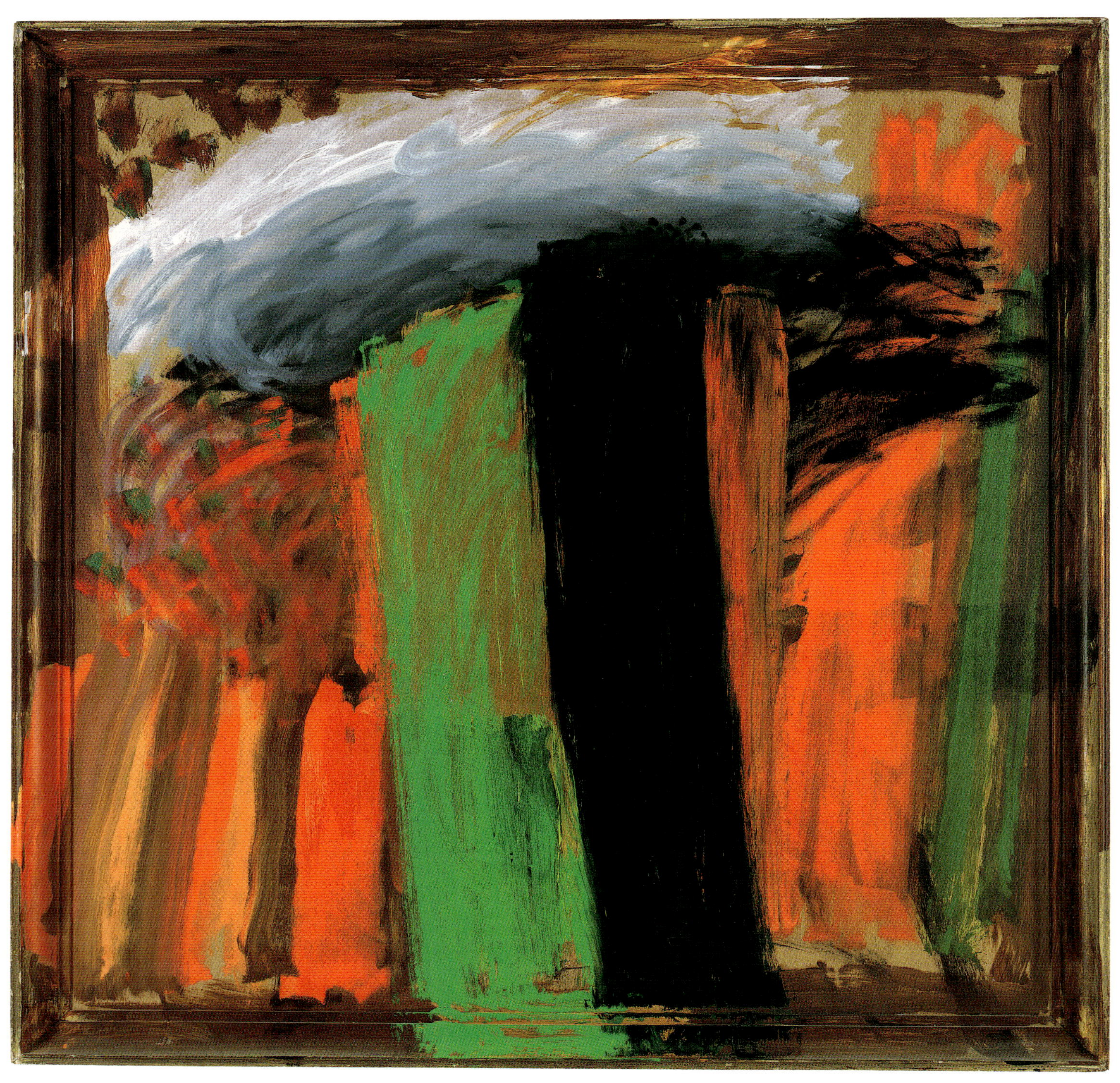

46. The Body in the Library, 1998–2003

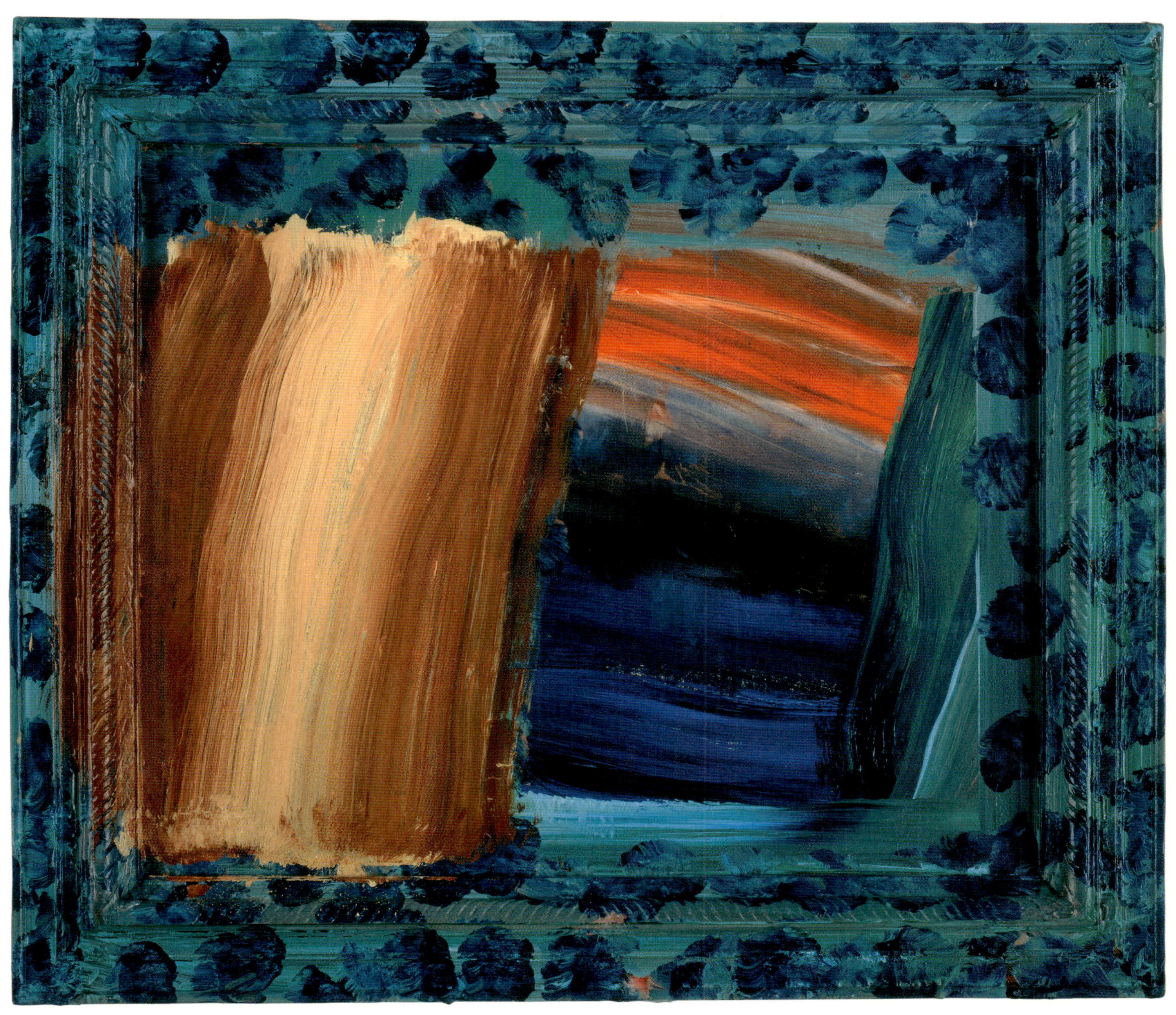

47. Moonlight, 1998–99

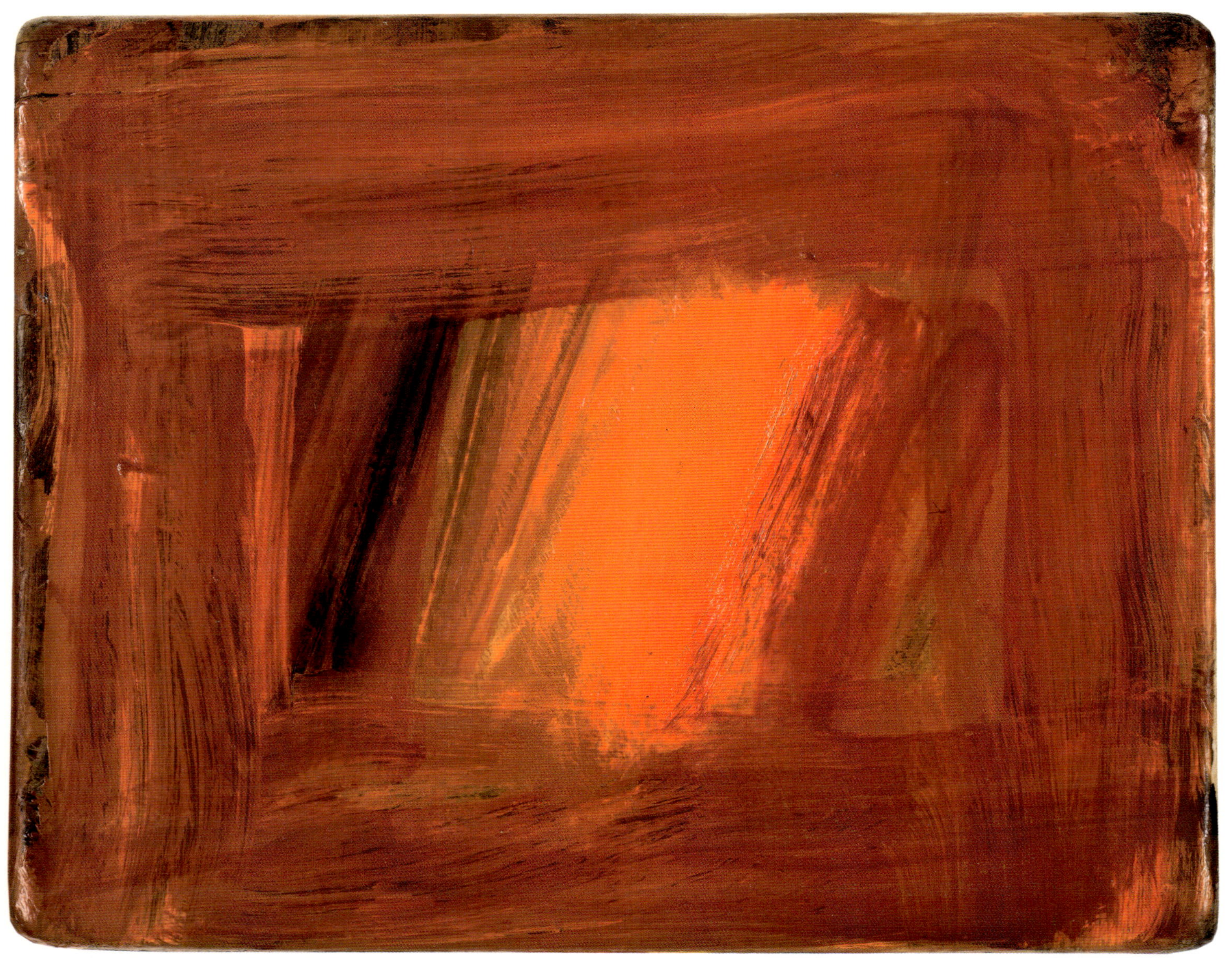

48. Keep It Quiet, 2000–01

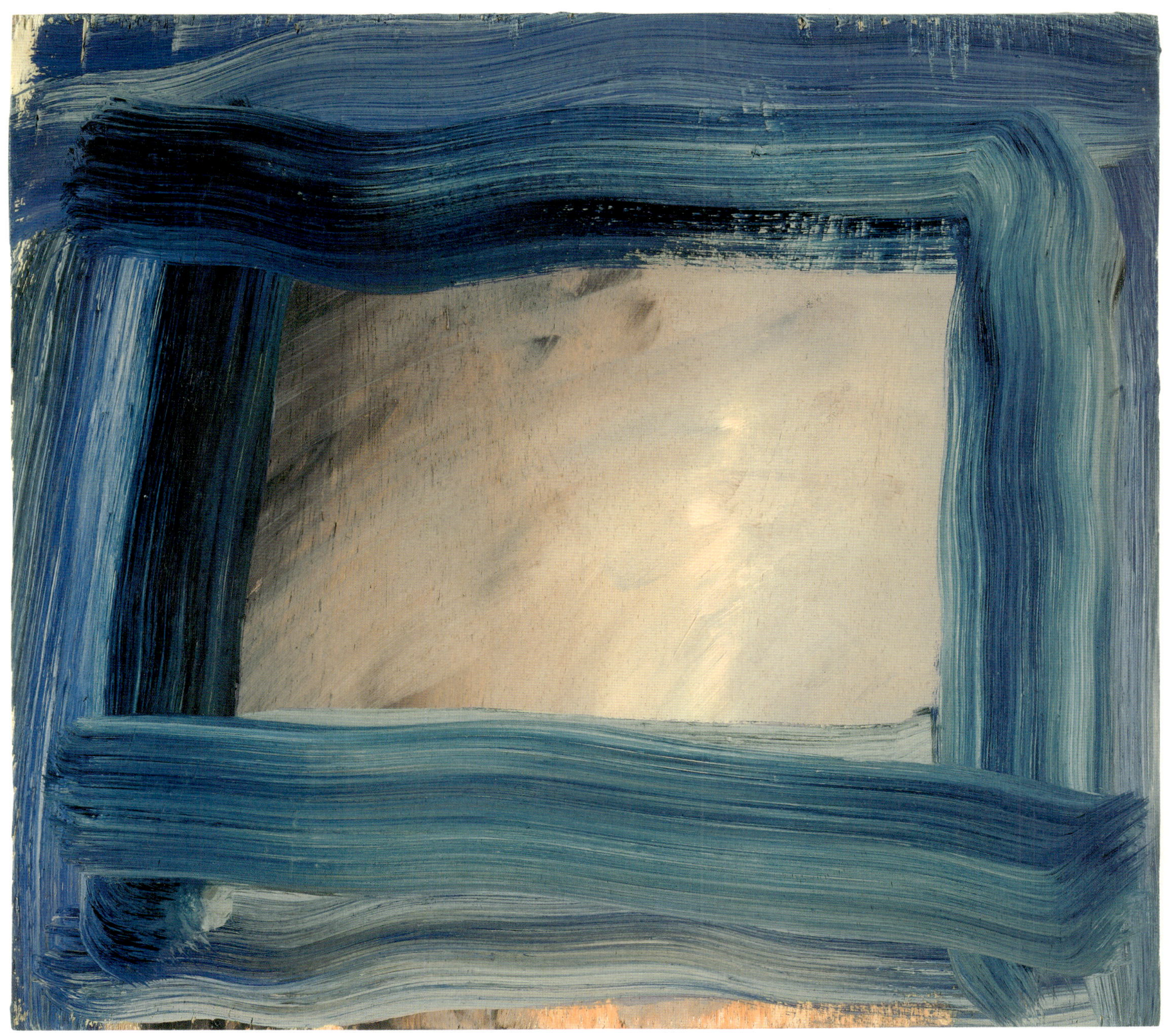

49. Fog, 2002

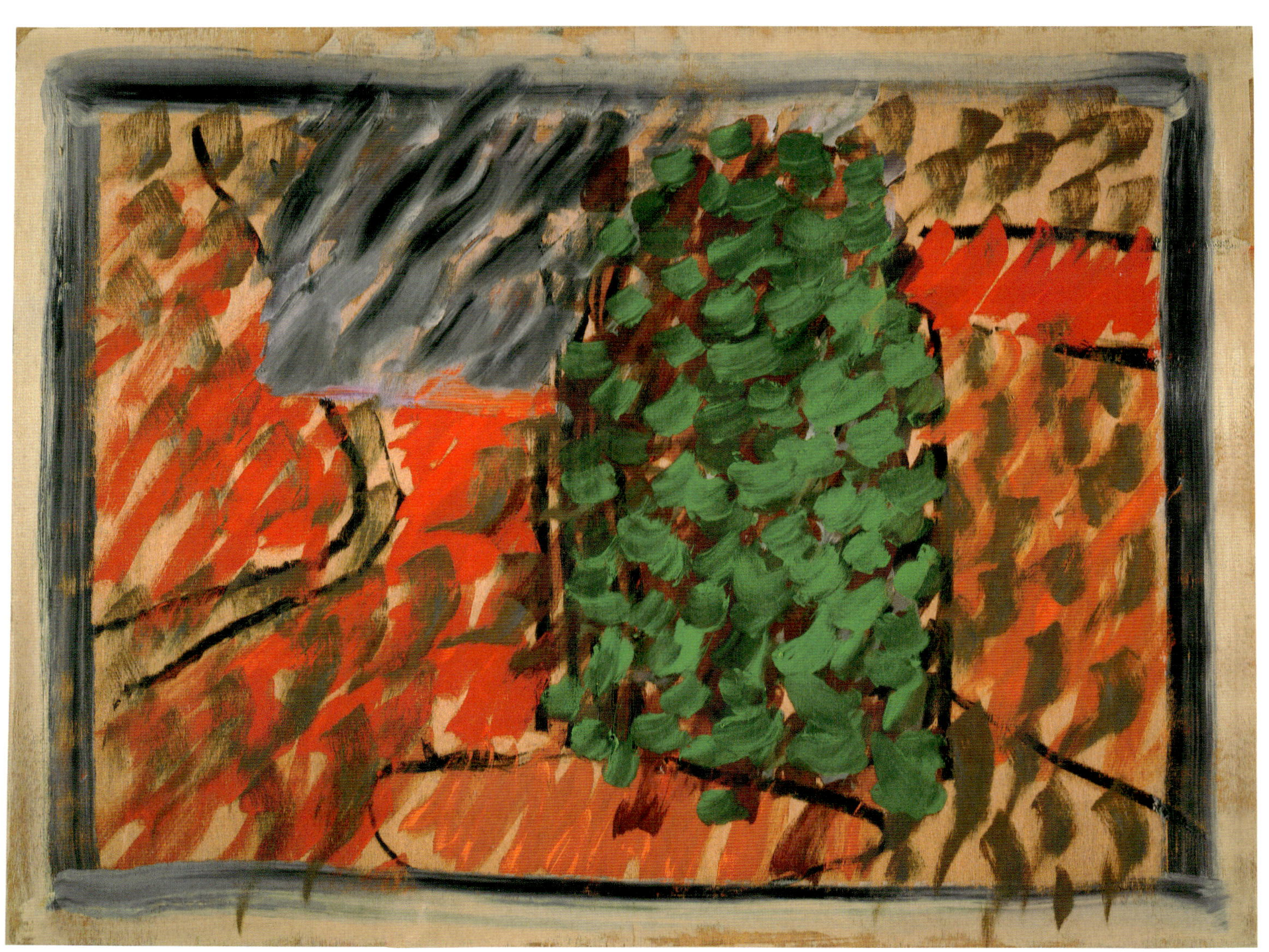

50. Clarendon Road, 2000–05

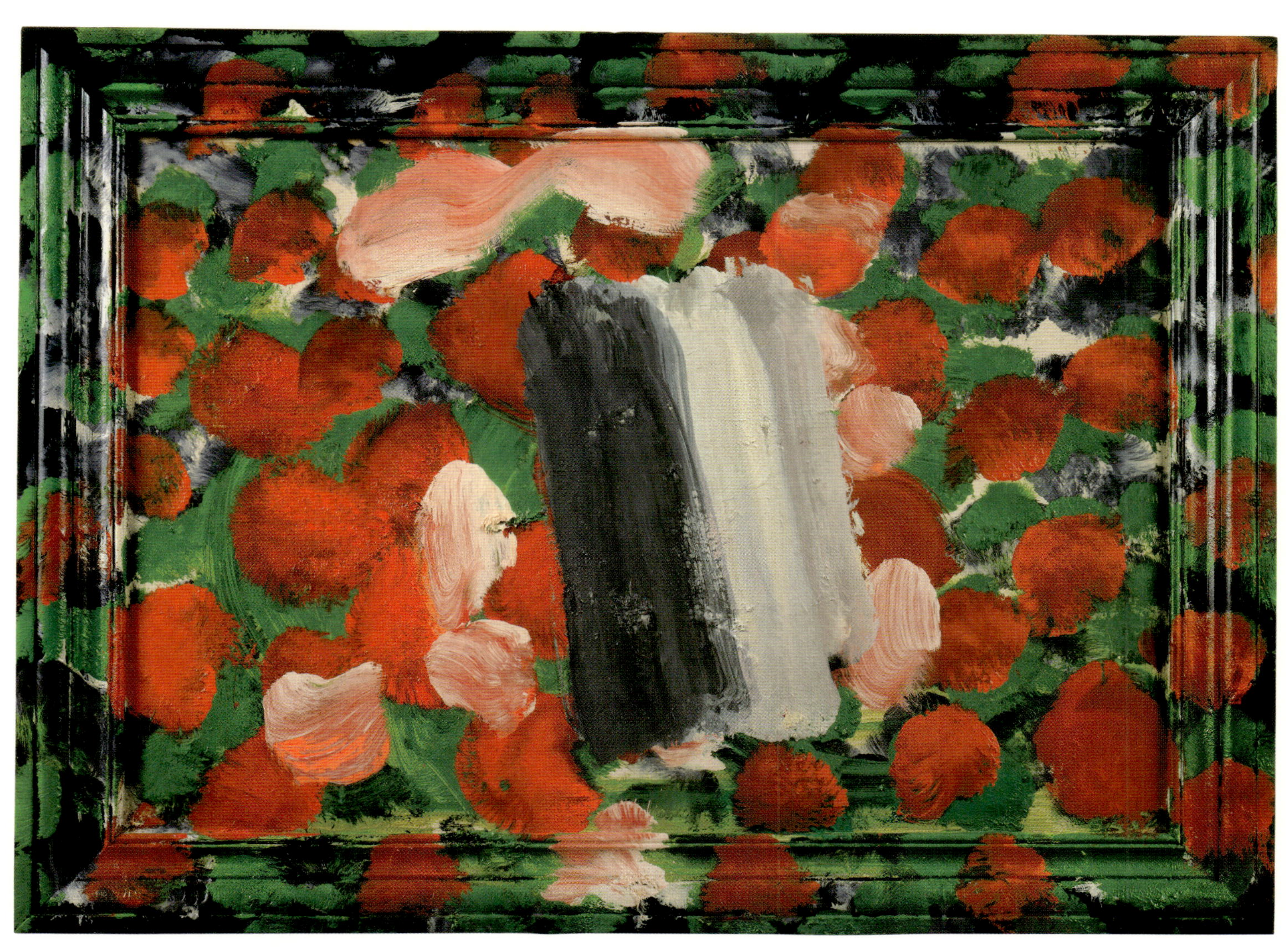

51. Flowerpiece, 2004–05

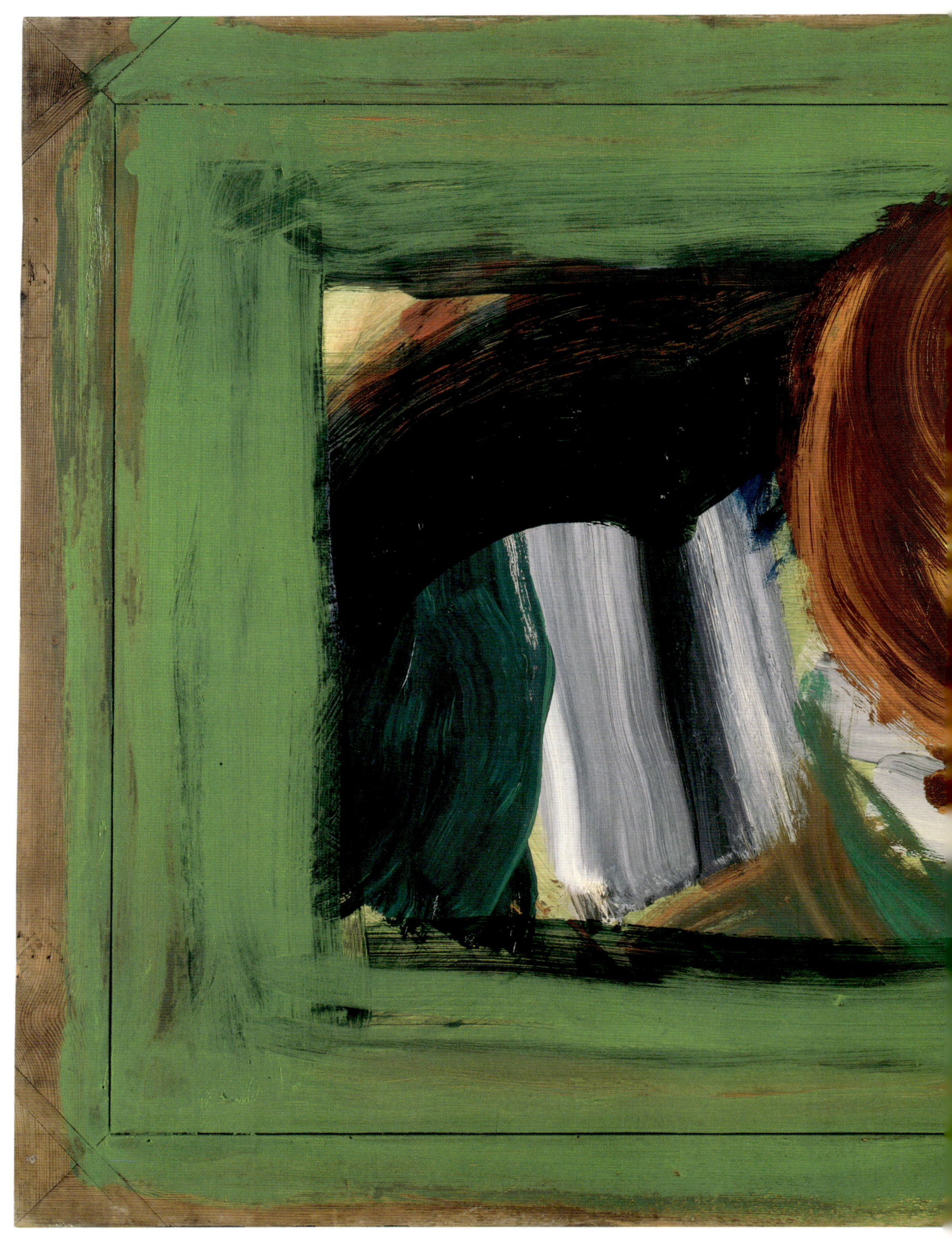

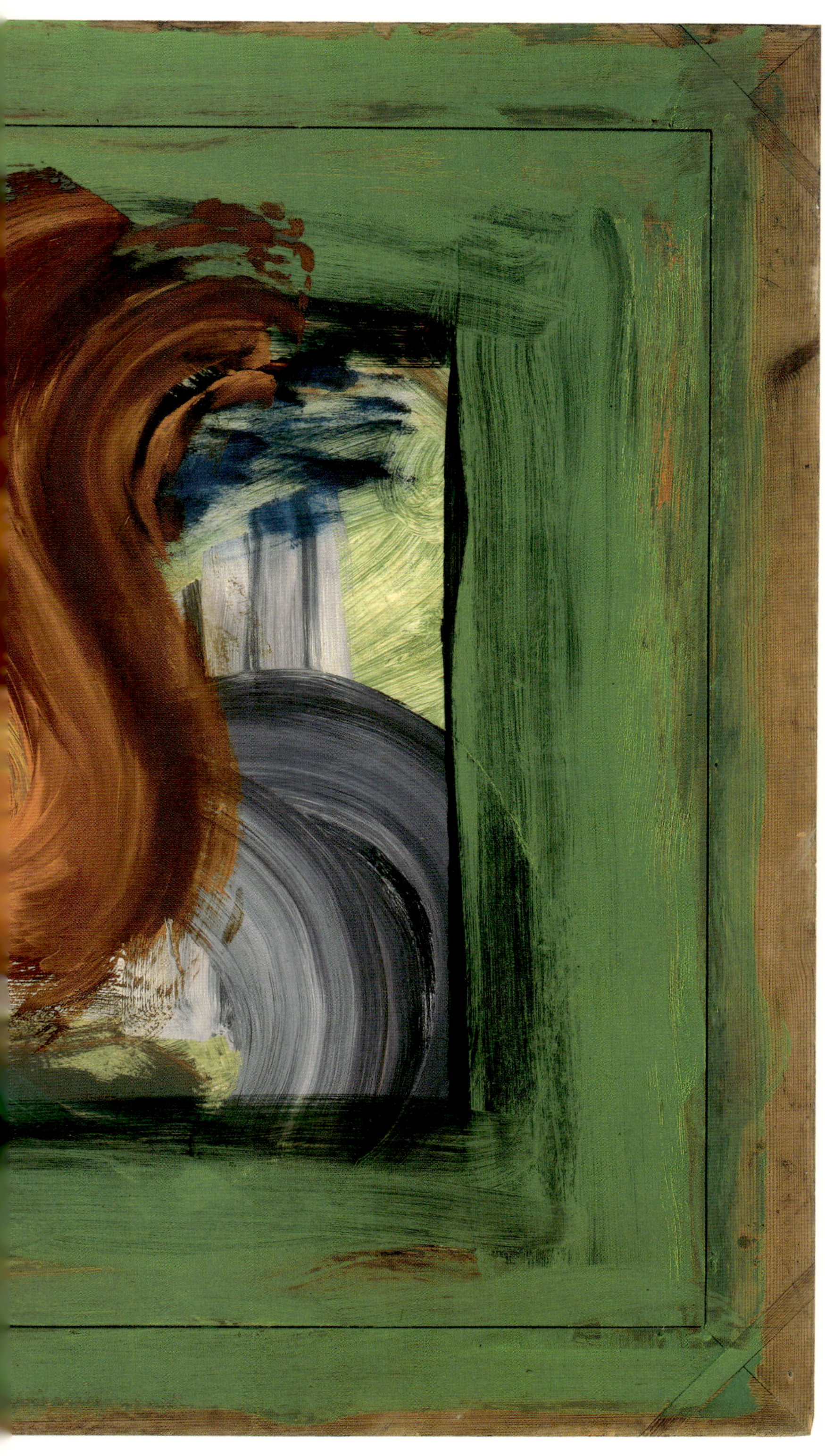

52. An Italian Landscape, 2003–05

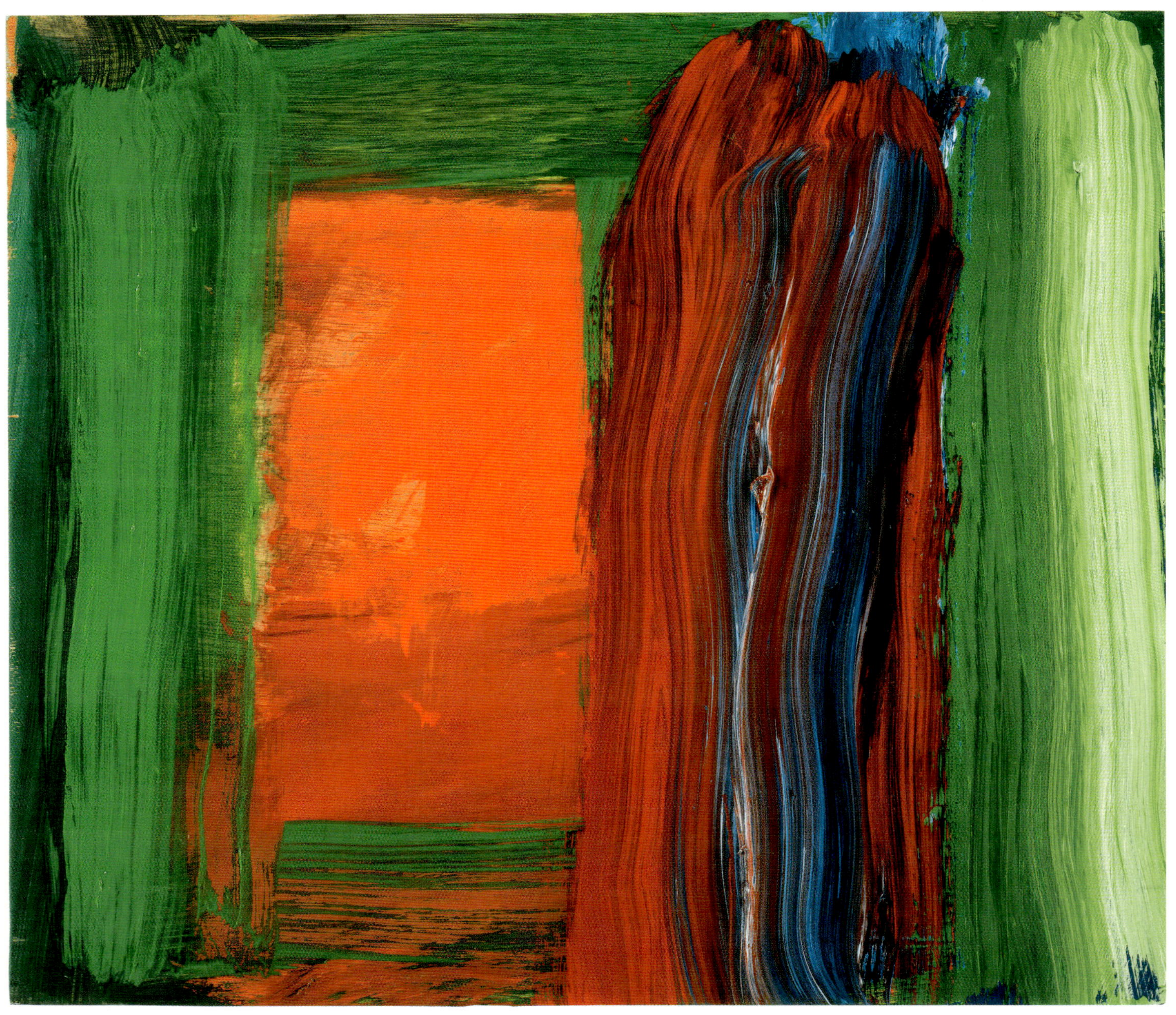

53. Pyjamas, 2004

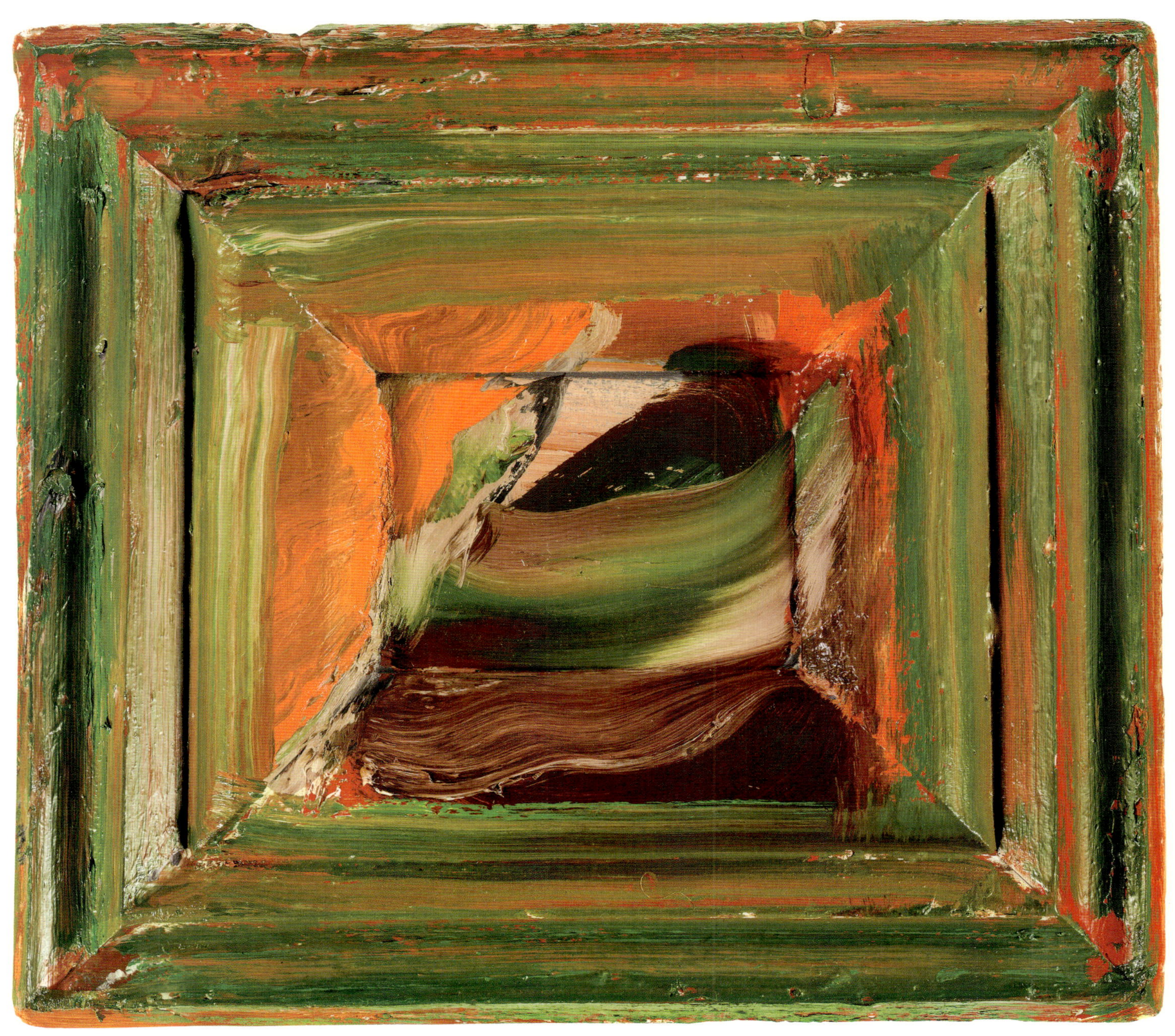

54. Venetian Landscape, 2000–03

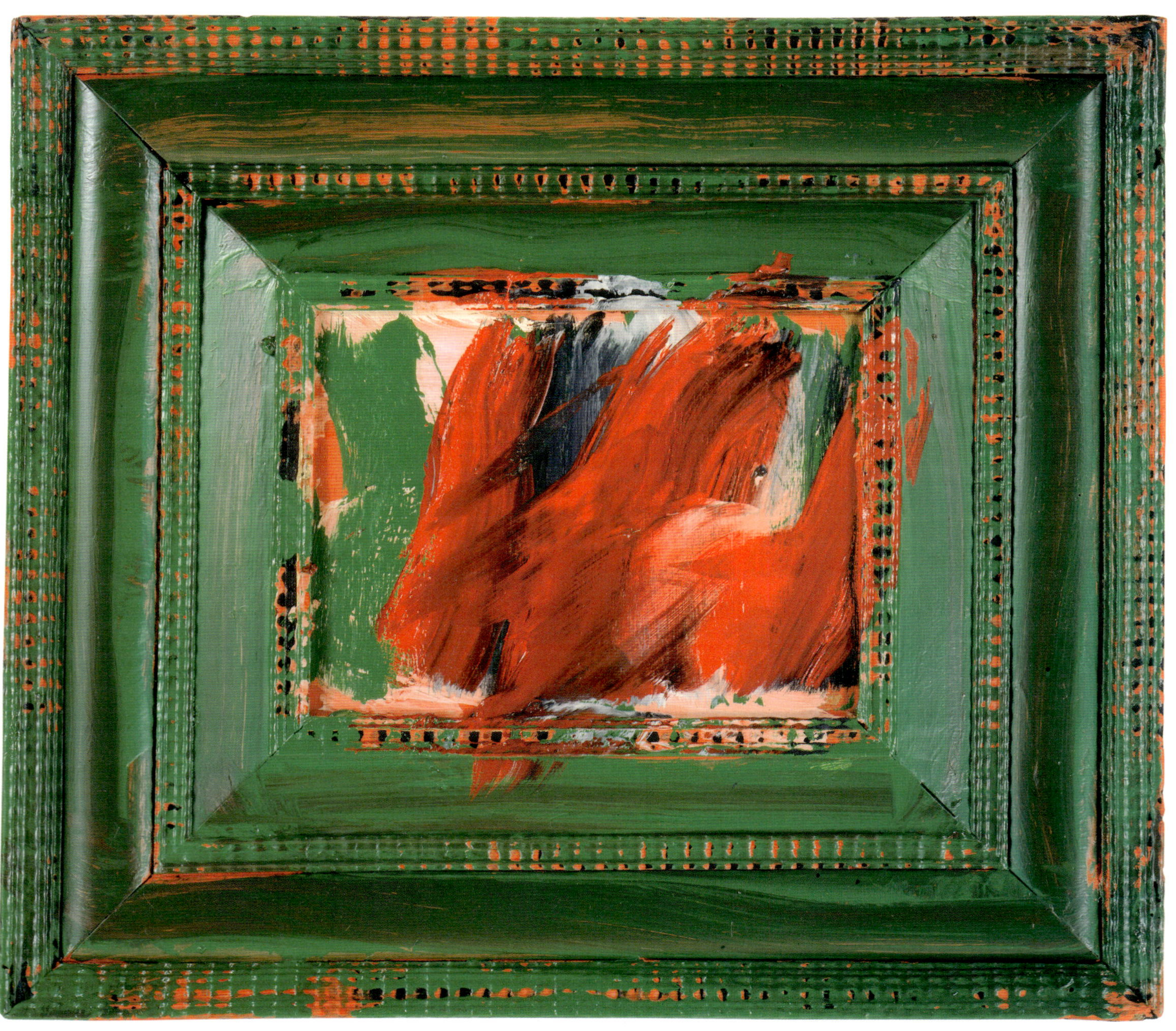

55. These Foolish Things, 2002–03

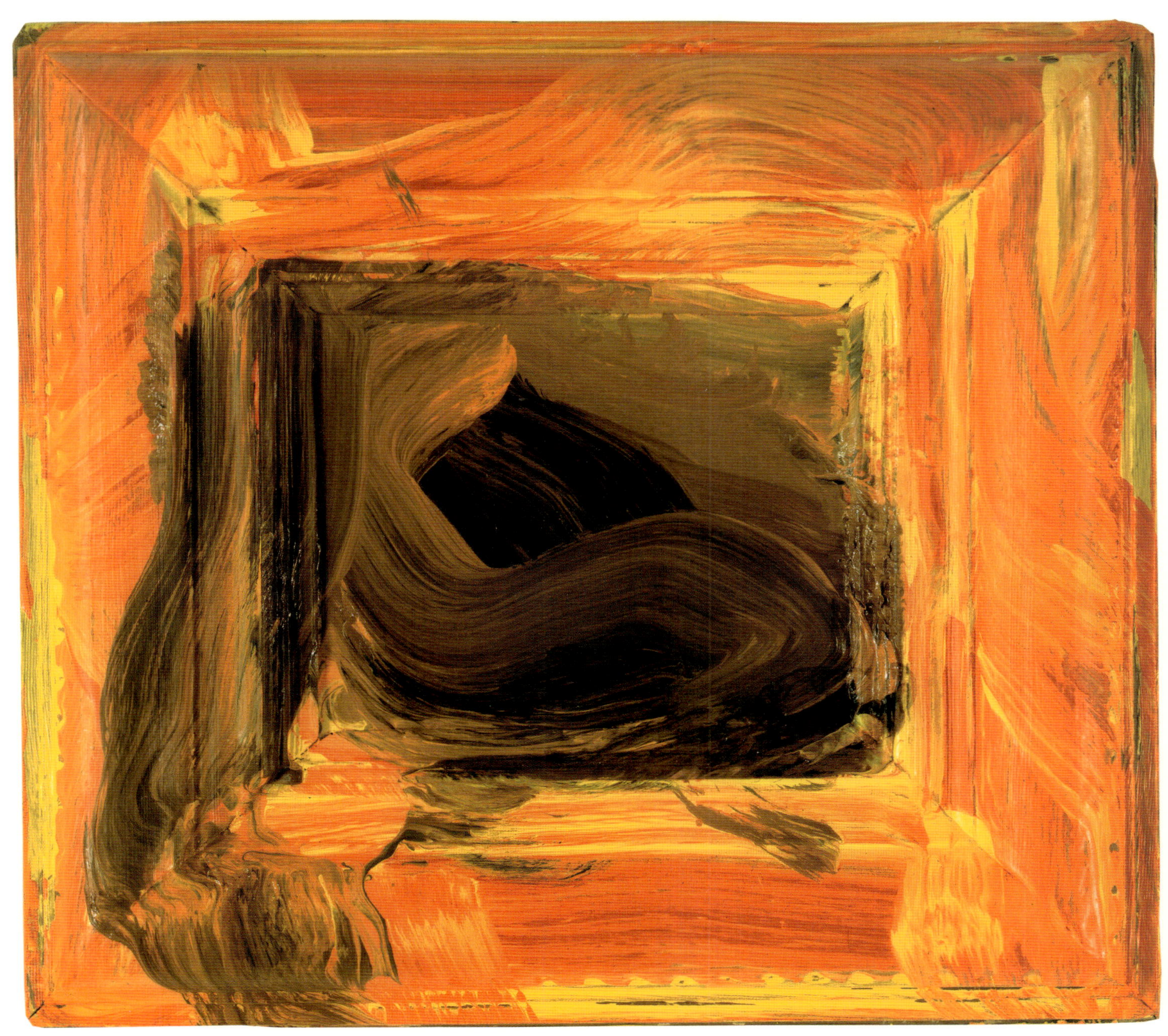

56. You are my Sunshine, 2002

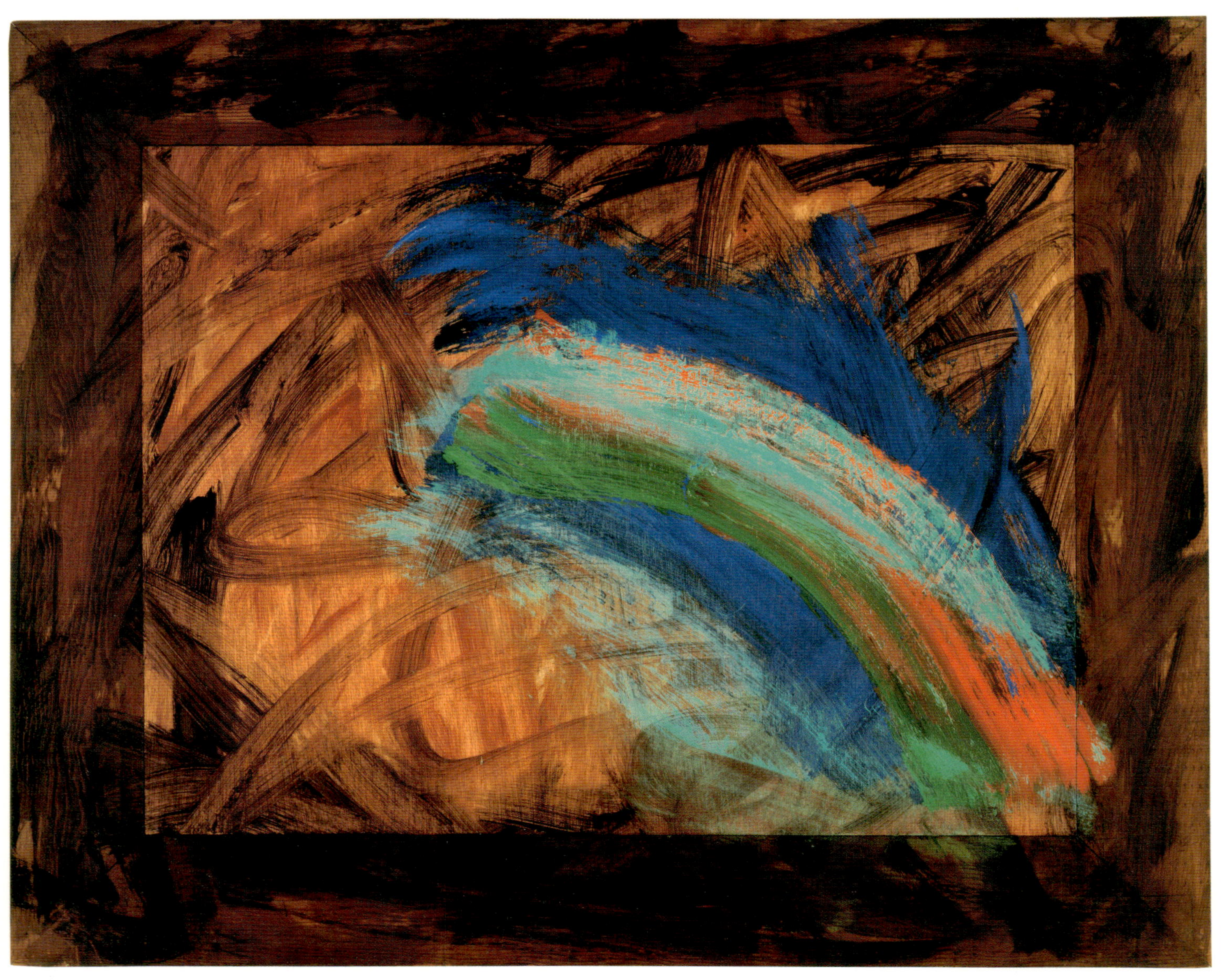

57. Falling Down, 2002–04

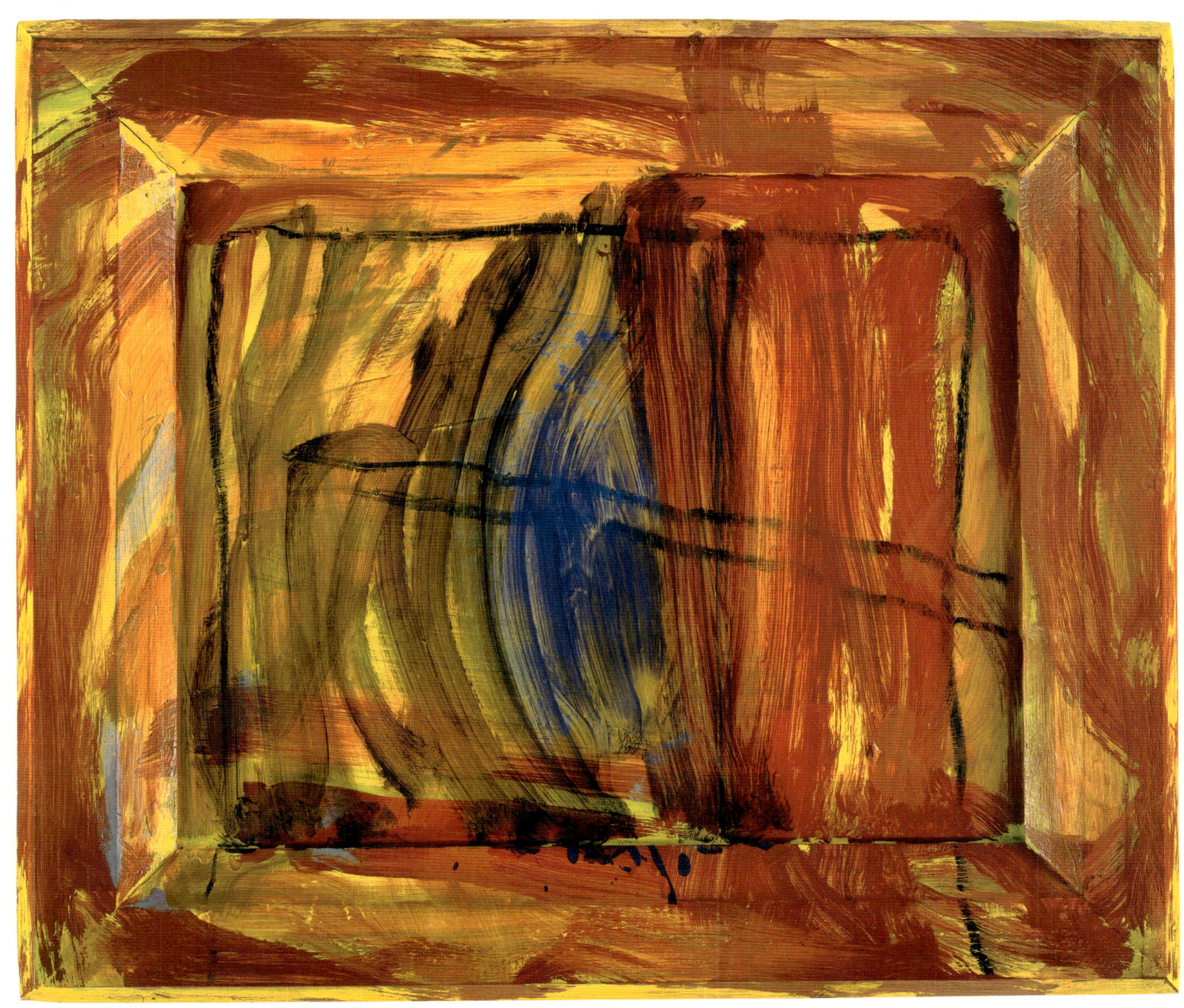

58. Hide and Seek, 2000–04

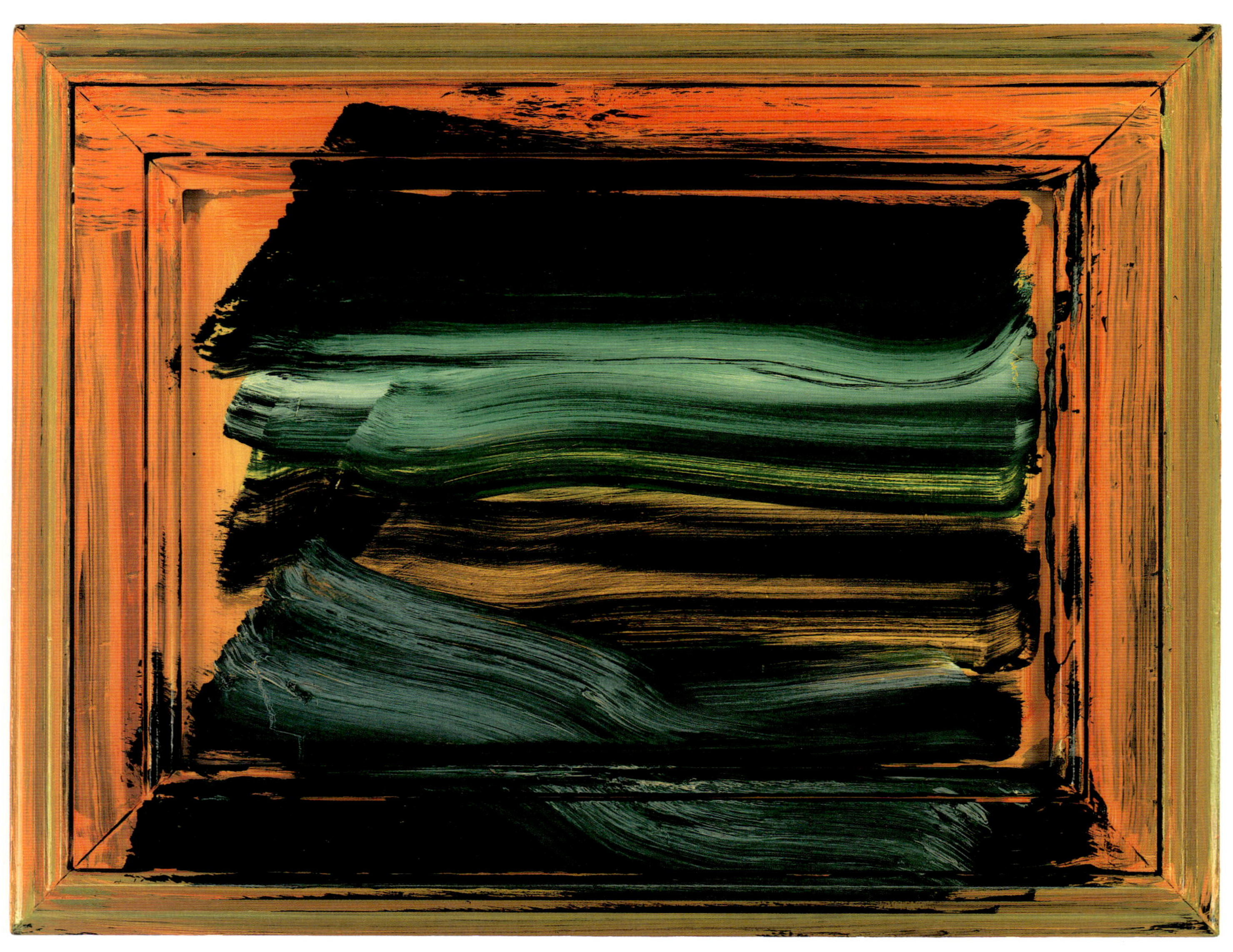

59. Old Books, 2006

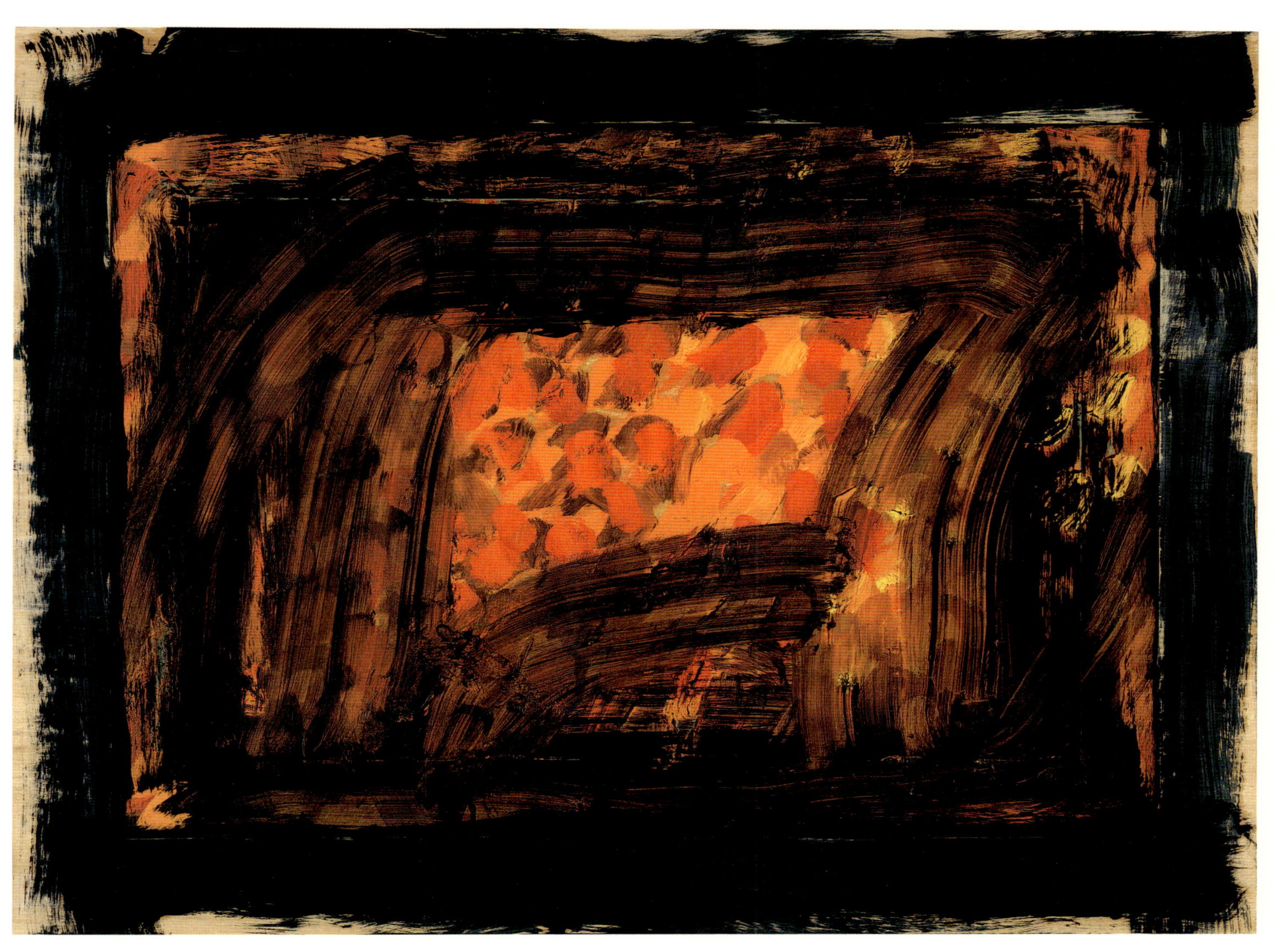

60. "Privacy and Self-Expression in the Bedroom," 2006

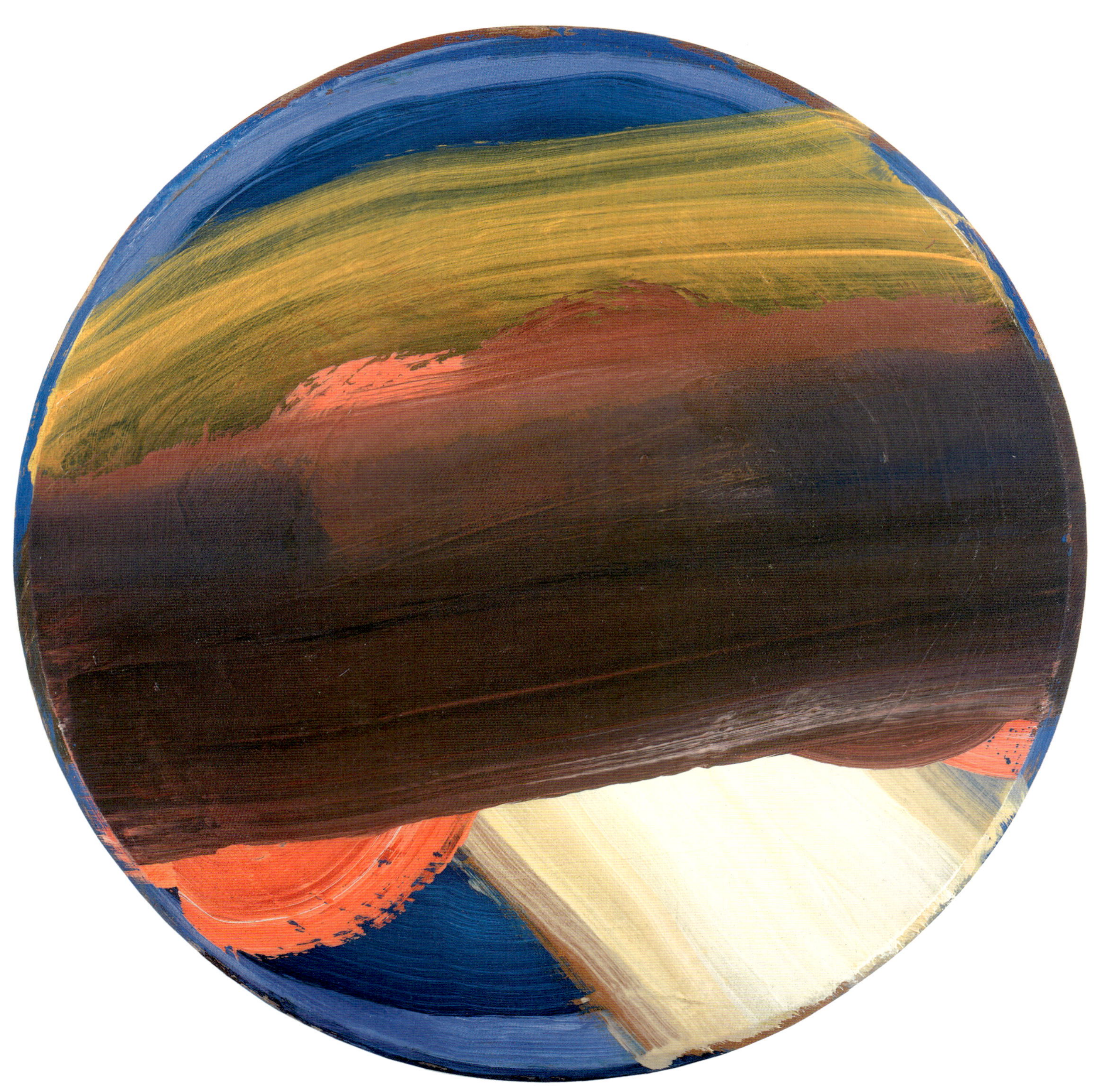

61. Small Chez Max, 1989–97

CHECKLIST

Works in the selection are arranged chronologically here. Their position in the gallery that precedes this checklist is indicated by the number at the end of each entry.

Small Chez Max
1989–97
Oil on wood
18 in. (45.3 cm), diameter
Courtesy of the Artist and Gagosian Gallery
no. 61

Venice Grey Water
1988–89
Oil on wood
10⅜ x 11⅝ in. (25.8 x 28.5 cm)
Private collection, London
no. 27
Fitzwilliam only

A Visit to Paul and Bernard
1990
Oil on wood
52 x 56¾ in. (132.5 x 144 cm)
Private collection
no. 6
Yale only

Bedroom Window
1992–94
Oil on board
43 x 54¼ in. (109.5 x 137.5 cm)
Kronos Collection
no. 8
Yale only

After Degas
1993
Oil on wood
26 x 30 in. (66 x 76 cm)
Private collection, London
no. 44

Afternoon Flowers
1989–95
Oil on wood
44½ x 54¾ in. (113 x 139 cm), horizontal oval
Private collection
no. 2
Yale only

Rain at Il Palazzo
1993–98
Oil on wood
59 x 75¾ in. (149.9 x 192.4 cm)
Private collection
no. 7
Not exhibited

Chinoiserie
1994–97
Oil on wood
16¾ x 18 in. (42.6 x 45.7 cm)
Collection: Edwin C. Cohen
no. 4
Not exhibited

Bamboo
1995–97
Oil on wood
23⅝ x 27⅛ in. (60 x 68.9 cm)
Herman and Faye Sarkowsky
no. 3
Yale only

Old Sky
1996–97
Oil on wood
15½ x 17¼ in. (39.4 x 43.8 cm)
Private collection, London
no. 28
Yale only

When in Rome
1996–97
Oil on wood
19 x 24 in. (48.5 x 61.3 cm), oval
Courtesy of the Artist and Gagosian Gallery
no. 5

After Vuillard
1996–2002
Oil on wood
43⅜ x 51 in. (110.5 x 129.5 cm)
Sir Evelyn and Lady de Rothschild
no. 45

Silence
1997–2004
Oil on wood
18¼ x 18½ in. (46.5 x 47 cm)
Courtesy of the Artist and Gagosian Gallery
no. 26

Evening Sea
1998
Oil on wood
69⅛ x 102⅜ in. (175.9 x 260.4 cm), oval
Museum of Fine Arts, Houston; Museum purchase with funds provided by the Caroline Wiess Law Accessions Endowment Fund, 2000.234.
no. 12
Not exhibited

Autumn Foliage
1998–99
Oil on wood
39 x 46½ in. (99 x 118 cm)
Private collection
no. 11

Moonlight
1998–99
Oil on wood
30 x 34 in. (76.2 x 86.4 cm)
Private collection
no. 47

Small Rain
1998–99
Oil on wood
17⅛ x 18⅞ inches (43.5 x 48 cm)
Caroline Conran, London
no. 9

Theatre
1998–99
Oil on wood
12¼ x 14¾ in. (31.1 x 37.5 cm)
Peter Simon Family Collection
no. 43

Autumn
1998–2003
Oil on wood
84⅞ x 120½ in. (215.6 x 306.8 cm)
Courtesy of the Artist and Gagosian Gallery
no. 39

The Body in the Library
1998–2003
Oil on wood
84 x 85 in. (213.3 x 216.5 cm)
Courtesy of the Artist and Gagosian Gallery
no. 46
Yale only

Walking on Water
1999–2001
Oil on wood
18¼ x 20¼ in. (46.4 x 51.4 cm)
Marion Stroud-Swingle
no. 42
Yale only

Thunder
1999–2002
Oil on wood
45⅝ x 53⅜ in. (116 x 135.7 cm)
Private collection
no. 30
Yale only

After the Storm
2000
Oil on wood
30½ x 34¾ in. (77.6 x 88.4 cm)
Location unknown
no. 18
Not exhibited

Out of the Window
2000
Oil on wood
38⅛ x 44¾ in. (97 x 113.6 cm), oval
Private collection
no. 15
Not exhibited

Please Explain
2000
Oil on wood
23⅝ x 29⅛ in. (60 x 74.3 cm)
Private collection
no. 10
Yale only

Torso
2000
Oil on wood
49⅜ x 52¾ in. (125.7 x 134 cm)
The Phillips Collection, Washington, D.C.;
Purchase, The Drier Fund for Acquisitions, in
memory of Robert Cafritz, 2001.
no. 16
Yale only

An Autumn Leaf
2000
Oil on wood
11⅝ x 13 in. (29.5 x 33 cm)
Courtesy of the Artist and Gagosian Gallery
no. 29

Keep It Quiet
2000–01
Oil on wood
12½ x 15 3/4 in. (31.8 x 40 cm)
Julian Barnes
no. 48

Echo
2000–02
Oil on wood
12⅛ x 13⅝ in. (30.8 x 34.6 cm)
Private collection, London
no. 32

Spring Rain
2000–02
Oil on wood
38¾ x 42 in. (98.4 x 106.7 cm)
Collection of James H. Duffy, New York
no. 31
Yale only

Double Portrait
2000–03
Oil on wood
42⅜ x 48⅛ in. (107.7 x 122.5 cm)
Industrial Petro-chemical, inc.,
President Edward L. Gardner
no. 14
Yale only

Memorial
2000–03
Oil on wood
74½ x 99 in. (189.8 x 251.4 cm)
Courtesy the Artist and Gagosian Gallery
no. 22
Yale only

Venetian Landscape
2000–03
Oil on wood
17⅞ x 19⅞ in. (45.4 x 50.5 cm)
Roger Thomas and Arthur Libera
no. 54
Yale only

Hide and Seek
2000–04
Oil on wood
41¾ x 48⅛ in. (106 x 122.3 cm)
Kay Harrigan Woods
no. 58
Yale only

Clarendon Road
2000–05
Oil on wood
53 x 69¼ in. (134.6 x 175.9 cm)
Irish Museum of Modern Art
no. 50

Dirty Weather
2001
Oil on wood
10 x 14 in. (25.4 x 35.5 cm)
Courtesy of the Artist and Gagosian Gallery
no. 34

Alone
2002
Oil on wood
18⅞ x 23⅛ in. (47.9 x 58.7 cm)
Collection of Bert Kaplan
no 37

Fog
2002
Oil on wood
13 x 14½ in. (33 x 36.8 cm)
Pat Kavanagh
no. 49

Low Tide
2002
Oil on wood
16¾ x 21⅝ in. (42.5 x 54.9 cm)
Mr. and Mrs. John L. Townsend III
no. 41
Yale only

On the Rocks
2002
Oil on wood
16¾ x 22⅛ in. (42.5 x 56.3 cm)
Mr. and Mrs. John L. Townsend III
no. 38
Yale only

Grief
2002
Oil on wood
35 x 45⅛ in. (88.9 x 114.9 cm)
Private collection
no. 33
Yale only

Mud
2002
Oil on wood
15⅜ x 18½ in. (39 x 47 cm)
Courtesy of the Artist and Gagosian Gallery
no. 25

You Are My Sunshine
2002
Oil on wood
12⅜ x 13½ in. (31.4 x 34.3 cm)
Nigel Slater
no. 56

Christmas
2002–03
Oil on wood
16 x 18 in. (40.6 x 45.7 cm)
Kathy and Keith Sachs
no. 40
Yale only

These Foolish Things
2002–03
Oil on wood
16 x 18 in. (40.6 x 45.7 cm)
Courtesy the Artist and Gagosian Gallery
no. 55

Chintz
2002–03
Oil on wood
13⅝ x 15¼ in. (34.6 x 38.7 cm)
Collection of Brian Balfour-Oatts, London
no. 17

Falling Down
2002–04
Oil on wood
35½ x 43½ in. (90.2 x 110.5cm)
Private collection
no. 57
Yale only

Navy Blue
2002–04
Oil on wood
31 x 27 in. (78.7 x 68.6 cm)
Stan and Gail Hollander
no. 23
Yale only

Visitors
2002–05
Oil on wood
24½ x 27¼ in. (62.3 x 69.9 cm)
Private collection
no. 19
Not exhibited

Little Venice
2003
Oil on wood
10½ x 13 in. (26.7 x 33 cm)
Adam Proujansky
no. 20
Yale only

Heat
2003–04
Oil on wood
20⅝ x 28⅜ in. (52.4 x 72.1 cm)
Collection of Luther W. Brady
no. 24
Yale only

Performance Art
2003–04
Oil on wood
39 x 76⅝ in. (99 x 195 cm)
Courtesy of the Artist and Gagosian Gallery
no. 21

After Samuel Palmer
2003–05
Oil on wood
10⅝ x 12⅛ in. (26.9 x 31 cm)
Courtesy of the Artist and Gagosian Gallery
no. 1

An Italian Landscape
2003–05
Oil on wood
53⅜ x 72 in. (135.6 x 182.9 cm)
Mr. and Mrs. Meredith Long
no. 52
Yale only

Ultramarine
2003–05
Oil on wood
13¾ x 15¾ in. (34.9 x 39.4 cm)
Collection of Brian Balfour-Oatts, London
no. 13

Déjà vu, Déjà Blue
2004
Oil on wood
12⅝ x 12¾ in. (32.1 x 32.4 cm)
Private collection, Courtesy Kristy Stubbs Gallery
no 36
Yale only

Pyjamas
2004
Oil on wood
14⅛ x 15⅞ in. (35.8 x 40.3 cm)
Private collection
no. 53
Yale only

Flowerpiece
2004–05
Oil on wood
26¼ x 35½ in. (66.7 x 90.2 cm)
Private collection
no. 51

First Light
2005
Oil on wood
14⅞ x 20¼ in. (37.8 x 51.4 cm)
Courtesy of the Artist and Gagosian Gallery
no. 35

Old Books
2006
Oil on wood
21⅞ x 28¼ in. (55.6 x 71.8 cm)
Courtesy of the Artist and Gagosian Gallery
no 59

"Privacy and Self-Expression in the Bedroom"
2004–06
Oil on wood
45¼ x 60½ x 1½ in. (114.9 x 153.7 x 3.8 cm)
Courtesy of the Artist and Gagosian Gallery
no 60
Fitzwilliam only

INDEX

Page numbers for works illustrated in the essays are given in italics. Numbers in bold refer to works in the gallery.

CREDITS

Photography

Every effort has been made to credit the photographers and the sources; if there are errors or omissions, please contact Yale University Press so that correction can be made in any subsequent edition.

Fig. 1: Ashmolean Museum, Oxford
Figs. 2, 3, 13, 27, 28: Prudence Cumming Associates Ltd
Fig. 4: © Southampton City Art Gallery / The Bridgeman Art Library
Figs. 5, 6, 26: Ken Cohen Photography, New York
Fig. 7: © The National Gallery, London
Fig. 8: © The Museum of Modern Art / licensed by SCALA / Art Resouce, NY
Figs. 9, 22: Private Collection / The Bridgeman Art Library
Figs. 10, 11, 18: © Tate, London 2007
Fig. 12: Beinecke Rare Book and Manuscript Library, Yale University
Fig. 14: Photograph © 1998 The Metropolitan Museum of Art
Fig. 15: © Bildarchiv Preussischer Kulturbesitz / Art Resource, NY, photo by Jens Ziehe
Fig. 16: Rob McKeever
Figs. 17, 31, 32, endpapers: Richard Caspole, Yale Center for British Art
Fig. 19: Réunion des Musées Nationaux / Art Resource, NY, photo by R.G. Ojeda
Fig. 20: © NGC
Fig. 21: Louvre, Paris, Lauros / Giraudon / The Bridgeman Art Library

All images in the exhibition selection are by Prudence Cuming Associates Ltd, except for no. 27 which is by John Webb

Works of art

All works by Howard Hodgkin are © Howard Hodgkin

Fig. 8: © 2007 Artists Rights Society (ARS), New York / ADAGP, Paris
Figs. 9, 10, 11: © Estate of Walter R. Sickert / DACS 2007
Fig. 12: © Estate of Vanessa Bell, Courtesy Henrietta Garnett
Fig. 14: © 2007 The Pollock-Krasner Foundation / Artists Rights Society (ARS), New York
Fig. 15: © 2007 Estate of Pablo Picasso / Artists Rights Society (ARS), New York
Fig. 16: © Jasper Johns / licensed by VAGA, New York, NY
Fig. 17: © 2007, Cy Twombly
Fig. 18: © 2007 Artists Rights Society (ARS), New York / DACS, London
Fig. 20: © Judd Foundation. Licensed by VAGA, New York, NY

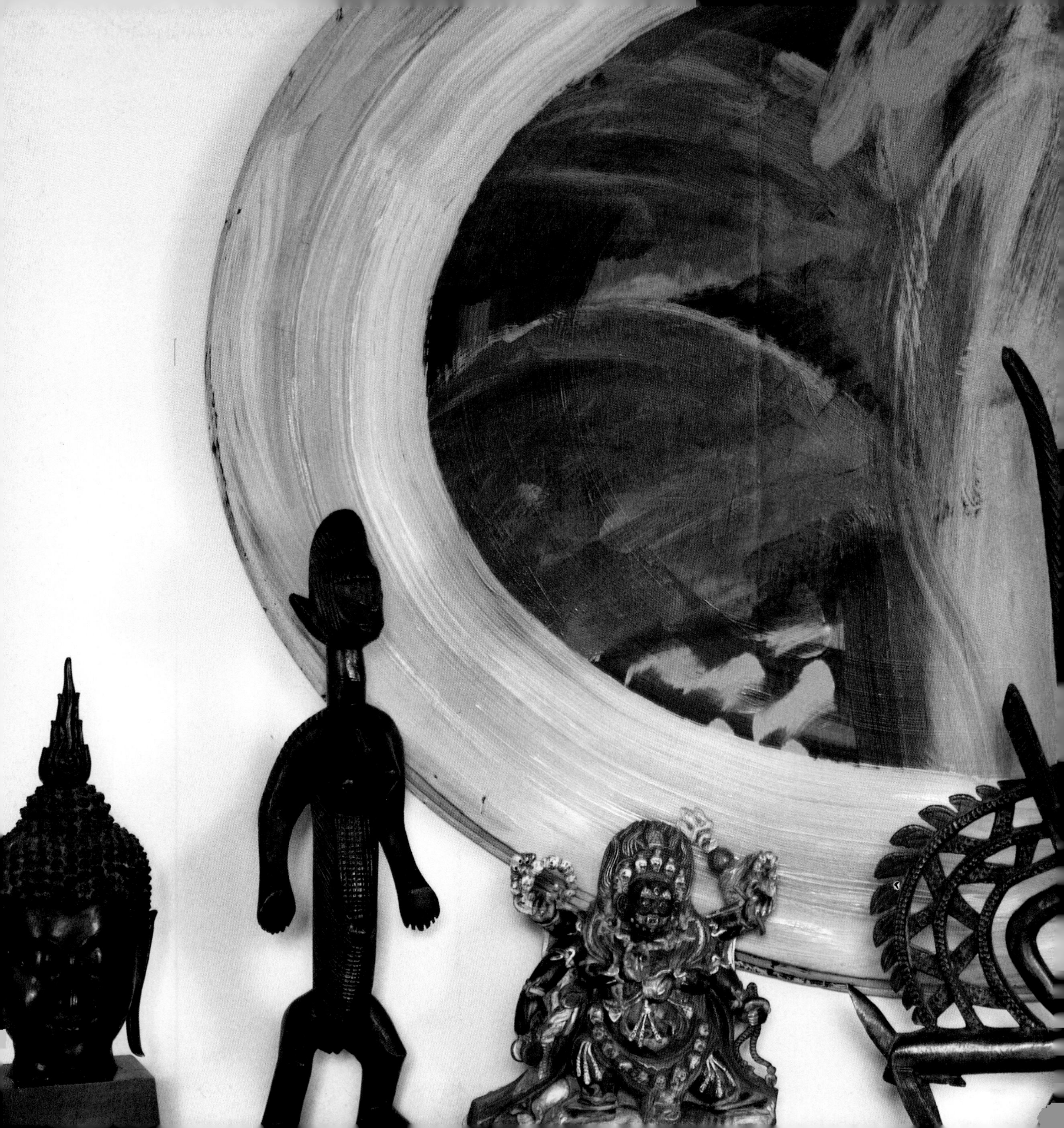